MISSION OF MALICE

My exodus from KwaSizabantu

ERIKA BORNMAN

PENGUIN BOOKS

Mission of Malice
Published by Penguin Books
an imprint of Penguin Random House (Pty) Ltd
Company Reg. No. 1953/000441/07
The Estuaries No. 4, Oxbow Crescent, Century Avenue, Century City, Cape Town, 7441
www.penguinrandomhouse.co.za

Penguin
Random House
South Africa

First published 2021

1 3 5 7 9 10 8 6 4 2

Publication © Penguin Books 2021
Text © Erika Bornman 2021

Cover image © Erika Bornman
Back cover image of KwaSizabantu courtesy of Koos Greeff

PUBLISHER: Marlene Fryer
MANAGING EDITOR: Ronel Richter-Herbert
EDITOR: Bronwen Maynier
PROOFREADER: Ronel Richter-Herbert
COVER DESIGN: Sean Robertson
TEXT DESIGN: Ryan Africa
TYPESETTER: Monique van den Berg

Printed by **novus print**, a division of Novus Holdings

MIX
Paper from
responsible sources
FSC
www.fsc.org   FSC® C022948

ISBN 978 1 77609 623 7 (print)
ISBN 978 1 77609 624 4 (ePub)

CONTENTS

I dedicate this book to my brother, Chris Bornman. You are my rock and my steadfast source of unconditional love. You helped me even when you needed help yourself. You have saved me, more times than you know. Thank you, I love you and I am so proud of you. My brother, you are my hero.

The single aim of such a hapless mother, howsoever tender and devoted she may by nature be, is to form her child after the one strict pattern her fate has set her – her master's will; since, otherwise, she dare not contemplate the perils which might overtake her treasure. Pitiful indeed, therefore, is the pitiless inflexibility of purpose with which she wings from her child's heart all the dangerous endearments of childhood – its merry laughter, its sparkling tears, its trustfulness, its artlessness, its engaging waywardness; and in their place instils silence, submission, self-constraint, suspicion, cunning, carefulness, and an ever-vigilant fear. And the result is a spectacle of unnatural discipline simply appalling. The life of such a child is an eggshell on an ocean; to its helpless speck of experience all horrors are possible. Its passing moment is its eternity; and that overwhelmed with terrors, real or imaginary, what is left but that poor little floating wreck, a child's despair?

– *The English Governess at the Siamese Court*, Anna Leonowens, 1870

FOREWORD

Sixteen years of investigative and crime reporting couldn't prepare me for what I was about to hear from the soft-spoken woman in front of me.

A few weeks previously, in early 2020, I received an email from an old journalist friend, Peter van Noord, telling me about KwaSizabantu Mission and the horror stories his friend Erika Bornman had told him about the place. Peter knew me too well; I don't have the ability to walk away from such a tip-off.

So I connected with Erika and set up a coffee date in a small boardroom called 'SHIFT' on the fifteenth floor of Media24's head office in Cape Town. It was February 2020. I opened my laptop and asked her to 'tell me your story'.

What I heard over the next two hours blew my mind. Having watched several documentaries on cults over the years, I asked Erika if she knew that what she was describing to me was a full-blown cult worthy of Netflix's attention.

Yes, she said. That's why she's been trying to tell the story for many years.

She told me about rape and sexual abuse, psychological and spiritual torture, the break-up of families in the name of religion and KwaSizabantu's link to the apartheid security apparatus that was yet to be fully revealed.

She gave me clippings of articles she had written for magazines almost two decades ago. I was horrified that nothing had come of these revelations and realised the power and impact a News24 exposé could have on this mission of depravity.

I opened a folder on my desktop and called it 'KwaSizabantu'.

I was aghast that the mission was still operating in a democratic country, governed by a Constitution and a Bill of Rights. There was overwhelming interest in exposing the truth behind the cult, and I immediately knew that we had found the perfect primary source for our investigation in Erika.

She understood journalism, had direct knowledge of years of abuse, had a vast network of people linked to KwaSizabantu and wasn't scared to speak out against Erlo Stegen and the mission's other rulers.

After our meeting, I walked straight to the desk of Tammy Petersen, News24's senior features writer, and told her that I had found the perfect story for her. Petersen also has a deep passion for social justice journalism and immediately connected with Erika.

We sat down with Erika, who introduced us to other sources and helped us unpack the structure and individuals behind KwaSizabantu. Investigative journalism 101.

Seven months later, we published *Exodus: Uncovering a cult in KwaZulu-Natal*.

If it weren't for Erika, this exposé would not have been told in the way we managed to tell it. She was incredibly generous with her time and didn't mind answering the same questions repeatedly. She realised the importance of telling the story to a broad audience.

After a few weeks, over one million people had read or heard about KwaSizabantu on News24.

Whistleblowers are the unsung heroes of investigative journalism. Erika had very little to gain from our exposé, besides a broad platform from which to tell her story. She was vilified for speaking out by her family and avid believers of the cult, but she persisted, driven by her burning passion for justice.

Her decision to speak out and our reportage led to a number of investigations being initiated into the activities of KwaSizabantu.

I am delighted that Erika has also decided to tell her story in her own words. I do not doubt that this powerful book will greatly assist in finding justice and peace for the survivors of KwaSizabantu.

ADRIAAN BASSON
EDITOR-IN-CHIEF: NEWS24

PROLOGUE

I'm clutching a large butcher's knife when my carefully constructed world caves in. Moments ago, the apartment was filled with the chatter and laughter of a group of friends gathered for a potluck lunch. Now the kitchen has fallen silent.

The afternoon starts out happily enough. I accompany my boyfriend, Samuel, and his sister to their friend's home. Around fifteen people mill around, the atmosphere is convivial. Most have gathered in the kitchen to get the meal going. I trail in behind Samuel, hoping to be invisible – I only know two people here and I don't want to get in the way. Then our host turns to me with a big smile and a bigger knife and cheerily asks, 'Hey, Erika, won't you make the fruit salad?'

My stomach drops as I take the knife and turn to the counter. Deep breath. I can do this. Then I spot a pawpaw and freeze. Oh no. No one has ever taught me how to peel or cut up a pawpaw. I'm going to mess it up and show everyone here that I don't belong in their world because they're going to see me cutting the pawpaw the wrong way and they're going to know that I don't know what I'm doing and that I don't belong.

I've been fooling myself. I shouldn't be here.

I'm a misfit. I'm a woman who doesn't know how to make a simple fruit salad. In this moment I see my whole life mapped out in front of me. I will never fit in. This society I long to be a part of will never be mine. I will constantly find myself in situations where, through my ignorance, I will reveal that I am not one of them.

Tears well up in my eyes and I cannot stop them streaming down my face. 'Everything okay, Erika?' No, everything's not okay. Everything's bloody terrible. I don't know how to do this, and I don't know how to admit to that. My rational mind tells me that any normal twenty-five-year-old would start chopping without a second's thought, but I know that I am not a normal twenty-five-year-old, and now everyone else knows it, too.

I'm bawling, a full-on ugly cry. I'm making a spectacle of myself and everyone is staring at me. Samuel looks at me with compassion – he has an inkling of what's going on.

I don't want to be here. I'm a fraud. I want to be back at the mission, where at least I knew how to act, I knew how to make cheese on toast, I knew my place in a room full of people. Much as I was dying there, I knew who I was. I was Erika, daughter of Esther, sister of Hanna. I was Erika, the girl who always smiled. I was Erika, the girl who never made a fuss.

Now? Now I am the woman who breaks down over something trivial in front of strangers in the kitchen of someone she's never met before. It's the biggest challenge of my life. And I'm facing it with an audience of baffled onlookers.

A public humiliation. I always knew this would happen to me. I knew that it was only a matter of time before I was shown to be a fraud. I will never fit in. I'll never be happy. Isn't that what Erlo told me when he put God's curse on my life? He said that I'd never be happy. I'm never going to know how to act. I'm never going to know what to do. I'm never going to know what the right thing is to say, and I'm never going to know how to cut up a bloody pawpaw.

I just want to give up and go back. At least there, a public humiliation and the prescribed apology is followed by acceptance back into the fold. Out here in the world, a humiliation is more likely to lead to a label: 'That emotional girl who's obviously very troubled.' No one will want to invite me ever again. I've made a fool of myself and Samuel.

I hate this. Why did I ever think it would be different? Who am I to think that I am strong enough and clever enough to make it in the world? I've been out here for more than three years and look at me – I'm an emotional wreck.

But no. I will not give in and I will not go back. Oh, they're waiting for me, I'm sure of that. 'She'll be back sooner or later like all the others. Just wait and see.' I know that's what they're all thinking back there, what they're hoping for. But I will not succumb. I may not know who I am, but I know who I don't want to be. And I don't want to be that submissive, smiling, emaciated girl ever again. I don't want to marry someone I don't love and bear his children and live a life of quiet desperation. I won't.

I also won't give them the satisfaction of killing myself. I won't have them preach about me for years to come. Use me in their sermons to terrorise children into blind obedience. I will not be one of their 'stories' – I'd heard too many of those growing up and I won't become one. I'll be a success. I have to be. I want to be. I know I have it in me, somewhere, if only I can breathe through this fear. Most days I think I get it right. I think most people think I'm normal.

What was I thinking, coming to this lunch? I've totally ruined it. I've ruined it for Samuel, I've ruined it for everyone, but that's what I do, isn't it? I ruin people's lives. I've ruined my mother's life, I've ruined my life, I've ruined everyone's life, and I don't know how I'm going to live, but I want to live. And I want this life and I want to know how to make a fruit salad.

I know tonight will be the same as every other night, except maybe worse. It's at night that the day replays in my head and I cringe at the many faux pas I'm sure I made. This lunch isn't a faux pas, it's a full-on disaster. The fear that usually visits me in bed at night arrives early: fully blown and overpowering. My chest constricts and I want to die. This fear is as much a part of me as my lungs and my heart, but

I can usually keep it at bay during the day. I live with it every day, commune with it at night.

I have no memory of what happens next. I leave my body, dissociating the way I often do. It's how my nine-year-old self coped. In the coming days, as I watch this incident with the malevolent pawpaw unfold over and over again in my mind's eye, I know one thing for sure. I have to learn to control my fear and up my game at pretending I'm okay if I'm to succeed in making people believe that I'm normal. Because I desperately want to be normal, even if it's only an act, don't I?

PART ONE

THE SHADOW CHILD

1

A FIRE IN THE GARDEN

Three kilometres is a long way to walk in the hot sun when you have little legs. My consolation is that I know the house will be cool once I get there, because in the summer my mother always makes sure to keep the curtains shut during the heat of the day. It's the end of 1979 and I'm eight years old. In 1979, in Natal, it is still safe for a little girl to walk to school and back, and besides, my brother Chris and sister Hanna are usually with me. Entering the house on Hellet Road is a relief. Something's off, though. My mother – Mamma as we call her – is gathering everything from her cupboard and carrying it out to the backyard. All her clothes. Her jewellery. Her make-up. Her shoes.

We've got a huge backyard. The house sits on a half-acre plot close to the Dutch Reformed Church, not far from the railway line. My dad is an avid gardener and he grows fruit trees, grapes, vegetables, you name it. So we eat healthy, good food because a lot of it we grow ourselves; well, my dad does. On weekends, my brother helps him in the garden and my sister and I do chores inside the house.

Mamma throws everything onto a big pile in the backyard and sets it alight. She burns all her clothes, jewellery, make-up, shoes … everything. The pile burns. It's not only *her* clothes that she burns. She burns some of mine too. My shorts and trousers, but not my dresses. I am a young girl, she says. I am not allowed to wear boys' clothing. My sister's clothes get judged as well. I don't remember any of my brother's or my dad's clothes making it onto the pile. Probably because, hey, they are meant to wear the pants in the house, being men and all. I would come to learn more about the differences between men and women in the years to come.

In one of my pockets, she finds a little note that a boy in my class has written to me because he likes me, and I like him. He's written me a little letter. As she opens the note and reads it, her face changes. She suddenly looks angry and tells me that this is just not on. I am not allowed to have anything to do with boys any more. This is just one more baffling element to the whole confusing afternoon. Not talk to boys?

Mamma explains to me that all the stuff she is burning belongs to the devil and we will not be wearing anything any more that doesn't glorify God. So I am no longer allowed to wear shorts or trousers or tracksuit pants, because those are men's clothes and somewhere in Deuteronomy it states that women may not wear men's clothes. (It's only years later that it strikes me: didn't men wear long, flowing robes in the times of Deuteronomy? So, basically, dresses?)

My mother has this sense of certainty about her. It is as though what she is doing today is nothing out of the ordinary at all. I have been raised to not question my parents. We're encouraged to ask questions about the world and other matters, but when the two of them say or do something, that's it. No questions asked; total obedience required.

For a while my mother recycles two outfits: a beige top and skirt with big orange, red and brown flowers, and another top and skirt that is a white and green-blue, paisley affair. She wears no make-up, and her only jewellery are her engagement and wedding rings and her watch. Apparently, women are temptresses, and everything we do to make ourselves look pretty could tempt a man into sin. The devil uses eyeshadow and lipstick and earrings to lure men into sinful thoughts.

Our little family of five has entered a new dispensation.

2

ONE MIDDLING HAPPY FAMILY

Rewind a few years. My dad is my whole life. He's playful and I've got him wrapped around my little finger. I play on that, little brat that I am. My poor brother. I'd start something with him, he'd retaliate, and I'd run straight to my dad and jump on his lap. My dad would just look at Chris and say, 'Chris, she's just a little girl. She's fragile and you have to treat her well.'

We're living in the Western Cape, first Rawsonville then Worcester, when I'm around four and five years old. All three of us children, Hanna, Chris and I, were born in Malawi, but we're back in South Africa now, where my dad is a teacher.

Sometimes Pappa is a lion, stalking me. One day, I am so wrapped up in our game that when the lion is about to catch his prey, I shriek in real terror. I fall to the ground. 'Garrakachok, I'm in my den!' I scream. Where that word comes from is a mystery. But it's a safe word both my dad and my brother honour. When I am fear-stricken, I shout it out loud, and that means you can't touch me and whatever you are doing has to stop right now, because I am too scared to continue. Eventually I simply need to say 'Garrakachok!', and everyone stops what they're doing immediately. The word keeps me safe when we play make-believe.

Words fascinate me. One day, when I'm three, I simply refuse to play with my dolls or anything else any more. I want to read. My brother is now in school and reading. My sister can read. So why do I have to play with dolls? I want to read. My dad was born in Kenya, so he did his schooling in English, despite coming from an Afrikaans background. We speak Afrikaans at home.

This is the 1970s, and my dad knows teachers don't like it when kids are already able to read before they start their schooling. So he comes up with a solution. He teaches me to read in English. I can't really speak a word of English, but I can read it. 'This is Jane. This is Peter. This is Pat, their dog.' Those are the first words I ever read, from a Ladybird book, and the pictures help me understand what it is that I am reading. I'm lucky when I get to school to have a teacher like Miss Greeff. She nurtures my reading instead of frowning at the fact that I can do so already. Because, of course, I easily pick up reading in Afrikaans.

Being the youngest, I finish school before my siblings. Our home is close to the Drostdy, where my dad teaches maths and science, and I spend many an afternoon in his lab. He makes things smoke and explode in test tubes for me and teaches me about physics and chemistry. He tells me science and maths are like ladders:

you have to step on and understand each rung before moving on to the next. If you skip a rung, you're not going to be able to make it up the ladder of knowledge.

Birthdays are special because that's when my mother bakes each of us an elaborate birthday cake. One year, I get a castle with four turrets; brown chocolate icing covers the building, the grass is desiccated coconut that's been dyed green, and the doors and windows are made from various sweets. The next year, it's Humpty Dumpty's turn. I'm a tad disappointed; the cake feels so plain compared to the previous year's masterpiece. Humpty Dumpty's big smile is painted on an ostrich egg and he's sitting on a wall. But oh, the delight when I lift him off the wall: a torrent of Jelly Tots and Smarties flows from his bum and covers the cake. I squeal with pleasure.

We don't own a TV. We're allowed to watch certain programmes at a friend's house, or with the neighbours, but in our home, we read books. On Sunday mornings, the three of us pile onto my parents' double bed with my dad. It's got a solid wooden frame with four drawers underneath the mattress. My dad had it custom-made in Malawi. My mother goes off to make breakfast while Pappa reads us a chapter or two from a book. A book he has to hide the rest of the week, mind you, maybe in one of those drawers. Together we read *Koning van Katoren*, the Afrikaans translation of *The Wind in the Willows*, and other classics. Breakfast arrives on a trolley, and afterwards we go to church. We walk to the Dutch Reformed Church, my sister and I wearing identical dresses that my mother has sewn for us, knitted white berets on our heads, clutching the coins we'll put in the collection plates later.

Our time in Worcester is the highlight of my childhood. I am safe; I don't doubt my parents' love for me. I am a happy, well-adjusted child who excels at school. We get a puppy and name her Patroon ('pattern' in English). She's a little black-and-white ball of fluff and love – a mix between a cocker spaniel and a Maltese poodle. There is enough love to go around in this house of ours.

And then everything goes pear-shaped. One fateful day, when I'm about seven, my mother goes to listen to someone preach. I find out much later that everything isn't as rosy as I think it is. My parents' marriage is in trouble. My mother hears that someone from a mission station in what was then just plain old Natal is coming to preach at the Goudini Spa, and she decides to attend. She returns with stars in her eyes and tells my dad that if there is anyone who can help her, it's these people. At a place called KwaSizabantu, they preach revival and repentance of sin and God's forgiveness. She has fallen under their spell.

I'm a little girl about to turn eight; I don't know how or why decisions about where we live are made, but in the middle of 1979, we all pack up and move to Estcourt in Natal, where my dad takes a job at the high school. And that's how we end up in that house on Hellet Road, one house away from the Dutch Reformed Church, where my mother burns our clothes one day.

3

THE PLACE WHERE
PEOPLE ARE HELPED

My mother goes to spend some time at KwaSizabantu Mission. Its name is Zulu for 'the place where people are helped'. I'm going to let you make up your own mind whether that is a good name or not. It's nestled in the Valley of a Thousand Hills, and it's beautiful there. Stunningly lush and green, right on the border of what was then Zululand.

We still attend the Dutch Reformed Church where my dad is the sexton, or *koster* as the position is known in Afrikaans. But over time, we spend more and more time at KwaSizabantu. (I'm going to shorten that to KSB for the most part from now on. People who have lived there call it simply The Mission, but to me the word 'mission' implies something benign, depending on your view of missionaries.)

On Sunday mornings, when we don't go to our local church, we pile into the car really early. We're a family of early risers, so that's not such a problem. KSB is 156 kilometres from our house. Today, Google says the drive should take one hour and fifty-five minutes, but back then it's more like two and a half hours. We need to arrive in time for the church service, which starts at eleven o'clock. You'd think that would mean the service would be over by twelve, right? Not so much. We're lucky if we're out of there by two o'clock.

From Greytown, the road is often covered in a dense mist. Headlights hardly cut through it, so my dad has to drive really slowly. We pass the time in the car by playing games. 'I spy with my little eye something beginning with …' Or seeing who can add the numbers of a passing car's licence plate the fastest. We turn at the sign that says 'KwaSizabantu Mission'. The security guard lifts the boom gate to let us through, we park and then check in at reception, as all visitors must do. And then we either go to the big hall or, if it's a large service, make our way to the tent. It's a blue-and-white striped affair with simple wooden benches filling most of the space – the chairs from the hall don't fill it all.

Ah, those chairs. They're better than the benches, but they're the most uncomfortable chairs I have ever sat on. Maybe that's just because I have to sit on them for such long stretches at a time. They're hard-backed and straight, and we are not allowed to fidget. To this day, I can sit still without moving for the longest time. And I don't fidget. It's not necessarily a good thing. Unless you're birding or being stalked by lions, of course. But if you're a normal human being, it's good to move. It's not natural for kids to have to sit still for hours.

The service is usually in two languages: Zulu and English. There is always a translator up on stage with whomever is preaching. At the back of the hall – or the tent – there is usually someone translating into German, and often translators speaking French, sometimes Dutch, depending on which overseas visitors are present.

My favourite part of the service is when the choir sings. Oh my word, it is beautiful. I am growing up in a home filled with classical music, and classical music has always been and will always be my soul music. The choir here at KSB sings lots of Handel, from his *Messiah* in particular. And the harmonies! I'm used to everyone singing exactly the same tune in the Dutch Reformed Church, but here, both the choir and the congregation harmonise so beautifully. Sopranos, altos, tenors and bass. The music is the one thing that makes the services bearable.

After the choir sings a few songs, the main event starts. Sunday services are taken by the founder and leader, Erlo Stegen, except when he is travelling. He is an imposing giant of a man. A South African German who speaks fluent Zulu, German, Afrikaans and English. He is eloquent and well spoken, super charismatic. An orator, for sure. He usually preaches in Zulu and someone then translates into English.

After not that many services, I know what the root of all evil is: premarital intercourse. Not that I know what intercourse is. Disobedient children are often under fire, too. And women! They – we – are the worst. You'd think that we should just be exterminated from the face of the earth because all we do is tempt men into sinning. So the sermons are fairly predictable. Erlo preaches about sin, God's judgement, lust, and having to repent in order to escape eternal damnation. He shouts a lot, and he gets really red in the face. Almost like a pufferfish that looks as though it's going to blow up any minute now. A red-faced pufferfish. Later, I learn that Erlo is allowed to get angry. For everyone else, anger is a terrible sin. But when Erlo gets angry, it's a righteous anger. It's a God-given, righteous anger. (I'll be bearing the brunt of that righteousness some years later.)

So, this red-faced man stands there and shouts at us in Zulu and then someone translates in a much calmer voice into English and then, eventually, after two or three hours, it all ends, mercifully. And the choir sings again, happiness. And then I rejoice because my numb little butt can get off that horrible chair.

The moment the sermon ends, the chairs are stacked up, quick-sticks, against the wall, trestle tables are laid out and food emerges from the kitchen – steaming pots of rice and stew – and we all queue up for the communal meal. And then, at some point, the five of us pile back into the car and make the drive back to Estcourt.

Soon, though, there will be only four of us going back home to Estcourt. KSB has various congregations around the world where people gather at one another's houses every Sunday to worship. All the other churches have it wrong, you see.

KSB's followers are the only ones who have the Truth and know the True Way, because God has shown it to them. Well, he showed it to Erlo, who showed it to everyone else. What's the point of going to any other church when they are all going to hell? Rather gather in each other's homes the way the disciples did. And so they do, all over the world.

One of these congregations is in Johannesburg, and some of the Joburg parents start talking about how the schools their kids attend are dens of iniquity. Or maybe it's the kids who are iniquitous. Whatever the case, they decide to send their children to live at KSB. From there, they get bussed the fifty kilometres to Stanger High School (a school like any other, I might add) every weekday morning and back again in the afternoon. In the evenings, they attend the obligatory church services. These are all white kids, because we are in the 1980s and schools are still segregated in South Africa. Apartheid, you know. I don't know whether it's my sister who tells my parents that she wants to join this merry band of itinerant kids (I can't imagine it being her decision) or whether it's my mother who thinks this is a good idea (I can't imagine my dad coming up with it). Nevertheless, at the start of her Standard 6 year, my sister goes to live at KSB, from where she gets bussed to school in Stanger.

I help her pack, and one of the items she's taking is a pack of sanitary pads, except I don't know what those are yet. I pick it up and playfully toss it from one hand to the other. 'What is this?' I ask her. She looks at me, then looks at my mother, who yanks it out of my hand, puts it in the suitcase and says: 'That is nothing that concerns you.'

And just like that, our family of five becomes four.

4

ABANDONED AND ALONE

My dad is a teacher, and a damn good one at that, but he's a missionary at heart. That's why all three of us were born in Malawi – he was teaching at a mission school there.

It's 1982. I am nine years old and Chris is twelve when my parents sit us down and tell us that they are going to France so that my dad can learn French, as he wants to serve as a missionary in the French-speaking African countries. My parents are able to do this because they know that they have a safe place to leave their children. Yes, you guessed it: KwaSizabantu. However, I will accompany them on this adventure because I'm ten years old and all the other kids at KSB are high-schoolers. (I think it helps that I'm the youngest, too.) Although my brother is only in his final year of junior school, he will stay behind. There's only room for one in this inn.

He'll be staying in the dormitory below the kitchen with the other boys. My sister is in a dormitory with the other high-school girls in the middle of the main building. Room 9, it's called. Right by the switchboard – some quite important people live along the corridors on either side of Room 9.

A short while before we're due to leave, however, my parents break the news to me that I will be staying behind after all. The two of them are going, and the three of us are staying behind at KSB. I don't remember being given a reason, but I'm devastated. I'm so little, and now I'm going to live in a dormitory with girls who are in high school.

I don't question my parents. If this is what my dad has decided, then it's the right thing, obviously. And it's obviously also God's will, because by now I've learned that God's will is the most important thing ever. When making any kind of plan, even if it's just what time you need to be somewhere, you have to add 'God willing'. I'll be having soup for supper, God willing. I'll do my homework when I get home, God willing. I'll see you on Sunday, God willing.

To make up for my disappointment, I am given new bedding. It's got a patchwork print and it's pink and white with lots of little flowers everywhere. My mother sews some curtains for me, because I'll be getting the bottom of a bunk bed. They're bright pink with delicate cream lace all around the edges. They're hung on white curtain wire that my dad stretches over the metal frame of the bed.

That first night in Room 9, after my parents depart, I close the curtains.

'Garrakachok,' I whisper to myself. It doesn't work – that night, I wet my bed. (Many decades later, my brother tells me that he wet his bed that first night, too.) It's the beginning of a pattern for me.

The shame is intense. Sometimes I am made to wash my bedding by hand. Punishment, I suppose. There is a very kind young woman living upstairs in Room 10. I'm not supposed to go into the room, but some nights I pop my head around the door and whisper her name. She always has a stash of clean, dry bedding for me, just in case. I whisper my thanks and go back down the stairs and make my bed, doing my utmost to be as quiet as possible.

The relationship between the three of us siblings breaks down pretty much completely. I can't speak for my sister, but I put myself in her shoes: she's in high school, and here's this kid who stinks up the dormitory with urine on a regular basis and is a complete embarrassment. I don't blame her for not knowing how to mother me. She isn't my mother.

I hardly ever see my brother and don't recall having meaningful conversations with him at all. In this place where our parents left us, boys and girls don't talk to each other. We're not allowed to. I'm sure KSB would counter this by saying that of course brothers and sisters were allowed to talk to one another, but that was not our reality. My brother and I sometimes see each other at breakfast and on the school bus, but boys and girls don't share seats, so we hardly exchange two words for weeks at a time.

I miss Patroon, too. We had to give her to another family in Estcourt when we moved here. With one or two exceptions, people don't have pets at KwaSizabantu, and there's no way the three of us, living the way we do, would be able to care for her.

Some of the older girls are kind to me, but I don't remember ever feeling seen. I do remember feeling absolute terror all the time. I don't know how to stop wetting my bed; I don't understand why this is happening to me. I stop drinking liquids at supper and I know that I need to go to the loo before I go to sleep. But to get from the dormitory to the bathrooms at the end of the building, I have to brave a cold, dark corridor on my own. And these are public toilets.

Even at that age, I hate public toilets. I hate public bathrooms. I'm a germaphobe, I always have been. Maybe it started here, who knows? I find it incredibly difficult to have to wash myself and go to the loo where I know lots of other people have been; where there is no cloth and detergent for me to clean the bath and toilet before I use them. Oh, the bathrooms and loos get cleaned, but usually only in the mornings.

I don't know how much of this contributes to my bed-wetting. Perhaps it's being abandoned by my parents in a place where there are no hugs. This is a community that frowns upon affection. There is no one to read my essays and tell me, 'Well done.' No one checks that I've done my homework. No one even checks that I am eating, although some of the bigger girls might notice if I don't turn up for breakfast, which we eat hours before everyone else because of the long bus ride – supper is a communal affair with the rest of the community.

I am bereft and alone and completely unimportant. I have not only lost my parents; I have lost my siblings, too.

As a group, we aren't left to our own devices, though. We are regularly called to meetings in Room 5 (down the corridor from Room 9) or the Upper Room (I'll tell you more about that awful place soon). In these meetings, we are told how evil we are. That we are sinners and that we are going to hell, and that if we don't confess our sins, if we die with one single unconfessed sin, we will go to hell for all eternity. Thinking about it now, this might have contributed to my wet sheets.

5

THE BURNING HELL

At KwaSizabantu in 1982, there are no radios, no TVs, no magazines. None that I know of, anyway. The outside world does not intrude here. At night, every single night, there is a church service we have to attend, where we may not fidget.

Some nights are movie nights. This is not as fun as it sounds. Everyone from babies to the elderly sit and watch these movies. When with the things of the world, age restrictions don't exist here either.

I am sitting next to my dad the first time I see the 1974 movie *The Burning Hell* – this is shortly before my parents leave for France. As the first people on screen scream as they fall into the flames of hell (some rebellion against Moses that got the earth to open up for them or something), my dad pulls me onto his lap and tucks my head into his shoulder. He averts my eyes from the screen because the horror is just … it's like nothing I've ever experienced. As he carries me out of the hall, pressing my head into his shoulder, I can still hear the screams and the wails and, I suppose, the gnashing of teeth.

But then my dad leaves for France and I'm on my own. The filmmaker depicts in graphic detail how he imagines people in hell are tortured. You see the flames all around them, the blood on their faces, and their eyes are wide and white as they stare and wail. You can hear the agony in their screams. And then maggots crawl out of their eyes and the guy who killed John the Baptist, he's in hell and he's crazed and he stands there shouting: 'He's still alive, he's still alive, but this time I'll kill him!' It's just agony and hatred. So much agony and so much hatred.

I'm not allowed to shut my eyes; I have to let the gruesomeness in. The savagery on screen teaches me what awaits me off screen if I don't follow the rules. This is what's going to happen to me if I do not obey them. As a nine-year-old child who grew up in a very protective home without a TV, I am not familiar with the concept of a movie being a mere depiction of an event. That what I see is not the truth, or someone's version of the truth, never crosses my mind. What I see is real. And it is terrifying.

I am a defenceless child and, to this day, I cannot watch horror movies. I find nothing entertaining about fear. They show us other movies, too. *If Footmen Tire You, What Will Horses Do?* teaches us about the awful and murderous communists. After premarital sex, communists are probably the worst evil in the world. They really hate Christians, whom they persecute and torture. Of course, the movie

17

depicts the torture. I don't think I will ever get the image out of my mind of a soldier forcing a bamboo stake through a boy's head from ear to ear, perforating his eardrums so he can't listen to the Gospel. 'You find this horrible?' the narrator asks, before warning that communists can do much worse things. They like to strip a Christian woman naked, he says, tie her head to one Jeep and her legs to another and tear her apart, limb from limb.

Oh, and there's *The Grim Reaper* as well. More terror and damnation. In one of the films, kids denounce their parents – I don't remember which movie, but I remember resolving to never do that. Not even if my parents go against God will I ever denounce them.

I later learn that other families, both friends and relations, offered to take us in while my parents were in France – they were not members of KSB, though. I guess my parents thought they were leaving us in the best possible hands, but I can't help wondering what life would have been like in a loving home with adults who cared about us. Not that I ever tell my parents how unhappy I've become. Neither does my brother, for that matter. If I were to tell them, I would be saying that my dad had made a mistake, that he shouldn't have left me here. And my dad knows best. He doesn't make mistakes. So, the fault lies with me.

We get to speak to my parents every now and again on the phone, and after a while my dad asks me: 'Erika, why aren't you writing to me any more? What's going on?' But I can't tell him that I don't know what to write because I am so desperately unhappy. It pains me that he maybe thinks I don't write because I don't care about him or I don't miss him. That is so far from the truth. I don't write because I don't have the words for what is happening to me. I might not be burning, but I am in hell.

6

SCHOOL SAVES ME

School is my escape. At school I can pretend to be normal, and I soon make lots of friends. I'm in Standard 4 at Stanger Primary. A bit of a teacher's pet, because I am that little girl who is always bright and cheerful and knows the answers to everything. I am charming and sweet and so desperate for attention that I actively participate in class. My hand goes up for every question. Pick me, ask me! Please!

I'm popular at school. I'm in the Afrikaans class, but I play with the English girls. I remember my teacher writing to my parents to tell them that I was the first girl who got the English and Afrikaans girls to play together. I'm a natural leader, and so I blossom at school. And I get really good at pretending everything is okay 'back at home', because I don't know who to tell or how to say that it's not. I'm ten years old; I don't have the tools for that.

There's a boy in my class, Thinus. I'm not allowed to talk to boys. I'm not allowed to like boys. But no one from KSB is in my class, so they don't have eyes on me when I'm at school. They don't know that we call ourselves ET – Erika and Thinus. Not that I've seen the movie *E.T.*, but I know that there is a movie called *E.T.* and that everyone is talking about it.

You can't call what Thinus and I have a romance: it is sweet and innocent and lovely, and yet entirely forbidden. I don't think we even held hands. I remember this friendship in particular because it was so illicit, and I knew that I would be in serious trouble if anyone found out I spent any time at all with a boy. (Thinus, if you're reading this, thank you. Your friendship helped me feel normal and that someone cared about me.)

Reading is another escape, and that is what keeps me alive. I visit the school library every afternoon because the junior school finishes before the high school and the bus doesn't depart until we're all out. I take out two books every day. I know how unlikely that sounds, but I'm a fast reader and I have many dead hours to kill. The librarian becomes my best friend; she knows I read two books a day, like clockwork. I read a book on the way back in the bus, then I read at night and finish the second book on the way to school the next morning.

Here's the one good thing about the lack of supervision. If I don't flaunt the books, no one checks what I read. I read all of Enid Blyton. I read the Hardy Boys. I devour Nancy Drew – she's so strong, so brave, so clever! I want to be her so badly and go on adventures and solve mysteries. Instead, every afternoon, I get on the bus and go back to hell.

7

JESSIE LEARNS A LESSON

Fear. What an inadequate word for what we experienced. If I were to write *Starting a Cult for Dummies*, a huge section would be devoted to how to instil fear. And there would be an entire chapter or three on public beatings. They're an excellent tool for controlling your followers.

I've made a friend at the mission. Let's call her Jessie. It's not her real name, but it's a name I love. And I love her too, so it feels appropriate to call her that. She doesn't go to my school, but her parents live at the mission and we sometimes play together in the afternoon. Well, I don't know about 'play' exactly, but we're sometimes together. Come to think of it, I don't actually recall playing per se – I don't really know how I whiled away the time when I wasn't reading or in a church service. Or in the Upper Room.

I guess that room got its name because you have to climb a set of stairs to get to it. Or maybe because it is grandiose. Also, 'The Upper Room' sounds like the kind of place where you'd have 'The Last Supper' if you were modelling yourself on Jesus and his disciples. The floor is carpeted. I know, because I sit on that floor quite often. There is another room next to it that is tiled, but I don't remember going in there very often. The room is supposed to be a meeting place. The co-workers – that's what the upper echelon of this community call themselves – regularly meet here. They're adults, though. When the kids are called in, you know there's trouble.

We get summoned there when someone has done something wrong and they are going to be punished. Or simply denounced, if they're lucky. The Upper Room fills me with terror. I have to force myself up those stairs because I know that whatever's waiting behind that door is not going to be pleasant. Every single time, I fervently hope that I'm not the wrongdoer.

For some or other reason, on this particular day there's quite a gathering of people at the mission. Jessie sees another girl put some toffees in a suitcase. It's the daughter of one of KSB's leaders. This girl and a bunch of others leave to go to the shop. Jessie can't join them, because she has not a single cent. She seldom has any money to buy sweets. Her parents aren't part of KSB's elite, and so they are desperately poor. KSB gets all their labour and they get a roof over their heads and communal meals. Lucky them. They certainly don't have money for Jessie to buy Wilson's Champion toffees. Jessie loves Wilson's Champion toffees.

And so she goes over to the suitcase and helps herself to some toffees that don't belong to her. Jessie is only seven or eight years old. She knows stealing is wrong, that it's a sin, but stealing is also only still a concept to her. This other girl has lots of stuff. Lots of toffees. She's even gone to the shops to buy more.

What Jessie doesn't know is that there is another girl in the room, lying on her bed, who sees this happening. And she snitches on Jessie. Don't be too harsh on this girl. She has been taught that it's her duty to snitch. If you know of a sin that someone else has committed and you keep quiet, you are as guilty as they are and as destined for eternal damnation to boot. Many of the services they hold with kids are for the sole purpose of getting us to snitch on one another. The snitching culture is huge. KwaSnitchabantu.

This is what brings us to the Upper Room today. An adult takes the floor. Let's call her Jenny, because that is her real name and she is still there. (In 2020, Jenny will testify at a commission convened to investigate human rights abuses at KSB. She will say that KSB is a wonderful place, filled with only good people, and that any allegations of abuse are lies.)

I'm prevaricating, because what happens next is simply too awful. There is a piece of orange plumbing pipe that the adults use to beat us kids. Jenny brandishes the pipe. 'No,' she declares. This sin is too grievous to warrant a 'simple' beating. She softly gives an instruction to a man we'll call David, because that is his real name, too. (May he rest in peace.) Jenny places the orange pipe on the banister and David disappears down the stairs. He returns holding a large butcher's knife.

'The Bible teaches us that thieves get their hands cut off,' Jenny pontificates. I have turned to ice. This cannot be happening. My friend is going to lose a hand. Maybe both hands.

'Choose,' Jenny commands, looking at my friend. 'The knife or the pipe.'

Neither Jessie nor I can remember what she said, or even if she spoke at all.

Today, more than forty years later, Jessie doesn't remember the beating that ensued. Her brother does. As do I. We remember it well. She was given a savage beating, the adults impervious to her screams. I am forced to look at her. I am not allowed to look away and I am not allowed to cry. I am not allowed to show any emotion at all. Because if I do, I will be next.

In a way, perhaps it's good that Jessie doesn't remember. This is what terror and trauma do. They leave black holes in your memory. Jessie dissociates, because staying inside her body is too unbearable.

Don't confuse these beatings with the hidings you might have got as a kid. I got hidings from my parents; sometimes they used their bare hands, sometimes a stokie slipper. These beatings are something else. One adult holds down the child's upper body or arms on the floor and another holds down the legs, while a third administers the beating. And it carries on and on. This is not 'six of the best'. It's a sustained assault on a minor child. I am so terrified of this happening to me that I become a little shadow who never warrants a second look. As a result, as far as I remember, I never get beaten in public – I am way too scared to ever do anything wrong. I can get away with talking to a boy at school, but I'm not going to do that here.

I get good at deception – especially because I fake normalcy at school and pretend everything is okay back at KSB. I am ten years old, what recourse do I have? I have no choice but to believe all the threats of damnation I am fed on a daily basis. I live with fear for so long that I sometimes think it has played a bigger part in forming who I am than my parents ever did. They left to go and learn French so that they could save people, when the people who needed saving the most were their three children.

THE LIFE THAT COULD HAVE BEEN MINE

My parents are at a language school in Albertville, learning French with a bunch of American missionaries. And these Americans are appalled at the thought that my parents left their three children behind. They are simply appalled. And so they get together and raise enough money for all of us to fly to France for Christmas.

We fly on Sabena airlines, and because we're all minors, the staff treat us like royalty. I haven't felt special in a while, so I lap it all up. We fly via Joburg, Kinshasa and Brussels and land in Geneva (the closest airport). There are my parents. My dad envelops me in a hug and I feel so, so safe.

What an amazing time we have. Thank you, America! I still have photographs of us sledding in the snow. Albertville is surrounded by mountains and we frolic and have so much fun. It's the first time I see snow and it's just unspeakably wonderful. My mother, my sister and I are the only people on the slopes wearing skirts, of course, but I have so much fun, it doesn't even bother me.

My parents take us into the language laboratories where they wear headphones through which they hear a phrase that they then have to repeat. One photograph shows me in the lab in a red turtleneck – the headphones are almost as big as my head, but there is happiness and joy beaming from my smile. I am entranced and start my lifelong love affair with the melodious sounds of the French language.

I love walking with my dad to the bakery in the mornings to buy a steaming-hot baguette. The Americans' generosity doesn't end with plane tickets. They book us into a cabin in the Swiss mountains, too. This could have been my life, I think. I could have been here with them. The grief I feel is intense, but I don't let on.

Christmas lunch is an educational affair. We are in France, after all. Everyone is gathered in the festively decorated dining room and all goes well until the plated main course arrives. There, lying on my plate, is an intact dead bird, its unseeing eye staring up into the void. I later find out that quail is a delicacy in France. My dad saves the day by removing the head and advising me to think of it as chicken. I like chicken and I love my dad and I don't want to embarrass him in front of all these people, so I tuck in. Dessert makes up for it – an ice-cream log that is beautifully decorated and sliced. Now, *that* I'm happy to devour.

The few weeks with my parents are a necessary reprieve, reminding me that I am loved, that I do matter. I return in January 1983 with a heavy heart, sad to say goodbye to them and filled with dread for having to head back to hell.

A CHILD'S DESPAIR

I wrote this piece, titled 'Just hold on a moment', in January 2003 – when I still felt very, very lost. I'd just come back to South Africa from a long stint overseas and had no idea where I was going to live or what I was going to do. I was staying with my friend's mother in Sedgefield, my second mother, Sheila. A British guy who liked me and thought he wanted to marry me had accompanied me back home. One day he overheard me chatting to my friend about something, I can't remember what. Afterwards, he sat me down and told me that I really needed to put my past behind me. Let it go once and for all. I was so taken aback and so very angry – he didn't know that much about me, as back then I only shared a select few details of my past with certain people. I understand today that he was just trying to help.

But I was livid. He just didn't get it. So I thought I would help him understand that 'letting go' is not at all simple. And that it's what I'd been trying to do. I sat down and over the next three days wrote him this. I don't remember ever giving it to him to read; we broke up shortly thereafter. This is the me in 2003 writing about the me stranded at KSB as a little girl. That young-adult version of me was closer emotionally to the girl child of the 1980s than the current version of me (who is a lot older and wiser), which is why I don't want to rewrite this as I am now. So here it is, raw and entirely untouched ...

I cannot put the past behind me for the past is living right inside me.

It is in the past where my character and my responses were formed.

And I get so angry when people tell me that I must move on. What do they think I've been doing for the last ten years? So please don't tell me to let go of the past. It is like telling someone on life support that they should try and breathe by themselves. Think they don't know that? Of course they bloody do. And I can guarantee you they've been trying. So have I. And succeeded to a large extent. Had I not done that, would I be where I am today?

It is fairly easy to let go of stuff that happened to me – what is not easy is to let go of the decisions I made about myself, the world and the people in the world as a result of that stuff happening to me.

I have come so far along this road already, and I won't be treated as someone who cannot let go of her past. Or as someone who is unwilling to face up to her problems. Or as someone who refuses to deal with issues – that is something I've been doing all my life. And when I say I am tired of struggling, it is because I really am tired. All the more because I know that it is not over yet, and may never be. And no, I am not indulging in self-pity, this is my reality. That's something I don't think anybody in my life really gets. I do battle with myself all the time. There is no respite. I know that my instincts and internal responses are not appropriate for my life now, but I do not have the tools to change them in an instant. It's a process. I know that I am not alone – I read books that other survivors have written. It gives me hope. But I also know that few people in my world have really and truly suffered and that is why I do not feel comfortable opening up. I do not trust them with my innermost thoughts precisely because they say things such as 'you should really let go of your past'. They display such ignorance in these matters (and lucky them that they are ignorant, I don't begrudge them that) that I do not feel I can portray my despair for fear that they will belittle it with trite phrases.

There is no doubt that the experiences I went through as a child have an impact on me still. But this is true for everybody on the planet. Take a moment to think of a nine-year-old child you know. Then think how they would cope if their parents left them without any warning in a place where they were told daily that they were evil and going to hell and a place where there was nobody to love them or hug them or congratulate them on their performance at school. That this child would survive is a given. The human spirit is awesome in its capacity to withstand hardship. That there would be mental scars and reper-cussions far into the child's life is also for sure.

Let us go a little further with our young child. In order to cope in this foreign, hostile world in which she suddenly finds herself, she would need to withdraw into herself. She is taught that everything human is a sin. Even friendship. For if she knows of a friend's sin and doesn't confess it (i.e. report it) then she is as guilty as her friend. So all friends are treated (after two or three times of her confidences being reported and she being punished as a result) with suspicion. She soon treats anybody who asks her how she is doing as someone who is trying to trip her up so that she'll reveal where and when she sinned.

In this particular environment, our child is correct in treating everyone with suspicion, for everybody there has lost touch with reality and blindly follows orders. We see that this child is starved of affection and recognition – as any other child would be. And we see how she gradually builds up a wall between herself and the world – feigning happiness and never complaining about any-thing. All her support structures have been taken away from her and she relies only on herself to make it through each day. Her older sister treats her as any other older sister would treat a younger sister: at times tolerating her, but mostly ignoring her. As for her brother, she only rarely sees him at school – back at the place she is now forced to call home, boys and girls (even siblings) are not allowed to be together. But through it all she stays fiercely loyal to the parents who abandoned her. Never telling anyone her plight, above all not her dad for she does not wish to distress him.

And this is how our little girl learns that she cannot trust anyone – a good thing because she really shouldn't trust anyone there. Being on the lookout for betrayal and masking her true feelings become her focus. As they should. She's living her life in a concentration camp where the other children are potential informers and the adults (the guards on whom her life depends) could turn at any moment and inflict whatever punishment they choose for any perceived misdemeanour. And no, this is not being melodramatic – any survivor of a cult will confirm that all-pervasive fear that rules every action you take, every decision you make.

The defence mechanisms she adopts are very appropriate for her. And because she is so very young, these defence mechanisms become part of her makeup, part of her character. Soon she cannot distinguish between who she really is and who she has had to become in order to survive. And now she's an adult with these self-same mechanisms holding her back.

I have just described my first few months at the KwaSizabantu Mission. My association with that dehumanising place lasted thirteen years. Thirteen years of confirming everything I learned in those first few months. It took tremendous courage to leave. It has taken courage to carry on. I could so easily have slipped into an easy life, not challenging myself, never daring to try and better myself. But that is not what I chose. I chose to face my demons, do battle with myself, and find out what makes me tick. Because I know that then I'll be in a position to help others. Help other children who were forced to give up themselves and their power in the same way that I was.

Right, we left our little girl in a concentration camp masquerading as a mission station. Its name, KwaSizabantu, is Zulu for 'The place where people are helped'. It should really be called the place where personalities are destroyed. It's nestled in the Valley of a Thousand Hills, in my mind the Valley of a Thousand Ills.

(It is hard to explain what went on there. So much of it is so alien to normal life that I run the risk of not being believed. And yet when I meet with someone else who grew up there and has left, I realise that I do remember events accurately and sometimes even get reminded of things that I had forgotten about. So suspend your disbelief for just a little while – such people really do exist.)

Day-to-day life consisted of getting up, eating breakfast, getting on the bus for a two-hour journey to get to school (and on the bus she had to sing hymns with the other children and if she didn't, then she was seen to not want to be part of the group, which meant that she did not want to do God's will, which meant that she was bad and a sinner, which meant that she would receive some sort of punishment. And no, people from the outside don't really get that 'logic' either.). Every now and again she managed to pretend she was sleeping, but only got away with this occasionally. When the older children were writing exams, that was the best time because then she got to read on the bus. The librarian at school knew her very well because she took out two books every day to read – fortunately the primary-school library stayed open until the high-school kids came out. She had nothing else to do. Schoolwork was no challenge and her homework was usually completed long before she got onto the bus back home.

Home. It still feels wrong to call it that.

And then when she got home (for lack of another word – isn't home the place where you go to after school? The fact that she didn't feel safe or loved there did not make a difference back then, so we'll just continue calling it home for the sake of this narrative). After she got back home till the next morning when she got back on the bus, our little girl's memory lets her down. Despite the fact that she was between the ages of nine and eleven at this stage, she cannot remember much of what went on there at all.

She remembers that there were regular meetings where children were denounced for their sins. She remembers the terror when one of the other girls had been caught stealing sweets and the adults held her down – one with a big knife in his hand and threatened to cut off her hand. The terrifying thing is that our little girl believed they were capable of doing that and she would not have questioned their right to cut off a child's hand. Because they would not do anything that was not God's will. That is how warped her idea of God, of humans had become. She believed them capable of such a horrible thing – cutting off the hand of an eight-year-old child for stealing sweets – and she would have believed it to be the will of God. That is one of the few memories our little girl has. Small surprise really that she does not remember the incidents she hears about now – perhaps she was there when it happened, but she does not remember how they stuffed bits of toilet paper between a boy's toes (who knows what sin he had committed, maybe swearing, maybe lying?) and then lighting those pieces of paper so that the boy could get a taste of what hellfire would be like.

Can you imagine the terror they instilled by such tactics? Our little girl (and all the other children there) were terrorised into obedience. Can you even imagine what that does to the human spirit? No wonder that her memory fails her when she tries to remember that time. No wonder that the one image she manages to conjure up is cold, dark corridors. That is what that time is to her – cold, dark corridors.

There was nowhere for our little girl to go. She had no resources of her own. She was a child, for god's sake. She couldn't even make a call or post a letter without someone's permission. This is the place her parents left her. She could ask nobody for help and this is most likely where she decided that she was on her own and could not count on help from anyone. Here she is, twenty years later and she'd still rather suffer than ask anyone for help. Not rational, she knows, but something deep inside her rebels when she wants to cry for help. She just cannot. She hates that about herself, hates the fact that twenty years down the line they still control her because she still responds in the way they conditioned her to respond. And then you wonder why she considers herself weak.

I don't presume to own the human emotions. I mentioned that I don't feel that people who haven't suffered can really understand me. But I acknowledge that hurt has no measure. And nobody can judge another's suffering. I also don't want to negate what anybody else has gone through. I just wish to adequately paint the picture of my experiences and thereby hopefully uncover some keys to unlocking the door with which I keep the world at bay.

How can I trust my feelings when I don't even know what they are? It is usually only in retrospect that I can express how I think I felt at any particular time. Ask me in the moment what I am feeling and I will be unable to answer you. I just do not know.

Perhaps it is because there is always the underlying feeling of fear – it could be that that overrides everything. Could be. I think it is more likely because I was denied the right to feel emotions such as anger and irritation and infatuation and lust. Forbidden to feel certain things resulted in a denial of all of my feelings. And so numbness set in. And because I was not allowed to feel or even name certain things, I stopped acknowledging any feeling whatsoever.

Let me tell you about these people that populate the mission. People who feed off the fear of children. Men and women (but mostly men) who grow more powerful with each person they coerce into submission. Men and women who engulf and enmesh others – themselves so weak that their survival depends upon the humiliation and obliteration of others.

I am not sure that I want to continue writing any further. I have never before dared to properly revisit and dwell in that specific time. And I have never felt it fair to burden anyone with this either. I'm writing it down but feel frustrated because I can't manage to convey the true horror of that place. And I'm only a little way into my story – I still have ten years to go – ten awful, awful years. Maybe now you can start to see why it is that I've never really wanted to let anyone close.

I'm not sure what I'll find inside me – what if they managed to instil something of themselves in me? I'm sure you would say that is not the case, but I have so many doubts. Doubts I cannot even articulate yet. But I fear that I carry them inside me and that if someone gets too close they will see that evil inside me that I don't even know is there.

I'm going to stop writing for now. There is so much, I don't even really know where to go from here. It is like there's a huge, deep lake, and I am diving from the side to try and retrieve pieces of a puzzle, but I don't know which area of the lake to start diving in and I don't know how many years I'm going to have to dive before I find all the pieces. I don't even know how many pieces there are. Maybe I'll just run out of oxygen.

10

A NEW BEGINNING

In July 1983, my mother comes back home after ten months, while my dad spends another three months in Switzerland. He sends us a postcard from there – a map of the country in which he's pricked a tiny hole to show exactly where he is, so when I hold it up against the light, I can place his whereabouts.

My mother moves into the mission. Neither my brother nor I can remember whether we moved in with her when she came back or stayed in our respective dormitories. But after my dad's return, we all move to Johannesburg, where he will work for Open Doors Mission. On our way, we stop at Estcourt and pick up Patroon from the family who has been looking after her. She's in the backyard and starts barking when she hears my dad's voice. He opens the door and her whole body wags as she runs to him. I don't know who is happier to be reunited, Patroon, my dad or us kids.

Happiness! We move into a four-bedroomed home on the corner of Kenneth Gardens Road and Botha Avenue in Kibler Park, one of Joburg's southern suburbs. Open Doors Mission is not at all affiliated with KwaSizabantu. I remember my dad's colleagues as kind, utterly lovely and genuine people. The organisation describes itself as a non-denominational mission supporting persecuted Christians all over the world. They work with local partners to distribute Bibles and Christian literature, give discipleship training and provide practical support, such as emergency relief aid.

My dad is back, and I'm safe again. It's the most wonderful feeling in the world. We're back in a family home. The five of us, together again. We're still walking – my dad walks to work, I walk to school. Chris and Hanna take the bus, as the high school is way too far to walk.

I watch for my dad every afternoon. Just after four, I see him walking down the street and I run out to meet him. Without fail, he picks me up and swings me around and around and around. It's a joyous cap to every weekday. His new job takes him into countries where South Africans aren't supposed to be in the 1980s. Mozambique, Madagascar and Angola are all under communist rule. White South Africans are not welcome at all. Because my dad was born in Kenya, he has a British passport. So, for example, when he goes to Mozambique, he flies to Malawi and then crosses the Shire River in a mokoro. To get to Madagascar, he goes via Swaziland, Maputo and Réunion.

After one trip, I overhear the adults talking and find out that he'd been captured by some soldiers in Mozambique. I am a child, so they shield me from most of the dangers of his job. I remember clearly, though, that every time we take him to the airport in our white station wagon, we don't know if he's coming back, as he is putting his life in danger.

He goes to these countries to meet with Christians, take them Bibles and tell them that the world hasn't forgotten them. He comes home from one trip to Mozambique with only the clothes he is wearing – he's given the rest away. He weeps as he shows us what he's brought back: a pair of pants and a vest made of tree bark. It is rough and must have chafed the wearer's skin. They have nothing, he tells us, his voice breaking.

The next time we visit KSB, which is just about every school holiday, he takes the vest along and Erlo shows it to the whole congregation one Sunday. This is what communists do, Erlo thunders from the pulpit. If we let them take over South Africa, this is what you and your children will be wearing, he warns.

It is while my father is on one of his trips that my class teacher, Mr Louw, pulls me aside. He needs to speak to my parents, he tells me. I'm in my final year of junior school, at Danie Theron Primary, just up the road from our house. I like it there. It's almost like a farm school that's been transported onto the outskirts of the city: we're allowed to go to school barefoot if we want. I often do, though not in winter, of course.

A few weeks before this, we did IQ and aptitude tests – I guess to help guide us in our subject choice when we get to high school. Mr Louw says he has fantastic news for me. There is this school for highly gifted children and they want to meet me. Mr Louw has seen how unchallenged I am by the schoolwork and has contacted the school on my behalf. He says that they may be prepared to offer me a scholarship if the fees are a problem.

He accompanies me home that afternoon. My mother is polite, but firmly tells him no. I'm astounded that she doesn't ask him to wait until my dad returns. She makes this decision on the spot. Erika will get a big head, she tells him. She's nothing special, so no. I wonder what Mr Louw thinks. I feel so ashamed. He is trying to do something good for me, something I suddenly want with all my heart, but no. After he leaves, my mother sits me down and tells me that if I achieve anything, it's because God is working through me, not because I am clever or special. That lesson is starting to sink in, don't worry, Mother.

Despite this, the overarching feeling is that I'm safe. My dad is here most of the time and I'm safe. Every Sunday, we drive to Krugersdorp, to Waldemar Engelbrecht's house. He is the head honcho of KwaSizabantu in the Joburg area. People from all over Johannesburg and Pretoria gather at his house every week to hear him preach. We squash into his lounge, and fortunately his sermons aren't as long as those at KSB. Afterwards, it's lovely when we all have tea and sandwiches. We also visit Waldemar once a week for an evening service. After the long services I'm used to, these are a breeze.

Later, as the congregation expands, we are given use of a church in Doorn-fontein on Sundays. It's here where I watch my dad participate in one of their 'fire services' out in the yard. It's a practice started during the Revival, when people who wanted to be set free from demonic control would bring items relating to witchcraft or anything else that took their focus off God to be burned. Books, TVs, clothing, tapes, you name it. If it's evil, it burns. It's weird for me to see my dad throwing books into the flames. At home, we've always been taught that books are sacred. You don't ever put a cup of tea or a glass of water on top of a book. Books are to be treasured. Today, they're being burned.

I don't remember being unhappy in this time. When my parents went over-seas, they gave KSB all their furniture. But there must have been some pieces they'd specified they'd like back again. My father's piano for one.

My dad was the youngest of six children. His mother sold eggs and kept some of that money aside to buy him a piano when he was a young boy. All she asked in return was that he play her a song every evening before she went to bed. The piano travels everywhere with us. It's heavy because its strings are encased in metal. The piano is made of dark-brown wood and features some carvings in the front. There are two copper candelabras on each side of the music rack, where you place your sheet music, because this piano dates back to pre-electricity days – that's how old it is. The ivories are not white any more, but they're proper ivory, slightly yellowed with age. This piano in our home is a testament to his mother. She died when he was only nineteen years old and he speaks of her with such love. I wish I could have met my grandmother.

That piano is one of two things that symbolise my childhood. The second is the bush of yellow daisies my dad always plants outside our front door whenever we move into a new house.

11

THE MISFIT

I'm not wearing my school uniform today. It's civvies day! I get on the bus with my siblings for the ten-kilometre drive to Hoërskool President, where I started high school in January 1985. Already on the bus, I notice kids looking at me. It gets worse when I get to school. It's still early in the year so I haven't really got to know everyone in my class, but I most certainly feel like I'm the person most stared at that day. The other girls are wearing jeans or short skirts – they all look really pretty. I'm dressed in standard KSB attire: a skirt that covers my knees, sleeves that cover my upper arms. Sedate. Modest. Everything most teenagers try so hard not to be.

Here, in high school, I am suddenly very, very different from the other kids. Way different. I still make friends, though, because that's who I am. That time at KSB didn't manage to break my spirit completely, and I'm blossoming because I'm back with my dad. My dad calls me '*die familie se kurkproppie*' (the family's little cork) because, he says, no matter what happens to me, I'm like a cork that, when pushed underwater, just bounces straight back up time and again. You can't keep Erika under, he says.

I have two parents. The one tells me that I'm special, believes in me, celebrates my wins with me. The other tells me I'm nothing special, any achievement of mine is God working through me, calls me out if I spend too long in front of the mirror. 'Are you titivating yourself again, Erika?' I know which parent I want to believe.

Because both my parents are so scared of evil influences, I'm not allowed to sleep over at a friend's house. I'm most definitely not allowed to go to any parties. So my interactions with my friends take place mainly at school. I don't want to invite them home; I don't want them to realise that we're weird. I don't have that much in common with them – there's always a lot of talk about what happened last night on TV, and I'm completely in the dark there. Luckily, there are some girls who are quite happy to hang out with the little misfit that I am. I do my best to fit in, but sometimes I fail miserably. Especially when we're not dressed in our school uniforms.

One day, in lowered voices, my friends discuss making babies. There's lots of sniggering and giggling as they talk about what they know. I remain silent. I know absolutely nothing, and I know this is dirty talk and I should walk away, but I can't. One girl says something about the man sticking something into the woman's hole.

'What hole?' I blurt out before I can stop myself.

'You know, the one down there,' one says, as the others shake their heads at my ignorance.

'Ah, that one,' I nod, feigning understanding. But I don't understand. Women have a hole? Where? How? What? Do I have a hole?

I figure this must have something to do with the conversation I had with my mother when I was around eleven years old. She had called me to their room, never a good sign. She had prayed, an even worse sign. When my mother prays before having a conversation with me, I know I'm in trouble. I don't know what I've done wrong, but I've done something wrong. I'm probably going to get a hiding now.

But no, not that day. That day my mother wanted to know if I ever play with myself down there. Down where? You know, there, where you are not supposed to touch yourself. No, I assured her. I don't touch myself down there, so how can I play there? I am baffled, but grateful that I can tell her what she clearly wants to hear. Good, she told me. Make sure you never do, because then you will burn in hell for all eternity.

I'm really puzzled. The hole they're talking about, if girls have them as well as women, must be down there, where I'm not allowed to play. I can't ask for clarification – they obviously all know what they're talking about and I can't show them I don't belong with them. I can't ask my mother or my sister either.

My sister says she was about ten years old when our mother informed her about sex. She says our mother gave her a book with very clear diagrams and information. My dear sister was lucky she turned ten before our mother came under the spell of KSB. I got nothing, nada, zero, zip. Shortly after this conversation with my friends, I notice a brownish-red stain in my panties one day. I don't know what it is, but it doesn't look good. It's there again the next day, and then it goes away. I sigh with relief. On both days, I wash my panties by hand – I'm scared my mother will think I soiled them by not wiping my bum properly. Even though I know that's not it.

It happens again, of course, sometime later. Now I'm seriously worried. I have stomach cancer, I decide. I'm going to die. And I'm probably going to hell because I know that I am not a good girl. The other day, we had a movie day at school and everyone had to bring R2 or R5 to school to pay for the privilege. I had lied to my parents about why I needed the money because I knew they would never allow me to watch a movie with this Mr Bond everyone was talking about. And I watched the movie with all my classmates. I sinned. God is punishing me with stomach cancer, and I'm going to die and spend all eternity in hell. I furiously scrub my panties in the bath. And then, the cancer disappears. Whew. God has decided to punish me another day.

This carries on for some time. I'm not sure how many months I get my period without knowing what it is. One day, my mother comes into the bathroom while I'm scrubbing away the cancer. She calls me to their room a little later. And yes, prays. Then she hands me a pack of sanitary pads and tells me that the 'cancer' is actually blood. You are having your period and it's going to happen once a month and it's normal and you must put a pad in your panties when it happens. I still don't know what's happening to me, but at least now I know it's called a period. (And that, dear sister, was the extent of the sex education I was given by our mother.)

We are pretty well educated in other aspects, though, and each has a good general knowledge that stands us in good stead at school. No TV, so we read a lot – in Worcester, in Estcourt and in Joburg, we visit the library every single weekend and borrow however many books each one of us is allowed. Back home, my parents vet each book and give it their approval. Or take it away if they don't approve. We whizz through the books we bring home and then share them around for the rest of the week until our next library visit.

There are ways to get around my parents' censorship, of course. They can't control what I read inside the school library during breaks. And one of my friends from school, Bernadette, is also an avid reader. She loans me books that I smuggle home and secretly read at night. I have a failproof plan, I figure. I sit up in bed, knees raised, with an open book balanced on top of my knees. This one is a book that is allowed. Against my raised thighs I have the other, forbidden, book. When I detect someone walking down the corridor, I quickly slam the top book over the other one and pretend to be reading that instead. The top book is always bigger than the one below it, I make sure of that.

Until one day, I'm not quick enough. My dad walks into my room. What's that second book, Erika, he asks. I burst into tears as I hand it to him. It's *Rich Man, Poor Man* by Irwin Shaw. My dad looks at the book, looks at me, looks back at the book. I have let my dad down; his disappointment feels much worse than my punishment. I don't remember if I get the hiding before or after one of my parents drives me to Bernadette's house that evening to return the book. One more layer of my facade to my friends has cracked.

I persist, though. Bernadette brings me Mills & Boon books now, innocent ones, just love stories. They're much smaller than Shaw's tome and much, much easier to hide. I can even sneak one into my pyjamas as I make my way to the bath.

One day, tragedy strikes. Patroon by now is an old dog. The family that looked after her in Estcourt didn't allow dogs inside the home, and so my mother decrees that that is how it should continue. Patroon is allowed in the kitchen, but not the rest of the house. Sometimes, when my mother isn't home, my dad breaks this rule. We can tell that Patroon is going a little blind and a little deaf. One day I don't go to school, as I'm not feeling well. I suddenly hear a woman wailing outside. Patroon had walked out in front of a bus and this is a bystander who witnessed the incident, now looking for Patroon's owners. I don't remember if my dad is home or if my mother calls him (his office isn't very far away), but I see him weeping as he cradles Patroon in his arms, taking her around the house to the back. When Chris comes home from school that afternoon, he digs her grave and buries her under one of the fruit trees in the backyard.

I don't recall my parents talking to us about death, not Patroon's or anyone else's. I do remember two funerals in Montagu when I was little: those of my grandfather and his brother. But we kids stayed on the farm while the adults buried the dead; I don't think we even went to the church services.

And so our life continues without Patroon. A friend's mother offers me a kitten, but my mother says no. I'm heartbroken that I'm not allowed to keep her – my sister had a kitten for a while, Katotjie, but she didn't live long, so I don't understand why I can't keep this little ball of fluff. My mother knows there are other plans afoot, of course. Because, one day towards the end of 1986, my dad sits us down. We're moving to KwaSizabantu, he announces.

Oh, no, please God, please, no! He's going to be principal of the school they've just opened – one of the country's first multiracial schools (we're still in the apartheid days, remember) – and I will attend, too. Chris will stay with family friends in Joburg as he's about to enter his final year of school and they've elected him prefect, so it makes no sense for him to be disrupted now. My sister has been awarded a bursary by Iscor, now ArcelorMittal, to study metallurgical engineering at the Pretoria Technikon, and so will also remain up north.

Unlike the French sojourn, when I was meant to go with my parents but then didn't, this time I know I will be joining them for sure. I'm going back to hell, with my parents. But it will be different, I tell myself. This time Pappa will protect me. He won't let them hurt me. It'll be okay.

PART TWO

THE SHRINKING TEENAGER

12

MY WORLD ENDS

I am fifteen years old when my entire existence collapses.

The day before it happens, my dad returns from Pretoria, after settling Hanna in for her first year of studies. I'd eaten a mango earlier that day, the way he'd taught me, sucking all the flesh and juices off the pip. The dried pip looks like a bearded wizard, so I let it dry completely and draw a face on it. A silly gift to give him when he returns. Which he does, without me knowing. I walk into the room and he's hiding behind the door and he jumps out at me. I get such a fright that I start crying. He instantly feels bad. He holds me and says he's sorry, over and over again.

Later that day, KSB calls him in and tells him they no longer want him to be principal of their new multiracial Domino Servite School. He is being demoted to a teacher. Because, I discover later, he won't go along with their policies. He had been so excited at the prospect of being put in charge of this new, pioneering school. I can only imagine his disappointment at having it so cruelly ripped away. Has he seen the darkness in the place he thought was light? Is that what he stood up against?

That night, it rains. No, it storms. Our rondavel is at the bottom, in the last row, and the water streaming past starts seeping under the door. We have to block it up to hold the water back. It feels like an adventure. Pappa says he'll fix it in the morning. Then we sit on the bed and sing the French hymn he loves so much: '*Quand les montagnes s'éloigneraient, Quand les collines chancelleraient, mon amour ne s'éloignera point de toi.*'[1]

And then he talks to me about my subject choice. School is starting tomorrow, the beginning of my Standard 8 year, and I have to choose six subjects. Maths and science, naturally, given my dad's background. I have a deep love for history, so that's a given. English and Afrikaans are compulsory. We debate whether the sixth should be biology or geography. My dad favours biology, but I can't face the thought of dissecting a frog. So we settle on geography, even though Pappa warns me that if I ever want to be a doctor, I need biology. I can't imagine ever cutting anyone open, so that's not a problem.

I'm going to do AdMaths as well, as a seventh subject, with my dad as my

---

1. 'Though the mountains be shaken and the hills be removed, my unfailing love for you will not be shaken.'

teacher. I got an A+ for maths at the end of Standard 7. We both know I won't find it at all difficult. I'm looking forward to calculus and trigonometry. I'm a star pupil and I'm so excited about having Pappa teach me.

We talk about what I'll study after school. I want to be an actuary. Statistics and predictions. I can't imagine anything better. My dad asks me if I won't get bored not working with people. He knows me so well.

The next morning, Pappa finds a shovel and starts digging a trench to divert the water away from our door. Together, we pick the spot where he'll plant the yellow daisy bush. Mamma asks me to do the laundry. I carry the basket up the hill to the bathrooms to do the washing by hand. I'm a skinny little kid and some of the clothes are difficult to wring out. I take my time. The basket of wet clothes is too heavy for me to carry, so I run down the hill to ask Pappa to come and help me.

Uncle Kjell passes me, running. Uncle Trevor passes me, also running. As does Uncle Fano. I don't know where they're going in such a hurry. When I get down to our rondavel, there are a few people milling about. Doctor Albu arrives, out of breath. Uncle Friedel, one of Uncle Erlo's four brothers, stops me from going in. He says Pappa is not feeling well. I explain to him about the laundry and he sends someone with me to help carry it down. I proceed to hang the clothes on the washing line behind our hut, carefully, the way I've been taught, to make ironing easier.

There is a flurry of activity out front and I see a kombi pulling away, fast. Mamma is sitting in the front seat, her face pale and drawn. She stares straight ahead. Uncle Friedel comes to find me and takes me inside the rondavel. Your father has had a heart attack, he says, we don't know whether he will live or die. And then he leaves, along with everyone else.

I lie on the bed and weep. I weep because I know Pappa is going to die. About a month before we moved back to the mission, I woke up one morning with absolute certainty that one of my parents was going to die. And I prayed. I said, Lord, please don't let it be my dad. Please, I couldn't live without him. Anyone but him. Please. And so now I know he is going to die. I know, because I wanted him to live. God is punishing me. Because by wanting my father to live, I automatically wanted it to be my mother who died. It is all my fault.

I'm alone for hours. I eventually cry myself to sleep. I wake up with Uncle Trevor sitting on the bed next to me. He tells me Pappa is dead.

It is 12 January 1987, and my dad, Daniel 'Tinker' Marthinus Bornman, is dead. He had a second heart attack and died on the way to the hospital, I'm told. He was forty-three years old.

Uncle Trevor takes me to Uncle Erlo's house. All I want is Mamma. But Uncle Erlo takes me into a room and asks me if I know what all this means. I say, yes, it means that Pappa has gone to heaven. No, says Uncle Erlo, what it means is that if you ever want to see your father again, you must make sure your life is pure. Then he tells me to confess my sins, because if I die with one unconfessed sin, I will go to hell. And I will never see my father again. This thought terrifies me more than eternal hellfire, so I confess God knows what. Then he takes me to Mamma.

I'm told the storm damaged the telephone lines and that is why my mother did not inform the mission about Pappa's death until their return. Either way, I discover, she was on the premises when Uncle Trevor gave me the devastating news. She let them drive her past the road leading to the rondavel where her child was waiting and then she sent someone else, someone I barely knew, to shatter my world.

Uncle Erlo drives us to his brother's farm, where there is still a working telephone connection. We call our relatives, then drive back to the mission, where Uncle Erlo and his wife, Kay, take us into their home.

I learn that Waldemar Engelbrecht, our old preacher in Johannesburg, has been dispatched to the families with whom Chris and Hanna live to inform my siblings and take them to the airport. My mom and I meet them at Durban airport.

13

'I'LL BE YOUR FATHER NOW'

We are taken shopping for clothes for our father's funeral. A white skirt and navy top with a scalloped embroidered collar for me. Getting new clothes is meant to be a happy occasion. I don't want new clothes now.

Everyone comes for the funeral. From the Cape, from Joburg. Pappa was so loved by so many people. My heart breaks for my brother. Chris is just a boy, but they make him a pallbearer. How can they make him carry our father's coffin? Only men should carry coffins. They bring the casket into the church. The top is open and we are made to walk past and look at him. Why? I don't want to see my dad dead. We take our seats in the front pew while everyone else files past my dad. All I can see now is the tip of his nose. For the whole service, I can't take my eyes off the tip of his nose.

The preachers drone on and on. We sing my father's favourite hymns. When we stand to sing, I can see more of his face. He doesn't look dead, just asleep. And then it's time to go to the cemetery. They make Chris carry Pappa out and then sit upfront in the hearse. It's so cruel. Why can't he drive with us? And then we are standing at the graveside. There's some more preaching and the choir sings 'Hallelujah' from Handel's *Messiah*. Pappa loved that song. I take my eyes off Pappa. For just a few seconds, I look at the choir singing. I look back, and he's gone. They've lowered him into the grave.

Someone tells me to grab a handful of soil, or maybe I pick some up off the mound next to the gaping hole in the ground, I can't recall. I approach the grave and toss the soil onto the coffin. Why am I doing this? Many of the others do it too. Is it a sign of respect, I wonder? It's the first funeral I've ever attended, so I don't know why I have to do all these things.

We walk away and they start filling the grave. I can hear the soil thudding on the wood and I don't want them to do it. I want to tell them to stop. But I can't. And then we're at someone's house for tea and sandwiches. How can anyone eat? Everyone keeps telling me that it's God's will that my pappa died. That's how I know I can't wail, can't make a noise. I have to keep quiet, because if they know how much noise I want to make for my dad, they will tell me I'm not following God because He took Pappa, so to cry is to rebel against God.

Uncle Manfred, another of Uncle Erlo's brothers, gives me a hug. He is the only person from the mission to do so. His daughter, Heidi, writes me a letter to say how sorry she is. Everyone else just tells me that it's God's will. Or that time heals all wounds. I don't know about that.

Later that day, Uncle Erlo tells Chris, Hanna and me that his home is now our home. 'You've lost your father; I'll be your father now,' he says on the day of Pappa's funeral. And despite what I've experienced at this place before, I believe him. And I feel special because, you know, Uncle Erlo is Uncle Erlo and he's such a busy man and such an imposing figure; everyone looks up to him and everyone wants a piece of him. I feel special and singled out, and I think that perhaps things will be okay after all if he's going to be protecting me now instead of my dad. There is still going to be someone looking out for me, safeguarding me.

14

I LOSE MY MOTHER, TOO

My sister stays with us for those few days surrounding my dad's funeral, so she is given my bed and I'm on a mattress on the floor. I'm not sure where my brother sleeps. I hope he's okay. One night, the pain is unbearable. I cannot hold it in any longer. I know I'm supposed to accept God's will and not grieve too much, but I can't hold in my sobs. I cry and cry and cry. After a while, my mother speaks from her bed: 'Quiet now, Erika, that's enough. You'll wake your sister.'

Then my sister and brother leave and it's just my mother and me. We move into a rondavel higher up from the one where my dad had his heart attack. Like the previous dwelling, it's really just a round room, with a section bricked off to form the small bathroom that contains a cramped shower, a toilet and a basin. My father's friend Tom has built a loft for us, and so now I have my own 'room', right up in the roof, the thatch forming my ceiling.

My mother has always been a fantastic homemaker and she can make anywhere a home, even a tiny room. She converts her sewing cupboard, with the door that swings down, into a kitchenette. It's where we keep our microwave, kettle and a handful of provisions. And an electric frying pan, should we want to cook. Cooking isn't necessary, as all the meals are communal in the big hall, where they hold the services. That's where I eat, anyway, with the other white kids whose parents aren't leaders and therefore don't have their own houses.

The main school hall and adjoining classrooms are still being built, so they convert Room 10 into our classroom. I'm studying in the room above the one where I used to wet my bed. This isn't the multiracial school my dad promised me. There's just a handful of white kids here. The black kids get taught elsewhere. I envy them; it's lonely up here. We don't even have teachers; we've all signed up through distance learning and I have Damelin books for my six subjects: English, Afrikaans, maths, science, geography and history. They construct cubicles for us and that's where we sit and study. There are three of us in Standard 8, and then some younger kids, too.

The entire school has assembly together every morning, though, which is really just another sermon. In the first assembly of the year, they announce the prefects. I just about die when my name is called. I can't be a prefect! I'm in Standard 8! None of these kids know me! Why have they chosen me? I don't want to be prefect over older kids. This is awful. Of course, I stay silent, walk up to where the others are standing and smile. I know it's supposed to be an honour, but it feels like a sentence. There's a Standard 7 boy who has also been made prefect. He's also white. It just feels so wrong. We're still so separated from these other kids, but I tell myself it's because my dad died. They needed to make a plan, quick. That doesn't make sense, though, unless the plan was always for my dad to teach us separately and now we just have to study through Damelin. Why can't we attend class with the other kids? No one ever explains it to me, and I, well, I just don't ask questions. I've learned that lesson well.

My academic lessons don't proceed quite as smoothly. I'm grief-stricken, lost and confused and I stare at the pages in front of me without taking in a single word. No one checks on us, no one makes sure that we're progressing through our workbooks. I guess they trust that we are. Maybe the other two are, but I'm not. I get stuck on the first page of my first science textbook. It talks about inertia and I'm unable to comprehend what that is. All my schooling up until now has been in Afrikaans and, while my English is good, this is new territory for me.

I have no idea what I do during the long hours at school, but I know that I ignore my maths and science books when I can't make heads or tails out of what they're teaching. I've always had a teacher teaching me and have never had to study by myself. It's only after a few months that it strikes me that I can look up the word 'inertia' in our dictionary in the rondavel. *Traagheid*. I know what *traagheid* is! Of course I do! I've understood that concept since I was a little girl, sitting in the car when my dad had to brake suddenly. He explained to me that the reason I jerked forward was because of *traagheid*. We were moving forward, then our vehicle stopped, and my body carried on moving.

The damage is done, though. I'm so far behind now that I'll never catch up. And all the joy has gone out of maths, once my favourite subject. I look at the pages and see numbers and squiggles and none of it makes any sense whatsoever. My mother is right, I'm nothing special. I can't even study by myself.

I'm sure my mother asks me if everything is going well and I'm sure I answer in the affirmative. She has embarked on a teaching career at Domino Servite and has thrown herself into schoolwork. She's obviously grieving (we grieve separately and never speak of it), and because this is the first time in her life that she is teaching, she has lots to learn. She's hardly ever home and we don't share many meals together. I can see she's happy, though, and that she likes teaching. Most nights, she works very late.

I lie awake many nights, convinced that my mother has slipped and fallen and is lying with her face in a ditch of muddy water and is breathing it in. She's drowning and I need to get up and go find her.

Before I go to bed, I fill the kettle and put a tea bag in a mug because she likes having a cup of tea before bed. Or I write a little note and pick a flower and leave it on her pillow so that she'll know I love her. I go to sleep only after I hear the door open. Oh, the relief. She's not dead.

15

A SHOWER GOES WRONG

I don't see much of Uncle Erlo that first year after Pappa's death. For someone who said that he'll be my father now, he's remarkably absent from my life. But I get it: he's our leader and he's a busy man. Everyone hero-worships him. He is God's mouthpiece on earth. In church, they say, 'Other people have the Bible, we have the Bible *and* the Revival.' It's clearly established that we're closer to God than other Christians. But how come?

Well, in 1966, God came down while Uncle Erlo was ministering to people in a cowshed in Maphumulo. They were praying when they heard a noise like a great wind – it was the Holy Spirit. 'Everybody was conscious of the presence of God. All I could do was to bow down and worship the God of heaven,' he tells people about that day, which became known as the beginning of the Revival.

The movement grew and KwaSizabantu was founded in 1970. Everyone knows how Uncle Erlo prayed for poor dead Lidia Dube – and then resurrected her from the dead. Everyone also knows what Lidia saw in heaven during her brief sojourn there – by her account, it's a pretty idyllic place. She was not the only miracle. Healings began to take place spontaneously. Sometimes the healed person hadn't even been prayed over; simply being in the service and hearing the Word had brought about their healing.

In 1981, the German pastor Dr Kurt E. Koch wrote a book about that time of Revival called *God Among the Zulus.* We all know the story about the sangoma (they call her a witch) who came to Uncle Erlo and his team for help. She knew no English, only Zulu, but when they started praying for her, she suddenly broke into fluent English. Shortly thereafter, she made various animal sounds – barking like a pack of dogs and grunting and squealing like a drove of pigs. The first hundred demons that had possessed her left with much shouting and screaming, then the second hundred departed and, finally, the third hundred. After all the demons had been cast out of her, her face changed completely – she now had the appearance of a saint who had been living in the presence of Jesus for many years. This is what we all still strive for today – to live in the presence of Jesus, to see the glory of God reflected in our faces.

The reported healings continued apace. In one service, ten blind people all got their sight back at the same moment. As did a blind woman who lived kilometres away. Paralysis, leprosy, kidney disease, deafness, infertility, tumours, addiction –

you name it, God cured it. Following their conversion, alcoholics reported becoming sick the moment they drank any alcohol. It was the same for smokers – after being cured of their addiction to nicotine, they'd feel ill if they lit a cigarette. God at work.

There were darker tales, too, of course. In the Revival, people living in sin and who were unrepentant were given warnings. Those who ignored the warnings sometimes died in accidents.

By the time my family joins The Mission, which is what insiders call the church, it has grown significantly and is funded by various projects: a pasta factory, a dairy (the yoghurt is yummy), a jam factory and a number of farming operations. Uncle Erlo is at its head. His closest advisors are three Zulu women, called the Mamas – Josephinah Nsibande, Hilda Dube and her daughter, Lidia-back-from-the-dead. They are responsible primarily, though not exclusively, for the black Christian community at the mission.

Alongside them is an ad hoc committee of elders who are responsible for the white Christians. Under the elders is a council of co-workers, which comprises all the preachers, including members of the famous KwaSizabantu Choir Number One. Below them is Choir Number Two, followed by Choir Number Three, then Choir Number Four, the KwaSizabantu Youth Choir, the Domino Servite School choirs and so on, right down to the various lesser choirs formed of different groups of individuals.

Then there are the masses of general workers, farm workers, shop assistants and builders who do not belong to any of the choirs and are therefore regarded as having made the least spiritual progress. The further you are from the top, the less you or your opinions matter. Choir Number One travels the world, singing and preaching. You want to be in their good books because they have a lot of power. And they're always on the lookout for people stepping out of line.

I'm not important because I don't belong to anyone important, so I mostly escape scrutiny. Probably also because I learned as a little kid how to be invisible here. So I get through the days without arousing much suspicion. Around a year after my dad's passing, I am showering in our rondavel. Even though it's summer it's quite chilly, so I close the window while I shower, and then I remember nothing.

My mother tells me that she was on her way out the door when she heard a moan, followed by a thud. Luckily, we don't lock doors in our home (who knows what nefariousness I could get up to behind a locked bathroom door!), so she came in and found me passed out on the shower floor. She pulled me out and called for help.

I am unconscious for a few hours. The adults figure out what happened. The little gas geyser's flame burned off all the carbon dioxide in the room and started producing carbon monoxide. I have carbon monoxide poisoning. I never think to ask, so I don't know why I wasn't rushed to hospital immediately. When I wake up, Uncle Erlo is sitting on my bed and praying that I will come back to life. He's raised someone from the dead before and I suppose they figured I was still breathing, so there was no need to seek immediate healthcare. Who needs a hospital, right? Let's just pray for this unconscious child instead. (Years later, Dr Google tells me that I should have been given oxygen therapy to minimise potential brain, heart and organ damage, but hey. Water under the bridge. At least they moved the geyser to the outside wall.)

So the first proper interaction I have with Uncle Erlo after the funeral is him begging God to spare my life so that I may serve him (would that be God or Uncle Erlo?). This episode marks the start of my many health issues. Over the course of the next few years, I suffer from severe migraines, sometimes more than once a week. I have severe stomach aches. I'm just really, really ill, and so every now and again my mother makes an appointment for me with Uncle Erlo and he prays for me and for my healing.

But I'm never healed. Despite these intercessions by the miracle man himself, the migraines continue, as do the stomach aches. But I've been well indoctrinated. It's not Uncle Erlo's fault that I'm not being healed; clearly there's something wrong with me. If God is healing all these other people and He doesn't want to heal me, the fault lies with me – in me.

And so, for now, this is the extent of my interaction with Uncle Erlo. He becomes an even more imposing figure. He is not my protector, though, not ever. I fear him. I'm taught that fear and love are the same thing. We fear God, and we love him. So it doesn't feel wrong to fear Uncle Erlo, but he doesn't become a father figure. Not at all.

I never feared my dad. Sure, I sometimes got a hiding from him, but I was never scared of him. I would never want to hide from him the way I want to hide from Uncle Erlo. My dad taught me beauty. To this day when I see a little wildflower growing on a mountainside, I think of him, because that is the kind of thing he'd point out to me. He taught me a deep, enduring love for reading. Not everything he read was serious; he loved the humour of the *Asterix* and *Tintin* cartoons. Reading, music, beauty, that's what my dad taught me.

I wish he hadn't died when he did. I have so many questions for him. Why, Pappa? How did you make the decisions you made? Explain to me why you left us here instead of with a family who would have cared for us. Why you would abandon us in the first place? Tell me, help me to understand.

16

THE DIMINISHING OF ME

One afternoon, I am lying reading upstairs in my little loft, my sanctuary, when the door opens unexpectedly and my mother comes in with two or three other girls. They're also prefects but I don't know them very well. They're here to go through my wardrobe and throw out anything that is too worldly. And so I sit on the stairs, watching as my wardrobe is raided and judged by strangers. I don't understand. My clothes aren't worldly. But they select quite a lot. The items are packed into a black bag and the girls leave. I don't know what happens to my clothes. They probably get burned at the next fire service. I crawl back upstairs and cry myself to sleep.

Many years later, one of those girls seeks me out on social media and, when we speak on the phone, she cries as she asks me to please forgive her. She says that that day has haunted her for decades. I tell her that of course I forgive her, if that is what she needs, but that, as far as I'm concerned, there is nothing to forgive. She says she should have refused. I refute that. We both know that when you were told to do something, you did it. Neither of us had a say in the matter. She recalls me crying out, 'But Mamma, other girls wear that too!' and begging her to allow me to keep one dress. 'You only bought that for me the other day, Mamma, why can't I keep it?'

I miss supper that night, but I'm not hungry much any more. I don't recall if I go to the church service that night, but chances are I did. I am only allowed to miss the service if I am actually ill.

Attending the evening service is compulsory, and you're only allowed to miss the Sunday morning service if you're so ill you can't get out of bed. On Saturdays, we have to attend three services: one in the morning, one in the afternoon and one in the evening.

There's still movie night, and the line-up hasn't changed. There's one that is a bit more fun than the others, *Pilgrim's Progress*. Pilgrim makes his way from the City of Destruction to the Celestial City despite many trials and tribulations and temptations. (Here is where I fall for Liam Neeson – it's his first movie ever and he plays the evangelist.)

Temptation is something I hear about often. It is to be avoided at all costs. The mirror in my bathroom is a temptation because I might admire myself in it. The boys around me are temptations. But they're not nearly as big a temptation as I, myself, am. Women are temptresses. They lead men astray. They lead men into sin. Lust. I hear that word so often and yet have no idea what it means, but I know it happens between a man and a woman and that it's evil and the woman's fault. Lust has to be avoided at all costs because it leads to premarital intercourse and that, I know, is the most evil of all the evils.

I start feeling really scared of being a woman. I don't want to be the cause of men sinning. That seems to be my destiny, though. I am going to become the person who causes men to sin. And then I'll definitely never see my dad again. So I do everything in my power to be invisible. I don't want to be seen. It doesn't happen overnight – I've always been that little sunshine child. The kid that adults who live in the real world look at and go, 'Ah, isn't she pretty?' or 'Isn't she adorable?' I'm naturally bubbly, naturally vivacious.

On the outside, I'm toned down, but on the inside I am still kind and loving. They don't manage to completely extinguish my spirit.

I shrink as the little shadow child reappears. No one living with me seems to notice.

My godfather, Martin, is a friend of my father's dating back to our Malawi days. Upon our return to South Africa, we lost touch with his family, but he visits KwaSizabantu during this time. When he leaves, I get a lift to Durban in the same car as him. This is the first time he's seen me since I was a little girl, and he can tell I am troubled and unhappy. 'You didn't say one word the whole trip, Erika. You sat in the backseat, quiet and withdrawn,' he tells me later.

He's right, I have been silenced. The *kurkproppie* has lost her buoyancy.

17

ANIMAL FARM

'All animals are equal, but some are more equal than others.' So writes George Orwell in his allegorical novella *Animal Farm*. The adults at KwaSizabantu love this book – see how those evil communists oppress and enslave others! They show the movie at school too, until some of the kids start drawing parallels between Orwell's farmyard and KwaSizabantu. Because some of the KSB animals are far more equal than others.

The leaders all have houses, of course. The higher up in the hierarchy you are, the bigger and nicer your house. They are all pretty well-off, too. Many of them own grocery-store franchises throughout the province.

My mother and I live in one of fifty or so rondavels – small, round face-brick structures with thatched roofs. We're lucky because it's just the two of us. Many of the rondavels house families of five or six. But even they are luckier than most, because they at least have their own bathroom. The rest live in dormitories. KSB is hierarchical, so your accommodation is directly proportional to your position on the stairway to heaven.

But even then, not all disciples are equal. If you're a married couple, you get your own room, but you still have to share bathroom facilities with many others. If you're unmarried and white, you will share a room with between three and seven others, but never more than ten. If you're an unmarried black man on the lowest rungs of the ladder, you can look forward to sharing a single dormitory with eighty other unmarried black men. If you're an unmarried black woman at the bottom, you'll be crammed in with a hundred of your sisters. No cohabiting here.

The school dormitories for the boarders, none of whom are white, are awful. Three-tier bunk beds, wafer-thin mattresses, and just a handful of toilets and showers. When I misstep, my mother threatens me with these dormitories. It's enough for me to toe the line.

How do they keep us all so faithful in such conditions? I don't know about the adults, but as a kid, I believe what they tell me. Joseph Goebbels famously said, 'A lie told once remains a lie. But a lie told a thousand times becomes the truth.' And that is exactly how KSB's brand of brainwashing works. Imagine you're a child, and you're told over and over and over again that you will amount to nothing. You're told that women are evil and exist to tempt men, who are their superiors. You are told that you are going to hell if you die with so much as one unconfessed sin. This becomes not just the truth – it becomes *your* truth.

I am brainwashed into believing only KwaSizabantu knows the one true way to get to heaven. Only Uncle Erlo and his cohorts have had the truth revealed to them by God. I am brainwashed into believing that I am headed straight for hell, and this is why I must go to church every single day, often more than once. Attendance is not optional.

'You have to break a child's spirit by the time it is three years old,' Uncle Erlo thunders from the pulpit. Others preach this as well, because where Erlo goes, we all follow. This lesson is ingrained in us. You have to break a child's spirit or that child will never follow God. Parents break their children's spirits with regular hidings. And the co-workers break the spirits of the Domino Servite School's pupils with an orange plumbing pipe. Public beatings of children are the order of the day. As a white girl, I'm spared that indignity. The threat of it terrifies me, though, and I modify my behaviour, my demeanour, my speech, even my thoughts, just so that I won't get beaten in public. And I don't. I'm lucky that I'm white or I would not be able to escape the orange pipe, no matter how good I try to be.

Much is made of how KwaSizabantu is a fully integrated society, but in my experience, racism is rife. The public beatings are just one example, albeit a horrific one. Virginity testing is another. After every holiday, the black girls are made to line up outside The Waiting Room, where some kind of test is administered. I don't know how you test for virginity; I just know that as a white girl, I'm spared this particular indignity. We also don't eat with the black kids. On the odd occasion, we might get the option to do so. But the food we get up at the hall, where we're allowed to eat with the visitors, is definitely better than the food the kids in the school hall are given. Also, eating there is no fun at all. You'd expect a hall filled with a few hundred schoolkids eating a meal to be noisy, right? Not here. Here you eat in silence, your life stilled and stilted.

My life is also stilted, but my mother's indifference to me gives me a certain kind of freedom. The black kids have no freedom. For people who claim to despise the communists, KSB leaders sure are good students of Lenin and Stalin. Conformity rules. Take hair, for example. Mine can be long or short, it's my choice. The black girls, not so much. To this day, if you look at the Domino Servite students, all the black kids have short, shaven hair. They have no choice in the matter and are shorn like sheep on a regular basis.

Another leaf they've taken straight from the communist playbook is restricting the flow of information. At school, the biology textbooks are censored – the chapters dealing with reproduction are literally cut out. I don't take biology, but even if I did, I would still have no idea how my body's reproductive system works. There are no radios allowed and no TVs, obviously. No newspapers. No magazines – although my sister sometimes brings me *Time* and *National Geographic*, which are allowed. Our only source of information is KwaSizabantu, and they only tell us what they want us to hear; everything else is censored.

Censored and censured. That's the way they like us, and the state in which they keep us. The happiest animals, after all, live simple lives.

18

THE THREAT OF A SUITCASE

'Have you got your note signed?' I sometimes hear one kid whisper to another. These are the notes from your counsellor to your teacher. Counselling is compulsory; you get punished for not going to counselling. If you're black, that is. I'm supposed to confess my sins, but no one ever asks me to provide a note. Then again, I don't have teachers, either.

Counselling in KSB-speak isn't career counselling or visiting what others might call a guidance counsellor. Nope. In this type of counselling, you confess your sins to a human being who has been deemed spiritual enough by the powers that be to hear confessions. This person listens to you, questions you, and then, when you have no more to say, they pray with you that God will forgive your sin. Because you go straight to hell if you die with a single unconfessed sin. Sermons are peppered with stories of people who thought they still had time, but God's mercy ran out and they are now in hell.

As a kid at Domino Servite School, you have no choice in the matter. You have to confess your sins to your counsellor at least once a week, otherwise there'll be trouble. I sometimes despair at just how much sin one child can commit in a week, considering that just about everything that might cause temptation – from movies, TV shows and magazines to books that aren't approved – has been removed from our lives. Just frowning at a classmate can get you in trouble. Having what a teacher deems a recalcitrant look on your face is a sin. We are to be serene, acquiescent, quiet beings, definitely seen (watched closely, in fact) but never heard (except in confession, the classroom and when screaming our repentance as the orange pipe rains down retribution).

It's a sign of just how unsupervised I am that I get away with not going for a single confession that first year after my father's death. But it catches up with me. It's the end of the school year when my mother comes home one evening, her face serious.

'Erika, we have to talk.'

I sit down on the bed, and she prays. Uh oh, I'm in trouble.

She tells me that the school board has met and has decided to expel me because not confessing my sins for an entire year goes against school policy.

Well, that's not so bad, I think. I don't go to class with any teachers anyway, so I could just continue to study through Damelin here in the rondavel, surely? I'd at least skip that dreary assembly every morning. But no, my mother hasn't finished yet.

'Because I am a teacher at the school and this is our home, if they expel you, I have no choice but to kick you out as well.'

I look at her and she looks straight back at me, her face calm and composed. She tells me to pack a small suitcase or bag. I mustn't make it too heavy, she says, because I'll have to carry it up to the main road, where I'll need to hitch a ride and go make a life for myself somewhere else.

I am sixteen years old, and all I have is a Standard 7 certificate, which will not get me a job anywhere. We're in the middle of nowhere, the nearest hamlet is twenty kilometres away, but there's nothing there. The two closest towns are each fifty kilometres away, but even if I got there, what would I do, where would I go? I plead with her, please don't kick me out, I'll do anything. Okay, she agrees. You have to be regularly confessing your sins by the time the school year starts again in January. Then you can stay.

The hunt is on for a counsellor, so I start auditioning them. I try out two, but I find them so cold and uncaring that I cannot imagine telling them my innermost secrets. Then, I think of someone. There's a man that's high up, he's one of the co-workers. When he preaches, I usually learn something – he doesn't just drone on and on about sin; he brings some world history into whatever he's exhorting us to do or not to do. I'll go to him, I decide.

Muzi Kunene is an intelligent, erudite man who speaks something like five languages. I ask him if he will be my counsellor, and he says yes. Whew. I'll be allowed to stay after all. And confessions with someone who is that interested in history can't be that bad.

Muzi is married with two kids, and I was right, very often the confessing of sins actually turns into a political discussion. He teaches me about apartheid and what it was – is – like for the majority of South Africans living in our country.

My parents didn't discuss politics at home. I'm lucky that I was raised to not be prejudiced, but my dad didn't teach me what was going on around us. In Joburg, I would sleep in my sister's room when we had guests over to stay so that they could have my room, and they were from all over southern Africa. There was Daniel from Madagascar – I loved the way he rolled his Rs. And another man from Angola, I don't recall his name. Our home was always open to all. I had a sense that it wasn't the case in the rest of South Africa, but I had no real knowledge of apartheid and what it meant.

Muzi sets me straight. He tells me about the *dompas*, that piece of paper all black adults have to carry when they are not in a designated black area. He tells me about segregated facilities, benches where only whites are allowed to sit, beaches where only whites are allowed to go. And then he teaches me about white theology and the teachings of certain Afrikaners that say that black people aren't as human as whites. That black people have smaller brains, etc. He shows me the correlations between this kind of thinking and the Nazi extermination of races and groups who weren't Aryan. I know all about the Nazis, of course. History has supplanted maths as my favourite subject and, seeing as history books are generally allowed at KSB, I read everything I can lay my hands on.

I hero-worship this man. And he laps it up. He's my father figure and just about the only person here who pays any real attention to me. I store up my sins, happily now, because at least I will have something to confess. I look forward to our meetings. Who knew confessing sins could be this much fun?

I come from a warm, affectionate family. But now, with my siblings far away and my mother present but distant, affection is in short supply. There's a lovely older Swiss gentleman who lives at KSB, Uncle Robert. He treats me with kindness and gives me a tape recorder when he realises I don't have one to listen to my father's classical music tapes. And then there's Uncle Erlo's brother, Uncle Manfred, and his wife, Aunty Evelyn. They don't live at KwaSizabantu, but they come to church here almost every Sunday. I look forward to Sundays because I know that I might get a few minutes of their time, and they both always give me a hug. Uncle Manfred gives the best hugs. He looks at me and smiles, 'Erika, my girl, how are you?' I live for these moments, and now I live for my counselling sessions, too.

Muzi holds most of his counselling appointments – of course, I'm not the only confessant he sees – in a small office along that cold, dark corridor that I used to dread so much. It's got a bed and a desk and an extra chair or two. Here's how confession works: you arrive, he prays. You confess however many sins you've committed since the previous time you saw him and answer any questions he might have about these sins. He then prays for God's forgiveness, and you're done. Except we keep chatting. I have so many questions, and I think Muzi quite likes having someone who hangs on to his every word.

On 24 August 1988, I've just turned seventeen and I'm confessing my sins. But I am emotional and crying because today is my dad's birthday and I miss him more than ever. I am bereft. When I get up to leave, Muzi gives me a hug to comfort me. Oh my word, it feels so good to be hugged. I melt into his embrace.

Hugs become the norm, and they make me feel so warm and loved. Muzi cautions me that people won't understand, so I mustn't tell anyone what happens between us. What we have is special, he tells me. I don't mind. I have no one to tell, anyway, and I don't want the hugs to stop.

19

SNITCHES DON'T GET STITCHES

Jessie and I rekindled our friendship when we moved back to KSB. Except, friends aren't friends at KwaSizabantu, not in the way that friendships work in the real world. We can't really confide in each other. I can't tell her about stuff that bothers me, and she can't tell me what troubles her.

If I know of a friend's sin and I don't tell on her, I'm as guilty as she is. The same goes for her. And if neither of us talk, and one of us gets found out and it emerges that the other knew about it, then we are both dealt the same punishment.

How can you trust your friends? They may agree with you today that something is weird or wrong or odd or laughable, but in two weeks' time, they might be sitting in a church service and God might speak to them and show them the error of their ways. And then they will go and confess this conversation you had. And you will be in so much trouble.

The art of snitching is encoded in Domino Servite School's code of conduct. In a subsection ('Expected Behaviour') of section 9 ('Administering Reward and Punishment') of the 2019 code of conduct we find:

- Exposure of irregular behaviour
- Admit a fault before exposure

The race is on. Will your 'irregular behaviour' be exposed before you've admitted to it? You've got to give the school board credit for being students of history. In the death camps of World War II, the guards relied on the kapos (the *Funktionshäftling*) and the informers to help them maintain control over their prisoners. Snitch or be snitched on. Those are your choices.

I do have friends, though. There's Jessie and Angie. There are my two classmates, and then there's a girl who's younger than me, Celempilo. She and I are kindred spirits. She is a ray of sunshine. And in such a dark, dismal place, a ray of sunshine is the most welcome relief.

At some point, we're moved from Room 10 to the school proper. But the three of us are still segregated from the black kids in our year. In the lower classes, there is assimilation, but not for us. We still don't have teachers, either, and are left to our own devices.

We get taken to Pietermaritzburg for exams at the end of the year. I don't understand why we have to go to a city that's 120 kilometres away instead of writing at the school, but I don't ask questions, I just do as I'm told. I study furiously for a few weeks before the exams. But maths remains a problem. It's like that ladder my dad explained to me all those years ago: if you miss one rung, you'll be lost. I have missed so many rungs and I am so lost. I get 17 per cent for maths. The shame. I pass all my other subjects, but that 17 per cent for mathematics ... I feel such a complete failure. My dad would be so embarrassed if he were here. I really am nothing special at all.

I don't know what my two classmates get, but I know it's nothing as abysmal as 17 per cent. Something about these marks must have shaken the school board out of their stupor because, when we get to matric the following year, we suddenly have teachers. I think they realise that they have failed us and that we are about to fail them, seeing as they prize their 100 per cent pass rate almost above anything else. If we don't organise some teachers, this kid is going to fail mathematics. I still study history on my own, but I feel such a sense of relief that finally someone is going to help me.

My two classmates are deemed advanced enough to write mathematics on higher grade, but I am relegated to standard grade. My black peers have no choice in the matter either. They are also told that they're writing standard grade – only the white kids will write higher grade. That damn 100 per cent pass rate affects a lot of kids' education. One of my black classmates tells me how she and another girl begged to be allowed to write English as a first and not a second language, as it would greatly boost their future job prospects (remember, we're still living under apartheid). They are both told that it's not possible. But they ask again and are given a Standard 8 English first-language exam to complete. They hand it in and never see it again, but are later informed that they both failed. And if they failed that, they are told, they will definitely fail matric.

A number of my peers fall foul of this 100 per cent pass rate. It's an open secret among us kids that if they don't think you'll pass matric, then you definitely won't pass Standard 9. Or you'll be told to take your subjects in standard grade or lower grade, not higher grade.

When my matric results come in, I pay no attention to the A (for English, second language, higher grade) and the B (for mathematics, standard grade). The three Cs (for Afrikaans, first language, higher grade; geography, higher grade; and history, higher grade) and one D (for physical science, higher grade) floor me. D. I should have seven or eight distinctions; I'm the kind of kid whose intellect is suited to school. Instead, I barely scrape together a university exemption. D in my dad's favourite subject. I am gutted. If only I'd worked harder, studied harder that first year. Looked up 'inertia' in the dictionary sooner. My hopes for applying for a bursary to study actuarial science are dashed with these results. I'm destined to stay at KSB.

20

A FUTURE ALREADY MAPPED

Three days after writing my final school exam, Uncle Erlo calls me in and says there is a man who feels it is God's will for him to marry me. I must now go and pray about it and see whether it is His will. How else are people going to get married when they're not allowed to talk to each other?

Boy sees girl, boy likes girl, boy prays about girl, boy proposes to girl via proxy. Girl prays about boy, girl accepts via proxy. Engagement is in church, Uncle Erlo stands between them, Uncle Erlo places ring on girl's finger. Wedding is planned. Wedding happens, Uncle Erlo stands in front of couple, allows boy and girl to exchange rings. Uncle Erlo pronounces them husband and wife. No kissing in public. In private, Uncle Erlo gives boy and girl The Talk. Boy and girl are alone for the very first time that night. Girl no longer belongs to her parents; she has been handed over to her husband. Intercourse is now no longer evil but mandatory, and she produces one child after the next. And they live happily ever after.

By now, I'm convinced that I don't have a relationship with God. He doesn't talk to me the way he talks to everyone else. I've sinned grievously and continue to sin, because Muzi's hugs have become uncomfortable. He holds on to me for too long. It doesn't feel right, and I know what doesn't feel right is definitely sin. I know that I'm going to ask God about this man who wants to marry me and He's not going to answer me. There's something wrong with me. But I obey and I go away and pray and, sure enough, God doesn't tell me anything. Nada.

This guy is from one of the prominent KSB families. He's not a Stegen, but the nearest thing to it, I guess. I would be guaranteed a place among the elite. But I simply cannot imagine myself married to this man. I still don't know or understand exactly what marital relations entail, so that's not what puts me off. The truth is, he's a dweeb. He has no personality that I can detect. There are so many great guys, why can't one of them ask me? And so I go back and tell Uncle Erlo that no, God hasn't given me the go-ahead on this.

Uncle Erlo, for once, is at a loss for words. I can see in his face that he is utterly gobsmacked at the gumption of this eighteen-year-old saying thank you, but no thank you, I'm not marrying this man. I feel relief, but also a flicker of pride, a tiny flicker, but it's there. I said no, and God did not strike me down with lightning.

It has been so ingrained in me that as a woman I am inferior to men that it is actually quite unthinkable to question this man who says that God wants him to marry me. I should immediately say yes, I know that. Be my husband, do with me what you want. Yet there is something inside me that says no, not this man. I guess I'm lucky that it isn't one of the hot guys who asks, because who knows what I might have done. There are two guys I have definite crushes on, and had one of them asked, I would have said yes right away, no prayer needed.

Over the course of the next two years, God impresses on two more men that it is His will for them to marry me (some months apart, of course – KSB has many quirks, but polygamy is not one of them). And because God doesn't talk to me, I can't ask Him why He keeps changing His mind about whom I should marry. The second man who proposes is a good man. I know I will have a good life with him if I say yes. I don't know him, but I can tell that he is kind. I agonise over the decision, because I know that this could be my best chance yet. But no, I simply can't. Perhaps it's all those illicit Mills & Boon novels I read in Standard 7, but the thought of marrying a stranger, no matter how kind he appears, terrifies me. I decline again. Uncle Erlo is not happy with me, I can tell.

My future is mapped out for me already, I just don't know it yet. My mother refuses point-blank to allow me to apply for a bursary to study anything anywhere. She will, however, allow me to study for a degree through UNISA. More distance learning. I have decided that I want to be a lawyer. I want to help people. All I have learned from Muzi about the injustices that have taken place in South Africa, that are continuing to take place, has strengthened my resolve that I need to do something about it.

But no. My mother won't let me study law. You'll be exposed to the ugliness of the world every day, she says. Become a teacher, she says. Everything inside me rebels against this. I don't tell her, but if I can't be a lawyer, then I want to be a translator at the United Nations. I'm good with languages and I long to be somewhere and do something that matters. And so, I enrol for Linguistics 1 and French Introduction, and then I manage to sneak one by her: African Politics 1. I tell her it's because I have to do a number of subjects just for a year and that I will only study this for one year. It will also help if I ever need to do mission work anywhere in Africa. I tell her that Muzi thinks it's a good idea, and that clinches it. He's a man of God, after all. If he thinks it's okay, then it must be.

Then she informs me what I will be doing at KwaSizabantu to earn my keep. I am eighteen years old with zero training, but that does not preclude them from giving me a teaching job at the very school from which I have just matriculated. In January 1990, I join the Domino Servite faculty. I am given forty-four cute little five-year-old Zulu kids and one little Afrikaans girl. I am told that they are now the English class. The idea is for them to learn English this year so that they may start their formal schooling next year in English rather than in Zulu or Afrikaans. It's a good idea, progressive even, as English is essential for future job prospects in South Africa.

Fortunately, over the past two and a half years I've spent many hours with a young girl, she's not even four years old yet, named Mirriam. She is the daughter of Muzi and his wife, and she is the sweetest child. She was born with muscular dystrophy, so her life is challenging and, I am told, she will not live long. Her limbs are as thin as sticks, and I spend hours massaging them and helping her move them around. I've been teaching her English, too. Her older brother is just as adorable. He's a bright little boy. These kids light up my afternoons and weekends. I've pretty much run out of books to read in the compound anyway, and this is way better than reading. I pour all my love into Mirriam. I research her condition and basically devote my life to her. She is a ray of sunshine and gives my life meaning. She loves me; her face lights up whenever I walk into the room or pass her sitting on the grass outside.

I love spending time with Mirriam, and the kids I'm about to teach aren't that much older than her. Maybe this teaching malarkey won't be so bad after all.

21

CLEANSED IN MUD

The day of my death dawns bright and clear and sunny. I've resigned myself to dying; I've had a few weeks to get used to the idea. I almost welcome it. Almost, except that I will never see my dad in heaven. I've given up on that, too. I don't have the peace they preach about. I don't have the relationship with God that they have, and that's how I know I'm going to die today.

A few weeks earlier, all the youth are called into a service. I'm in the first half of my first year of teaching. We are told that there will soon be a mass baptism, and that we need to get our lives in order with God and one another. 'Remember,' the speaker admonishes, 'if you know of someone's sin and you don't confess it, you are as guilty as they are in the eyes of God.'

A flurry of snitching ensues, and for a number of weeks there is a frenzy. We all want to be chosen to be baptised, and so if I even look at someone askance, I confess it and then apologise to them. But even as I go through the motions, I know I'm not going to make the cut. God will never allow it. He knows full well that I am not one of them and he's sure to punish me for it. He likes public displays of dissatisfaction, and he is going to make an example of me, for sure.

The God of KwaSizabantu is not the benevolent New Testament God. Sure, I'm told all the time that he loves me, but he only loves the righteous, and I fear him with every fibre of my being. He's a masculine monarch who scrutinises my every thought and deed.

'There is nothing concealed that will not be disclosed, or hidden that will not be made known,' we are warned daily, so best you make it known before someone else does! If you sin and confess, all good and well. But if you sin and try to conceal it, woe is you. 'Even the very hairs of your head are all numbered.' God is omnipotent, omniscient and ominous.

No part of me measures up to God's scrutiny: I am irredeemably bad because, after a decade of trying, I have no relationship with him. I am a fraud. God doesn't speak to me the way he speaks to everyone else. He is silent when it comes to me. There's definitely something wrong with me. My inner ears don't work. My inner voice is silent – I can't even pray any more because no one listens.

I go to bed scared that he will take my life overnight. And then I will spend all eternity in hell with not a chance to make up for what I've done wrong.

And so it comes as an enormous surprise when my name is read out with those

61

who have been deemed worthy of being baptised. How did I make the cut? Does God actually approve of me despite his silence? Am I okay after all? But no, it can't be. I can't be.

I pass the next few weeks in abject fear. Those who didn't make the list are excused from the regular meetings with The Chosen. Jessie's name wasn't on there, so I have to go to the meetings without her now. There are many of us, between thirty and forty, at least. The intensity of the meetings ramps up as we get closer to the big day.

One evening, one of the preachers tells us about a woman whose life wasn't right with God but who insisted on being baptised regardless. There, in the river, she was struck by lightning and died (going to hell, of course). And that's when I understand my fate. A lightning strike during my baptism. (Of course, science doesn't enter into all this fearmongering. Did the oke baptising her also die? If he was touching her, he should have. And even if he wasn't touching her, water conducts electricity, so surely he should have been fried too?)

The Sunday morning of my baptism dawns bright and clear and sunny. I dress in the clothes my mother has carefully selected. There will be no nipple stands as I emerge from the water. No wardrobe malfunctions, either. We must not lead men into temptation, so the onus is on me to ensure that, even when soaking wet, as little of my body is on display as possible.

I line up with my peers on the shore of a muddy dam. There are a number of co-workers, all men, waiting waist-deep in the brown water with Uncle Erlo. Visibility decreases the more people walk in, get dunked and then emerge, reborn.

I patiently wait my turn in this production line of salvation. The moment a man releases his newly baptised quarry, someone else takes their place. Finally, it's my turn. And I realise my fate is sealed. The person awaiting me is Uncle Erlo himself – the man who has God's ear, who hears God's voice. Surely God will tell him not to baptise me? Or maybe God will just strike me down with lightning. Either way, there's no way Uncle Erlo won't realise something is very, very wrong with me.

I make my way to him. He prays and then dunks me. Nothing happens except that I swallow a mouthful or two of brackish water. And then it's over. He lets me go and I stumble to shore, stunned. I'm alive! God has obviously decided to defer his punishment to another day. Whew.

That night, as I lie in bed going over the day's events, I feel the first seeds of doubt about Uncle Erlo's divinity. If God speaks to him, how come God didn't tell him not to baptise me? Is he as in touch with God's proclamations and commands as he claims to be? What is it that I'm missing here? Something doesn't add up.

22

SLUT

Muzi is still my counsellor, but something has started to change. I don't know it yet, but I'm a frog in a saucepan filled with cold water while the hugging phase continues for a few months. Then the flame is lit and the kisses on the lips start. For an Afrikaans girl, it's not really a stretch and it does not feel at all inappropriate. In my culture, we kiss people hello and goodbye on the lips – closed lips, of course. This continues for a while, until I'm comfortable in my saucepan of now-warm water. Then he cups my bum with his hands when we go in for a hug. I remember stiffening the first time he does it and crying in bed later. What is going on? But he's a man of God. I say nothing.

And so, when Muzi uses his tongue to open my lips and he penetrates my virgin mouth with his adult kiss, I have no defence. I have allowed everything up to now, how can I pull away? Am I allowed to pull away? In time, as the water heats up more, I start feeling a tingling sensation when he kisses me. Why does it feel so good but also so wrong?

He starts calling me more often than our weekly counselling sessions necessitate. We don't have phones, so he sends his maid to come and get me. I go to wherever he is, and sometimes this is the room he shares with his wife. I am so conflicted. Even though I have had absolutely no sex education whatsoever, I know that something is not right. Sometimes I feel something in my body and I have no idea what it is. I'm being aroused, of course, but I have neither the words nor the understanding to say what is happening to me. I just know that it feels different, sometimes even good, but it also feels very, very wrong.

Muzi is a man of God and therefore he can do no wrong. Besides, I am so indoctrinated that men are superior to women, the thought does not even cross my mind that he is acting in any way inappropriately. Something isn't right, though, and that can mean only one thing: the fault lies with me.

I don't know what to do about Muzi, but I want this to stop. I want to go back to simple hugs, when things weren't complicated and I looked forward to spending time with him. I want him to be my father figure again, not this man that feels me up and sticks his tongue in my mouth. Even though it feels good at times, it mostly feels wrong. And so I come up with a plan. If I tell him this is making me sin, then he'll have to stop, because he won't want me to sin. It's a good plan, I think. Foolproof.

The next time I see him for confession, I say that I've got something difficult to tell him. This thing, this lust that they preach about, I'm not sure I understand exactly what it is, but I think that it might be what I feel for him and I'm not sure we should continue what we're doing because I'm having these sinful feelings towards him. He doesn't hug or kiss me that night, and I am relieved. My plan has worked.

Oh boy, am I wrong. Muzi makes an appointment for both of us to see Uncle Erlo. We go up to his house and there I sit, in one of Uncle Erlo's lounges, with the two men facing me in their armchairs.

'Please will you tell Uncle Erlo what you told me,' says Muzi.

Hang on, isn't confession meant to be completely sacrosanct? Yet somehow, here I am, trying to put words to something I don't understand myself. Haltingly, I repeat what I told Muzi. But also, at the back of my mind, is Muzi's admonishment from all those months ago that I must not tell anyone about our special relationship. So I don't say that he kisses or fondles me. Instead, I tell Uncle Erlo that I think I may have feelings of lust towards this man, and I know that it's wrong and I'm really sorry. And Uncle Erlo, knowing full well how innocent and uneducated and ignorant his rules have made those adolescents under his care, rails at me. He tells me that I am a slut. I am a whore and a Delilah and a marriage wrecker. I am evil, trying to trip up a man of God. How dare I try to make a man sin. I am doing the devil's work.

And there sits Muzi, silent as the grave. He knows full well that if I have any feelings of lust, it's because of his actions, but he just sits there, listening to Uncle Erlo vilify me and saying not one word in my defence. He looks at me intently, though, throughout the tirade.

And then Uncle Erlo pronounces my sentence. I am no longer allowed to have anything to do with Muzi. We may not speak to each other, and we certainly may never ever be alone together, not ever. Understandable, but it's what comes next that shatters me. I am no longer allowed to have anything to do with Muzi's family, either. I may no longer speak to Mirriam or Msebenzi, his adorable children.

Uncle Erlo concludes by forbidding me to speak to anyone about this. Not even your mother, he warns. No one.

23

AT WAR WITH MYSELF

I have no idea what I am doing with the kids in my class, and there is no curriculum to follow, but we have a lot of fun. I'm really still a child myself. After my first few days on the job, I'm hauled over the coals. My kids are making too much noise. I need to control them better, and I'm handed the method of controlling them. An orange plumbing pipe.

I have to come up with a better plan, and I do. I develop a special kind of deafness. When the kids speak too loudly or shout, I can't hear them. I can only hear them when they whisper or speak softly. Then I lavish them with attention.

I get the basics in terms of stationery, and also the use of a screen and video player, plus a couple of cartoons that have been deemed okay for them to watch. We watch these often. We play a lot. I take them outside and also to the swings by Uncle Erlo's house where we have swinging competitions to see who can swing the highest.

My heart is filled with so much love for these kids. I have no idea how, but at some point they start speaking English to me, even the shy ones who wouldn't say boo or bah when they arrived. It is a genuinely happy time for all of us, I think. I hope.

But nothing lasts forever. I get called in again. Why am I not giving these kids hidings? Because they're good kids, I say. They're not naughty.

'Erika, these kids have been placed in your care. It's your responsibility to show them the way, to drive the devil from them. It is your God-given duty to give them hidings when they transgress. How else are they to learn?'

To my eternal shame, I start giving hidings to these sweet, innocent little kids who look up to me, who have been given into my care to protect. I will regret this to my dying day. I am eighteen years old, and I have become one of them. I have gone from being the abused to the abuser.

To the English classes of 1990 and 1991, I am so sorry. I wish you could see me weep as I write these words. Please forgive me for ever raising my hand to you. It was wrong. I was wrong.

Corporal punishment is still legal in South Africa in those years, and I never give anyone an excessive hiding – I know this because I find the whole idea so abhorrent. Nonetheless, I do it. I am told that God wants me to. And because God doesn't speak to me, I have to trust what I am told.

I don't realise this, but I am at war with myself. I am giving children hidings against my will, but I am still doing it. I am kissing Muzi against my will – he has not stopped calling me, despite Uncle Erlo's directive – but I am still doing it. I hate myself. I am evil and I can't believe that everyone else can't see it. I don't belong here. After more than a decade of trying to be like them, I am not like them. I don't fit in. I don't have a relationship with God; he never speaks to me. I don't feel the peace they preach about; all I feel is turmoil.

My weight plummets. I was already too skinny (I don't much like the food here, and with no one checking whether I'm eating or not, it's been so easy to skip meals), but now I'm anorexic. At my unhappiest, I weigh forty-four kilograms. I'm 1.76 metres tall, which gives me a BMI of 14.2, which would be a serious problem to anyone outside KSB. But no one here pays attention. My health woes increase as my weight drops. More migraines, more often. And my stomach is now so thin that when I get that serious tummy ache, you can actually see a lump on the right side below my navel. A palpable, visible manifestation.

24

BETWEEN TWO MEN OF GOD

I have one man of God telling me I'm not allowed to have anything to do with another man of God. But this second man of God is still calling me to come and see him – often late at night.

I don't know that I can say no. I'm nineteen years old by now, but I do not know that I have any power to resist. I never ignore Muzi's calls, I always go to him, even though I hate it. It's weird: I still like that he is giving me attention, but I am no longer aroused by his kisses or caresses. I just stand there, passively allowing this man to paw me. I do express my misgivings a number of times – I have Uncle Erlo to fall back on now – and I do tell him that I don't want to continue doing this. But he tells me that I mustn't worry, that Uncle Erlo doesn't understand. And so I do nothing to resist his advances.

I've been sworn to secrecy by Uncle Erlo, so I cannot speak to anyone about this. I briefly contemplate going back to Uncle Erlo, but what will he do to me if he knows I defied him? It doesn't bear thinking about it.

At one of our meetings, Muzi gives me a handwritten poem. It's on a lined, A4 piece of paper and covers the entire page. It's titled 'The Pearl'. And the poem is about a pearl, a precious, precious pearl. I think it's lovely, but then I would. Despite my very complicated feelings, I still hero-worship this man, my molester.

I am caught between these two men of God. All I know is that this is all my fault. One evening, Muzi and I are in his study when we hear Uncle Erlo's voice in the corridor. I panic and bolt out the door (the windows have no burglar bars – I should have gone out there) and run away in the other direction. But Uncle Erlo spots me. The next day, he calls me in and I get the dressing down of my life. Slut, whore, Delilah, marriage wrecker. All that and more. I must repent. I just sit there numbly and agree to everything he says.

Here's the odd thing, though. I am never publicly shamed. And by rights, I should be, considering my alleged crimes. No one ever reprimands me for not confessing my sins, either. Because that has stopped. Muzi doesn't even pretend to want to counsel me for my spiritual welfare any more. And no one has taken his place as my counsellor.

A few weeks later, Muzi asks me to return the poem. I do. And then I get summonsed by Uncle Erlo, who waves this piece of paper at me and asks: 'Do you know what this is?'

'Yes, that's a poem about a pearl.' And off he goes again. I'm a slut and a whore. He loves those words. He bandies them about like they're sweets every time he sees me. And he tells me that I am the pearl in this poem and that Muzi has written this poem about me, saying that I am a precious pearl to him. Uncle Erlo reckons this is just about the worst thing I've ever done because I am not Muzi's wife and how dare I be that person to him. But I didn't write the poem. I didn't even understand its meaning. Even so, I take on everything Uncle Erlo says. Yes, I am evil, I am irredeemably bad. Not even God talks to me the way he talks to everyone else.

I descend into further despair. I eat half a slice of bread every second day or so. I can't stand this body that is getting me into so much trouble. I don't want to be in this body any more.

I still wear my game face, though, my ready smile. Except on the odd occasion when I pass by Mirriam. I've taken to walking the long way round to get to our rondavel, instead of the path that leads me past where she sometimes sits.

'Miss Bornman, Miss Bornman!' Her face still lights up every time she sees me, despite the fact that I've abandoned her. And I keep walking. 'Hi, Mirriam,' I wave, and I keep walking as my heart breaks all over again.

One day, Muzi does something out of the ordinary. He comes to me for a change. I'm alone in our rondavel when he knocks on the door. He closes the door behind him and locks it. Then he asks, 'Erika, do you love me?'

What am I supposed to say? 'Yes, yes, of course I love you,' I reply.

Then he says, 'Well, in that case, please get undressed.'

Wordlessly, I go into the little bathroom. You don't ever get undressed in front of a man. I'm wearing a white dress, printed with blue and pink pixelated flowers. It's got shoulder pads and buttons all the way from the neckline to the dropped waist. I am wearing a white bra underneath. Slowly I unbutton the dress, but I don't take it off. With it unbuttoned but still on, I come out of the bathroom. I look at Muzi and say, 'I don't know what it is that we're doing but I don't think that I can do it.' Muzi gives me a long look, unlocks the door and leaves.

Maybe God does hear me, after all.

25

A SAVIOUR

Each of my parents has five siblings. My dad was the youngest of six. His brother, Chris, is twelve years his senior. Between them are four sisters. Growing up, I got to know and love all my dad's sisters, the younger one Iris in particular, but I've never met my uncle Chris. He emigrated from South Africa many decades ago and now lives in Sweden with his wife, Janet. My sister started corresponding with him while we were living in Joburg, I think. After my dad died, he wrote us a beautiful letter. A few months later, I pluck up the courage to write to him, too. And so starts a beautiful relationship. He responds graciously to this young niece he has never met, and the letters fly between Sweden and KSB. Well, not fly exactly.

'Your correspondence reminds me of the South African climate,' he writes teasingly. 'Long periods of drought followed by intense thunderstorms and rain.'

Towards the end of 1991, Chris comes to South Africa and the Bornman family hold a reunion in Pretoria. We all drive up. By this time my sister has married a man called Marius. There was no romance, of course. My mother called me to the rondavel one day and told me that my sister's engagement to Marius would be announced in church that day. I sat there, stunned. Not him, surely? I can't believe my beautiful sister is marrying Marius – a man with no redeeming qualities that I have been able to spot.

When I first meet my uncle, I can hardly speak to him. He's a bit shorter than my dad, but his mannerisms, the way he holds his head, the way his face moves, his inflections, wow. It's like I'm looking at a different version of my dad. The reunion is a fantastic day – reconnecting with long-lost cousins and chatting to my aunts, whom I haven't seen since my dad's funeral.

A few days later, Chris pays us a visit at KwaSizabantu. After he leaves, he contacts me with an offer that will change the entire trajectory of my life. 'You're learning French and you speak German, but you know the very best places to polish those languages are France and Germany, right?' Chris and Janet offer to buy me a plane ticket to Europe, as well as a three-month Eurail Pass that will allow me to travel on trains and busses. I later learn that, after his visit to KSB, he said to my aunt Iris: 'We've got to get Erika out of that place.' Thank you, Chris!

I am beside myself with joy. When I'd finished school, I'd wanted to au pair somewhere in Europe. I had done the research and even got some forms to fill in for an agency, hoping my mother would allow me to go. But someone had to teach the English class, and that someone had been me.

I have to get my mother's permission, of course. The age of majority in South Africa is twenty-one, but that is not the only reason. At KSB, a young, unmarried woman remains under her parents' jurisdiction until they hand her off to her husband. Then she becomes his problem. I cannot leave the compound without my mother's permission. I can't even make a call to my brother without my mother's permission. She has begrudgingly allowed my correspondence with my uncle, but only because I don't think she feels that she can deny me this when my sister set the precedent.

Miracle of miracles: my mother agrees! With conditions, of course. KSB has a huge number of supporters and followers in Europe: Germany, France, Switzerland, the Netherlands. They're a valuable source of income and are treated like VIPs when they visit. I may go, but only if I spend my time with KSB people. Uncle Robert and I get to work. He's Swiss and is so good to me. He helps me organise people to go and visit. I am so excited!

26

MY BODY IS A BATTLEGROUND

Before I get to go, though, there's the ongoing issue of my health to sort out. My mother has finally realised that there's something seriously physically wrong with me. The lump in my stomach, and the accompanying pain, has not gone away. Uncle Erlo still prays over me every now and again, but I think even he has given up on me. I'm not coming to the party by being healed by God, so my mother turns to medical science. I've been for so many tests, but no one can find the problem. They've checked my kidneys. Nothing wrong. They've given me the most humiliating, invasive and awful test investigating my bowels, still nothing.

One day, my mother tells me that I'm going to see yet another doctor. My brother is in the army in Durban by now, officer's training complete, and he will be taking me. He drives the 120 kilometres to KSB, picks me up and takes me to St Augustine's Hospital in Durban. There are some pregnant women in the waiting room with me, and I don't quite understand why I'm here. I am definitely not pregnant. At least, I don't think I am. I don't know how you get pregnant, but I know you need a husband for that, and I don't have one of those (not yet anyway).

The receptionist gives me what feels like an enormous amount of water to drink and then I get called in for the examination. The doctor is an older man with kind eyes. He takes some gel and puts it on my tummy and moves an instrument all over it. He explains to me that it's an ultrasound. Yes, he says, it looks like there's a small cyst on one of your ovaries. I don't know what an ovary is, but that doesn't sound good. I ask him if it's serious. No, it's small and it's quite normal, he responds. It should disappear on its own. He looks at me, frowning. Don't ever let anyone cut you to get it out, understood? I don't, but I nod.

He puts on some gloves. I'm going to do the internal examination now, he tells me. His nurse helps me raise my knees and open my legs. I freeze. This feels wrong. I am so exposed. Tears start forming in my eyes.

'Don't worry,' the man with the kind eyes reassures me. 'It will be over real soon.'

He puts some gel on his glove and then he puts a finger inside me. I had no clue that my body has an opening where someone's fingers can go. I feel violated and my reaction is visceral and immediate. I vomit out all the water I drank a short while ago.

As the nurse rushes to clean me up, the doctor takes my hand in his. 'I am so sorry, my dear,' he says to me. I'm crying now, from humiliation more than anything

71

else, because he didn't hurt me. 'I didn't realise you were a virgin, no one told me, and I don't see many virgins your age any more, you know.' I can't quite comprehend what he is saying, but it doesn't matter. The nurse helps me get dressed and leads me to another small room that has a bed. She puts a blanket over me and strokes my hair as I weep. I think I fall asleep. I've forgotten all about my brother, who is waiting for me in reception.

I don't tell my brother what has just happened, the shame is too deep. He eventually takes me home. My mother does not ask me how it went. She must have known that I was going to see a gynaecologist. She must have known what he was likely to do. She definitely knows that I have no understanding of how my body works – she's made sure of that. Yet she did not prepare me for the appointment at all. She just told me that I was going to see another doctor. I will never understand how she could do that to me. Yes, I am nearly twenty years old, but I'm still her little girl, aren't I?

None of these doctors can figure out what is wrong with me, so a surgeon in Pretoria who is affiliated to the mission agrees to examine me. My mother accompanies me this time. He tells her that I'm dangerously underweight. It's the first time I remember someone commenting on my weight. I don't remember what my mother answers. I don't know why or how, but he decides that there is nothing for it. He's going to have to cut me open, take everything out and examine it.

I remember what the lovely doctor in Durban said to me, but I have no say in what happens to me or my body. I am to be cut open from my navel to my pubic bone.

I don't know who pays for the operation – we don't have medical aid, and this is a really lovely hospital. Maybe the doctor? Who knows? I come around after the operation and I'm told that all they found was a slightly inflamed appendix, which the surgeon removed, and a cyst on my one ovary, which he also removed. The cyst, that is, not the ovary. But he could not find what is making me so ill and causing me so much pain. I recuperate at a cousin's house near Centurion for a few days before going back to KSB.

In no time at all, I'm on a plane to Europe. My scar is vivid and red, a slice down the centre of my stomach. A constant reminder of my powerlessness.

Before I leave, Uncle Erlo calls me in again. A third man has heard God telling him that we should get married. I don't know him at all, but I know his brother, who's a man I detest. Uncle Erlo tells me to go away and pray, and I respond bravely that my answer is no, I don't need to pray about it. Uncle Erlo nearly bursts a blood vessel. Explain yourself, he demands. I simply tell him that I cannot see how God would want me to marry a man like that. What I don't say is that nothing is going to stand in my way: I am going to Europe and no man, nor God Himself, for that matter, is going to make me stay.

27

LIFE BEYOND THE COMPOUND

Europe is a revelation. Everywhere I go, I am treated with so much kindness and warmth. None of the condemnation I'm used to back home. Sure, these people are part of the KSB community, but they represent everything that is good about it, with none of the fear and criticism I've become accustomed to.

Uncle Robert comes to Europe and takes me to visit a wonderful family in Brienz in Switzerland. They live right by the lake, and we're surrounded by mountains and beauty. I end up staying with them for about three months. They speak to me in English and *Hochdeutsch* (high German, which is the kind of standardised German all speakers would recognise), but I seem to have inherited my dad's ear for languages and soon figure out the many ways Swiss German differs from German and can start understanding them better when they speak their native language.

I blossom in Brienz. I regain my taste for life, and my taste for food. One day, we're high in the Swiss mountains in a cabin. There are a number of people, and on the table inside is what appears to me to be a feast: cold meats and cheeses and breads. It's the first time in a long, long while that I enjoy eating food. There's this one particular cut of cold meat I really like. It's tender and melts in my mouth and is so delicious. I can't get enough of it. Then I hear someone say, 'Should we tell her what she's eating?' Oh no, it's horse meat. I've been eating Black Beauty!

I get to Brienz late in April 1992. A few months later, I visit Chris and Janet in Sweden (my mother cannot forbid me from seeing my benefactors, after all). It's high summer and beautiful. They live in the south of Sweden, just outside Landskrona. This is one of the first times since I turned fifteen that I am in the home of anyone not affiliated with KSB. They drink wine, they watch TV, but they treat me with such kindness and care that I cannot imagine that they are headed for hell.

I spend my twenty-first birthday in Germany somewhere, surrounded by more love and kindness than on any other birthday I've had in recent years. I visit the Althof family in Berlin. Ah man, could their mother please adopt me? She is so kind, so loving, everything a mother should be. I feel like an alien who has been dropped into a world where she has no right to be, but where she desperately, desperately wants to stay. There is such abundance: of food, chocolate, love, laughter (how did I not realise how much I missed laughter?).

At some point, I make my way to the Jaeger family in Annecy, France. Again, so warm and welcoming. I spend many wonderful months with them.

Here's the thing about the average person who gets involved with KSB: they are really, really good people. The environment on the compound in South Africa is oppressive, but here in Europe, people's natures are allowed to shine through more. They're still repressed, and many of them are going through their own private hell, but I'm blissfully unaware of all that. I am loved and cared for, and I am starting to find my way back to myself without the constant monitoring and policing I experience at KSB. My uncle was right. I needed to get out of that place.

I write to my mother about once a week. I get frequent letters from her too, and from my brother. My sister also writes, but she has her hands full with her first child, the cutest little girl with Hanna's dark hair and dark eyes.

As is their wont, there are regular visits from Uncle Erlo, his brother Friedel and other KSB co-workers. Mercifully, not Muzi, from what I remember. We still correspond, but I am so grateful he cannot send his maid to call me any more. I feel free.

And then one day, we're in a church service. It's a Sunday and we're somewhere in the south-east of France. I'm surrounded by people where I sit in the middle of a row. Suddenly, I feel a pain in my chest that radiates into my upper back. It's so intense, I gasp audibly. It's clear something is wrong, and I'm not sure whether I make it out of the room by myself or if I'm helped out. Is this what happened to my dad? Am I having a heart attack? Am I going to die? I'll be going straight to hell, I know this. I haven't confessed my sins in months. There is a doctor present, and he immediately rushes me to hospital.

An X-ray shows I suffered a spontaneous pneumothorax. He explains to me that my one lung has collapsed, which was the cause of the excruciating pain. He looks at me and says: 'Erika, if you don't start eating, you are going to die.' This jolts me. For the first time in my life, I actually understand that I need food to survive. I've never made that connection before.

They determine that no surgical intervention is required, but that I do need to remain under medical supervision. I don't have medical insurance, and so this kind doctor and his wife welcome me into their home. He monitors me and she cares for me. The kindness of these strangers towards this young woman from another country amazes me. They look after me while I recuperate and never, not once, make me feel as though I'm any kind of burden.

It's a while before I'm allowed to fly again, and so my next visit to Sweden has to be postponed. When I get there, it's winter – a magical snowscape of wonder. Chris and Janet have some serious discussions with me about my future. It's the first time any adult has shown an interest in what I want to do with my life. I start thinking that maybe I can make plans, maybe there is hope, maybe I can find a way to be happy.

I tell them about my dream of being a translator at the United Nations. A few days later, they sit me down. They offer to pay for my tuition at Maastricht University in the Netherlands, as that would be a good place to study languages and translation. I would need to get a job to help with living expenses, but they want to help me achieve my dream.

I am beside myself with joy. I call my mother, all excited.

'No, Erika, you are coming home. You promised me you'll return in January, and so you are coming back in January. You have a job here and people depend on you. You are not allowed to stay in Europe.'

I don't know that I'm allowed to make my own decisions now that I've turned twenty-one. I'm officially an adult, but I am not aware of the significance. I am unmarried and therefore still have to obey my mother. Crestfallen, I bid Chris and Janet farewell, return to Annecy and pack up my stuff.

I resign myself to the fact that I will now have to get married. But it will be okay. I can see how happy my sister is now that she has a baby, so I can make this work. I have to. I return to teach at Domino Servite. And yes, I'll probably get more marriage proposals, and, at some point, I will have to accept one. Then I'll have kids, and there it is. My life is mapped out for me. I just need to obey and do as I am told.

28

EXODUS

As sad as I am about leaving Europe, there is joy in arriving back home. I get to see my mother, my sister, Jessie and my adorable little niece.

And then, I go to greet Muzi. He's in a new office that has been built in my absence. It's a lot nicer than his old dingy little room. Nothing else has changed, however. He pins me against the wall and kisses and fondles me, and I let him do what he does.

I can't sleep that night. I can't do this any more. The next day I phone my dad's sister Iris, who lives in Pietermaritzburg.

'Tannie Iris, please can I come visit?'

And she says: 'Of course, my child, come.'

I have to ask my mother for permission to get a lift, but she cannot rightfully deny me the opportunity to see my father's sister. I tell her that I have a gift from Chris and Janet for Iris and that I'd like to give it to her, which is true.

I pack a bag with minimal clothes. I only have a handful of toiletries, so that's easy. Shampoo, soap, toothpaste, toothbrush, body lotion. I'm only supposed to be going for the weekend, and if I pack too much, my mother will know that I have no intention of returning. I can't allow her even a tiny bit of suspicion, so I leave behind most of what I own. Although it not much, let's face it, it's still mine.

With my mother's permission, reception arranges a lift for me to Pietermaritzburg. I don't have my licence and I definitely don't have a car. I've never been taught how to drive, so I am completely at their mercy.

When I get to Iris, I break down. 'I cannot go back there,' I tell her.

And this beautiful angel says to me, 'Erika, you don't have to. You can stay with me for as long as you need.'

That night, I phone my brother. He's living in Durban, and I say to him, 'Chris, I'm not going back.' I'm crying and can hardly talk. It's late at night, but he gets in his car and drives through. We talk until the early morning hours, the three of us. I don't tell Chris everything that has happened to me, I don't tell him about Muzi, but I tell him enough for him to agree with me: 'Don't ever go back there.' Having his support means the world to me.

Iris makes the call to my mother on the Sunday morning, the day I was supposed to return to the mission. I sit trembling next to her. She tells my mother that

I will not be returning to teach at the school, but that I will be staying with her in Pietermaritzburg for the foreseeable future instead.

I may be going to hell, but I am no longer living there. I was going to hell anyway, even while at KSB. I may as well go to hell doing things my way for a change.

PART THREE

THE UNEASY MIMIC

29

THE ROAD TO INDEPENDENCE

I am one of the lucky ones; I escape by choice, and I have an aunt who takes me into her home. Also, an uncle who helps me realise that there is life outside the compound, and a brother who gives me his unwavering support from day one.

My schoolfriend, Celimpilo, is less lucky. Like me, they threaten her with expulsion, but at only fifteen, she's a year younger than I was when my mother threatened me with that lonely road out of KSB. Celimpilo's crime? Accepting a bar of chocolate from an adult male, a man who is her father's colleague. When confronted, she exacerbates the situation by refusing to acknowledge that she's in a relationship with this guy (she's not). She's just a girl-child, and now her original transgression has expanded to include insolence, insubordination and not showing remorse. They expel her from the school. Just like that. Her parents disown her (they choose to, sure, but they also have to, as their livelihood depends on the mission).

Celimpilo takes the road leading out of KSB. Unlike me, who'd at least had the promise of a suitcase, she leaves with only the clothes on her back and not a single cent in her pocket. Her parents take her belongings – including a much-treasured stamp collection – back home. They drive right past their little girl trudging up that lonely road, and they keep going. Celimpilo finds shelter from the harsh sun under a tree at a nearby store. Kind strangers give her a bed to sleep in that night and the next day she carries on, unwashed and on foot, to try to make a life for herself. Celimpilo is not the first to be kicked out like this and she will not be the last. That's how I know how lucky I am to have a home.

That first Sunday morning, waking up in Iris's house, feels surreal. I'm not getting ready for church and, as I lie there, wondering what I'm to do now, I vow to myself that I will not be like the countries I've read about, the countries I've studied in the African politics course I sneaked past my mother. I will not be an ex-colony that thirty years after liberation still blames the colonial power for all its problems. I will take charge of my life; I will make a success of it. At twenty-one years old, I'm filled with dread, but also hope.

What I don't realise is that I've bought into the victim-shaming culture propagated by the apartheid government – my African politics course was in 1990, before the fall of that regime. It's not that simple to let go of the past, and especially so when that past was designed to keep you subjugated. What do I know of the petty bureaucracy ingrained by the oppressor, the systemic lack of education that hampers progress, the instilled fear that stops dreams from germinating? I don't know that the struggle does not end when you declare independence. It's not over when you replace the oppressor's flag with your own. What I do know is that I am free – at last!

My first priority is finding a job. I've got matric, but no other qualifications except for half a bachelor's degree that is meaningless until I complete it. Sure, I spent the best part of two years teaching English to five-year-olds, but with no training. I know that no other school will employ me without the necessary qualifications. I basically have a matric certificate and a bubbly personality that they haven't quite managed to extinguish. I also have the debilitating fear that I am worthless, not good enough, and will never amount to anything.

Every morning, I read every single job ad in the *Natal Witness*, circling the ones in pen that might take me. My very first interview is for a dentist's assistant. I am shaking with fear as I walk into his rooms for the interview. No surprise, I don't get the job. My second interview is for a receptionist's position at an insurance broker. I feel a bit more confident about this one, as there is no medical equipment in sight. And I get it!

Within two weeks of leaving KSB, I am a salaried employee. It's a tiny salary, for sure, but it's a darn sight better than the R150 a month I got at KSB for teaching. I am on the road to independence. The job itself is not hard. I spend my weekdays making appointments, fielding calls, taking messages. What is hard is that I'm scared every moment of every day that I'm going to mess up because no one has taught me how to act in this world.

My new office is in a small complex, with an optometrist next door. Iris works at the Natal Museum and drops me off at work every morning – and I get a ride back home with her every afternoon. Back at home, Iris introduces me to Nana Mouskouri's music. There's something about her voice that soothes me, heals me. I listen to those LPs on repeat. Iris, bless her heart, never complains.

My health improves dramatically – while I still get the occasional migraine, I don't experience that intense abdominal pain any more. I'm still skinny, but at least now I'm wearing an adult size eight instead of clothes meant for girls aged twelve and thirteen.

Believe it or not, I still go back to KSB on the odd Sunday. Not often, just every now and again. I go back to visit my mother, but I have to sit through the Sunday service to do so. She is my mother, after all. And my sister and niece. How I adore my niece! At this point, I still believe KSB walks in the light of God. I am the evil one. I do hope I'll find redemption one day, though I can't see how.

I notice that people at KSB are not quite as warm towards me as before; it's as if I am walking around with the mark of the beast on my forehead. They haven't quite figured out what to do with me yet: Is Erika an apostate? Has she rejected us, or is there still hope that we can lure her back?

I never spend another minute alone with Muzi, and my relief is intense. He will never again get to run his hands over my body or put his tongue in my mouth. On Sundays, KSB is too busy, too full of people for him to have a chance to be alone with me.

And I always get back in the car in the afternoon and I always leave. There are enough people in and around Pietermaritzburg who go to church there for me to get lifts with them. What gives me the courage to go back to KSB is that Iris knows where I am. They can't keep me there. They have to allow me to leave, and it feels kind of good to flaunt my new-found independence.

A HEATHEN IN JEANS

One of the insurance brokers at my new job is a young guy, let's call him Gareth. As he gets to know me, he teases me about the old-fashioned way I dress. He calls me 'Koeksister'. I laugh, but it hurts. I know that if I'm going to fit in, I'm going to have to change the way I dress, but I'm completely clueless as to how to go about it. One Friday afternoon, Gareth gets permission for me to leave work early. Get in the car, he tells me, we're going shopping for a pair of jeans for you.

He takes me to Truworths and starts collecting jeans for me to try on. I put on the first pair, come out and show him. Nope, that won't do. We eventually find a pair he approves of.

Gareth insists I leave the shop wearing my new purchase. He can't be seen walking next to me in my old-fashioned clothes, he laughs. And, for the first time in my life, I feel sexy. Not that I know that's what I'm feeling – sexy is most definitely not a word that is in my lexicon. At the same time, I feel ashamed and sinful. And I'm convinced that once I step out onto the street, a bolt of lightning will come down and God will strike me dead for wearing this evil piece of clothing. And so we walk down the street and I do my best to stay under awnings. But the lightning bolt does not come.

As Gareth drops me at home, he turns to me and says: 'You're wearing that tonight and I'm taking you out.'

We're going to a bar. A bar with alcohol and loose women and men intent on sinning. I am so conflicted. On the one hand, I feel as though I'm finally living but, oh my word, if I die tonight, I will go to straight to hell and then I'm never going to see my dad again. My desire to experience life and to taste the forbidden fruit wins the internal struggle. I know I'm evil, and if I'm going to go to hell for wearing a pair of jeans, I may as well go to hell for drinking alcohol too. My idea of sin doesn't stretch much further than that. Not yet anyway.

Gareth comes to pick me up that evening. I'm wearing my jeans and a top I think goes with the jeans. I've never set foot in a bar in my life, and I know Gareth doesn't really get that. I've also never had any alcohol. Gareth calls me over; he's bought me a cider, plus a shot of something. He tells me to down the shot and shows me how. I follow suit and am instantly overcome – coughing, tearing up and breathless. The idiot bought me a shot of Stroh rum – eighty per cent proof. He realises that he's screwed up and is so apologetic. Once I've recovered, I laugh it off because I'm now buzzing beautifully.

But then there's another obstacle. Gareth leads me onto the dance floor. I have devoted my entire life to denying my body, to not feeling my body. I was not allowed to even acknowledge that I have one. Now I'm on a dance floor where people all around me are moving as though they like their bodies. They inhabit their bodies. They're comfortable in their bodies. They're shimmying and they're shaking and they're having fun. I am frozen to the spot, completely overwhelmed. I feel so insignificant, and I know that I am never, ever, ever going to fit into this world that is so foreign to me. I so badly want to be part of it, but how will I ever be able to move like that?

I whisper to Gareth that I've never danced before and that I don't know how. He gives me an incredulous look. Maybe the Stroh-rum episode helps convince him. Just mimic everything I do, he tells me. And so, Stroh rum and cider buzzing through my veins, I try. I manage to move my feet, somewhat anyway. Then Gareth shows me that I need to move my hips too, but my hips don't want to sway. They're locked and I feel like the biggest fraud ever.

Other people seem to be so at ease in their own bodies. I see it on the dance floor that night, but I see it on the streets too, and I see it at work. Everywhere I go there are people inhabiting their bodies with ease. It's as though they know who they are, and they have confidence. They walk upright and they look me straight in the eye and smile.

I just keep asking myself silently where they get such confidence. How do you know who you are? How do you inhabit your body with such ease? How can you show off your shoulders and your hips and your curves? How can you wear a bikini? How *do* you wear a bikini? How do you show off your body? How do you smile and talk to a man without wanting to hide?

The people I watch – and now mimic – show me how completely alienated I am from my body. I take Gareth's idea from the dance floor into the rest of my life. I don't know how to live in this world, but the people around me do. And so I decide that all I need to do to fit in is to act the way they do.

However, I cannot shake that feeling of being an impostor. I didn't fit in at KSB, and I don't fit in here either. I don't know how to live in this world. I don't know how to talk to men. I don't even know how to talk to women. I don't know what to say. I don't know how to act. I don't know how to dress. Everything about this world is foreign to me.

Back at KSB, I knew who I was – I was the girl who always smiled and never complained. I was dying inside, sure. But now that I'm outside, in the world, I still feel as though I'm dying, because I know that the moment I show people who I am, they will see that I don't belong in their world. At KSB, I lived in fear of putting a foot wrong because the punishment would be awful. Out here, I can't discern any proper punishment, except maybe scorn. I'm so scared that people will scorn me for not knowing how to live in their world.

I'm not happy in my skin. It's not that I want to die, not at all. I just don't know how to live. But I also know that suicide will send me straight to hell. I'm going to hell anyway, but I'm so confused. I know that if I kill myself, I'm definitely doomed for all eternity. But I'm hoping that if someone else kills me, God might look favourably on me, and still allow me into heaven, where I will get to hang out with my dad.

And so I spend many nights thinking of ways in which I can die without being the one who kills me. I decide the best way would probably be to wander about the more dangerous streets in Pietermaritzburg in the dead of night. Maybe some thug will kill me. I hear stories of women getting killed for being out at night. But my fear of first getting raped before getting killed is fairly huge. I'm still a virgin and don't quite know what rape is, but I now have an inkling of what sex is about, because now I can read any book I want and watch TV. So I'm starting to kind of think I understand what happens between a man and a woman, and the thought of getting raped terrifies me.

Thoughts of my brother stop me too. I can't do that to him. And I don't want to become one of the stories KSB tells kids. They love their stories: drug addicts who repent but then turn their back on God and overdose. Other people who have been shown the truth and the way but turn their back on God and die – in a car crash or by lightning strike – before they have time to repent. God's mercy has run out on them.

I shelve my plans to get murdered for now. I just have to figure this out. I can do this.

31

FACE-OFF

Uncle Erlo hears of my defection and sends for me one Sunday when I'm visiting my mother. I think I know what's coming, and so I walk up the road to his house as if I'm going to my doom. Once there, I am directed to a room I know well. This is where he sat next to Muzi and told me that I was a slut, a whore and a Delilah and forbade me to discuss it with anyone. Also where he told me that I was going to hell for being a stumbling block to a man of God after he happened upon Muzi and me that one night. It was in this very room that he told me about three different men who said it was God's will that they marry me and that I needed to go and pray about it. No, this room brings back no cheerful memories whatsoever. I know today will be no different.

As always, Uncle Erlo is impeccably dressed. It's after church, so he's taken off the suit jacket he wore at the pulpit and loosened his tie. He greets me as I take a seat across from him.

'How are you, Erika?'

'I'm well, thank you, Uncle Erlo.'

Then he tells me that he hears I have taken a job in Pietermaritzburg, and that I won't be returning to teach the English class at Domino Servite School. That's correct, I confirm. I'm now a receptionist at an insurance brokerage. He asks me where I'm staying and I tell him at my aunt's, my father's sister, who has taken me under her wing.

'So, Erika, is this really God's will for your life then?' he asks me, frowning.

I gulp. This man still has such a hold over me. I'm filled with dread and fear, but his grip has loosened slightly after my time in Europe and these few weeks away from his compound and followers. I also know I will leave here this afternoon – Iris is expecting me, there's no way they can keep me here. I look him straight in the eyes.

'Uncle Erlo, I didn't consult God on this one.'

Boom. The volcano erupts immediately. His face turns red, and he raises his voice as he berates me. He rebukes me for all the care and kindness that KwaSizabantu, that he personally, has shown me over the years, and how I am throwing it back in their faces. He admonishes me for leaving the one true way. I am one of the luckiest people in the world because so many never get the chance to hear the word of God, but I have been hearing the word of God for years now. And I am choosing to leave the one true way God has shown – I am deliberately walking away from a life with God.

He tells me that I am worse than any heathen. The heathens don't know any better, but I do. I am definitely going straight to hell because I am turning my back on the truth – the only truth. He warns me that I have been seduced by the pleasures of the world, but that the wages of sin are death.

He carries on doing what he does so well: telling me what I should do with my life and why I am so very bad. And I do what I have done so often: I leave my body. I am looking at him, listening, but I don't feel as though I'm even there. The only thought in my head is that I am leaving this afternoon, that I'll be returning to Pietermaritzburg. There's a car waiting for me, to take me away from here. To take me to a life that I don't understand yet. A life that I don't deserve. I don't know how I'm going to live this life, but it's different from the one he wants me to live.

I'm leaving, I'm leaving, I'm leaving. I'm leaving. I'm leaving.

Uncle Erlo's tirade ends. He's condemned me to an eternity of burning in hell, and now he is silent as he looks at me. I can't quite figure out if he's sad or still angry, but when he speaks again, his voice is calm.

'Erika.'

'Yes, Uncle Erlo?'

'You will never be happy. And, one day when you marry, your husband will sleep around with other women.'

Uncle Erlo gets up. This conversation is over. At the door, he turns to look at me. He has one last thing to say to me.

'God's curse is now on your life, Erika.'

32

DISOWNED

I take God's curse back to Pietermaritzburg with me. Along with my mother's engagement ring. Now that I'm earning a salary, I'm able to do something I've long been wanting to do. When my dad proposed to my mother all those years ago, he had very little money. She has a delicate engagement ring with a tiny diamond, but a few years after my dad died, the diamond fell out and was lost. I know where my mother keeps the ring; I take it and hide it in a pocket.

Later that week, I show it to a jeweller in town. He replaces the diamond and adds a bit of gold to the band at the back where it has worn thin. That's what I do with my first paycheque, and my heart bursts with pride as I hand my mother her fixed engagement ring a few weeks later. She can wear it again, this symbol of my dad's love. I might be cursed, but that won't stop me from trying to repair our relationship.

Six months after I start my job, the owner of the business tragically loses his life in a car accident. He has a wife and two young sons and it's devastating. The optometrist next door comes over and says he's been watching me and would like to offer me a job as one of his receptionists. I gratefully accept.

By now I've moved away from Iris and am living with a family in Wartburg, a small town about thirty kilometres from Pietermaritzburg. I get a lift in and out every day. It's Uncle Erlo's sister and her husband who have taken me in. That family is so kind to me, and I'll be forever grateful that they gave me a home for a while. But Wartburg is far for someone without a car (or licence), and so I leave to board with the widow of my former boss and her two boys. The family is grieving, yet it is a warm, loving environment. She introduces me to the music of Anne Murray. I now listen to Nana and Anne on repeat.

I haul out my UNISA textbooks – I have registered again to carry on studying for that bachelor's degree I don't really want. I don't have it in me to decide what else to study right now. And then I find I don't have it in me to study at all. Tomorrow, I'll study tomorrow.

I have a regular visitor – a guy my age who is still part of KSB, but not quite part of KSB. Let's call him John. John and I have always been friends; I don't quite know how we managed it. I guess it's because he's from one of the prominent families, so he gets away with a bit more, plus his family doesn't actually live at KSB, they just visit regularly. And my mother wasn't that invested in what I got up to. I remember one afternoon, when I was still living in her rondavel, how John and I sneaked in a visit to my little upstairs loft. It was entirely innocent, but terribly illicit.

Now, he can visit freely and there's genuine affection between us. As I get to know him better, I develop a proper crush on him. I'm twenty-two years old and I've never been kissed by someone I wanted to kiss. Until John and I kiss one day. It never really goes any further than kisses and some fondling, as John is as clueless as I am about matters of the flesh. And he's a sweet guy who doesn't push me to do anything I'm uncomfortable with. Our fledgeling, innocent relationship gives me hope that maybe I can find someone who loves me. I just don't think it is likely to be John. I'm an apostate now, and I can't imagine that his family will ever accept me. And so my heart is already breaking, because I know that if we continue, one day he will have to choose between his family and me.

And still I return to KSB, less often now, but I haven't given up on the possibility of repairing my relationship with my mother. Some Sundays, Chris drives up from Durban, picks me up in Pietermaritzburg, and then we go on to KSB together. We have lunch with our mother, see our sister and nieces (a second sweetheart has joined the first), and then we return the same way. Chris has to drive 400 kilometres every time we make that trip, but he never complains.

On one such visit, our mother sits us down. She is gravely concerned about our spiritual standing with the Lord, she tells us. She is deeply worried about the way we are living our lives; we know that it's not the right way. We are deliberately turning our backs on God, and we need to know that God's mercy is going to run out on us one day.

My mother says that she cannot go along with our way of life any longer. She cannot turn a blind eye to her children sinning with such abandon.

Either Chris or I let something slip about one or other leader at the mission – it's not complimentary. We question how she can blindly follow someone who has done something so wrong. Our mother is aghast. How dare we speak ill of a man of God?

'Until you acknowledge Uncle Erlo as your spiritual leader, you are not my children,' she tells us.

By now I have mimicked my way into feeling as though maybe, just maybe, I can live out in the world, and I feel strong enough to say to her: 'Uncle Erlo is not my spiritual leader.'

'Then you are not my daughter.'

33

EXILED

I knew when I left KwaSizabantu that people who leave are disowned. Excommunicated. Cast out. Banished. Exiled into darkness.

So why did I think I would be any different? I am an evil girl who is now living in an evil world – by choice. My only family is my brother. Iris, Chris and Janet, too, of course – I don't really know my other uncles, aunts and cousins any more.

I have to make peace with the fact that I am doomed for all eternity. I have to see if I can make something of my life. I don't know how, though. I'm floundering. As disconnected as I am from my feelings and from my body, I can recognise that I'm not okay. Except I don't know how to ask for help. Pretending to be okay has been my coping mechanism for so long that I simply cannot show anyone the depth of my despair.

All I need to do is sit down with Iris and tell her that I'm not coping. That I don't know how to be alive any more. I find myself unable to do even that. As much as I know she loves me, I cannot let her in.

Trying to survive takes up so much energy. Every time I look at my stack of university books, I want to cry. I didn't want to do this degree in the first place – I wanted to study law or actuarial science – but now that I have half a degree, I should just finish it. French in particular is a challenge – there isn't a single person around me who speaks French. This is long before the invention of YouTube or anything like that, so I don't have any way of immersing myself in the language. It seems an insurmountable mountain, this course.

I should be able to do this, I berate myself over and over. But I don't put any genuine effort into my studies and so I stop doing the one thing guaranteed to help me make something of my life: getting a degree. I don't write my exams that year and never sign up for another course again. I am self-sabotaging, but I don't understand that this is what I'm doing, and I don't realise its ramifications for my future.

Jessie, by now, has also left KSB. Her parents don't disown her in as many words, but she is estranged from her family. She works in a town about fifty kilometres away from me, but she has a car, so she visits me. Our friendship blossoms, and while we often talk about what happened to us back at the compound, we don't talk about what Muzi did to me or what her counsellor did to her. Jessie understands me in ways that my new friends don't, because how can they? What I went through is so foreign, so unusual, that I don't think they can ever really understand.

A thought strikes me a few months after leaving. What if I wasn't the only one? Muzi is counselling countless young girls and women. God knows what he might be doing to them. If I speak up, I could save them from what happened to me. So I do what I really, really don't want to do. I make an appointment to see Uncle Erlo and I go back there to speak to him. He's in his study this time, not the room where we had all our previous meetings.

'Do you mind if I record this?' he asks.

I have no problem with that, no. I tell him what actually happened between Muzi and me. I am starting to understand it was grooming, though I'm not familiar with the term yet. But I do know now that I was innocent. I tell Uncle Erlo how Muzi told me not to tell anyone because what we had was special. How he kept calling me to come and see him even after Uncle Erlo himself forbade it.

He listens in silence. That is not good, he agrees. He tells me that Muzi will be stripped of all his power, positions and privileges, and that he will not be allowed to counsel young girls or women any more. I'm relieved. I've done the right thing.

Two weeks later, I open the *Natal Witness*. There's a huge photograph of a beaming Muzi. The caption proclaims that he's the founder of Christians for Truth (an organisation he told me was designed to go underground when the communists took over South Africa). The article is flattering, and I am nauseated. I'm at work, but I don't care. I place a call to the KSB switchboard. I don't know if they've been told to put me through or whether it's pure fluke, but I get Uncle Erlo on the other end of the line. I tell him about the article I'm looking at and ask him how it's possible after he told me that Muzi would be censured and stripped of his position.

'Remind me what we spoke of?' My skin crawls. 'I don't remember,' says this man of God.

That's it. I'm done with that place. They're protecting the person who molested me and pretending they know nothing. I'm done.

That December, my brother Chris and I embark on a trip to Europe. It's so lovely, despite our severe lack of funds. Chris and Janet help pay for our tickets – they really are like my fairy godparents. We fly to London via Amsterdam, where we meet insurance-broker Gareth's mother and spend a few lovely days with her and her partner. Then we hire a car and drive up to Scotland to see one of Chris's friends. It's freezing cold. But it's oh so beautiful. I fall in love with Scotland and its ancient castles and mountainous landscapes.

Back to Amsterdam we go, where we spend a few nights in a youth hostel. One cold night we take a walk through the red-light district. My eyes are wide with amazement the whole time. Once again, I see women who look so comfortable in their bodies. I know I should despise them for being whores, but I don't. I admire them for their confidence, for their brazen display of who they are. Here I am, a naive young virgin. I know nothing about the darker side of their world, of course; the trafficking and coercion. What I see are empowered women. How far

I've fallen, I think to myself. Maybe Uncle Erlo was right. Maybe I am one of them. Because look at how much I admire them, how I wish I had their confidence. By now I have a better idea of what sex is. I know now that a man has a penis. And I know more about that hole that the girls were talking about back in Standard 6. But sex – the actual act – is still a mystery to me. An enticing mystery, but scary as all hell.

We catch a plane to Copenhagen, after which it's a short hop across the channel to the south of Sweden, where Chris and Janet and their warm, welcoming home await. We spend the most wonderful Christmas with them. This is family, I think. This is what other people get to experience every year. There's a Christmas tree and many, many presents. They are so warm and lovely. Is this what unconditional love feels like, I wonder?

And then it's back to South Africa, back to work. Back to my job at the optometrist.

34

WHORE

I have made another friend at work, let's call her Shelley. Shelley is a sweet young woman, quite shy, but she has a fantastic sense of humour. We bond and soon become fast friends. She knows tragedy too, and is sensitive to the sadness that runs like a vein through my days.

Chris has moved into digs with two other guys in Durban. I still don't have a car, so he always has to make the most effort. And he does – I see him often. He's the athlete of the family and swims the Midmar Mile. Then he trains for and runs the Comrades marathon with his housemates. I really enjoy hanging out with my brother – I've always been proud of him, but never more so than now. And I like hanging out with his friends, too.

One of his housemates invites me to a concert. Laura Branigan is coming to Durban, and he thinks I might enjoy it. And boy, is he right! He gets us good seats, close to the stage, and I am enthralled. I cannot take my eyes off her – Laura Branigan *owns* that stage. I've never seen anything like it. She is unashamedly, unapologetically and exuberantly herself. And she's a woman. The only people I've seen with that level of confidence are men standing behind a pulpit – and they are restrained by comparison. This strutting around on stage is such a revelation to me. I want to be like her so badly my chest hurts.

She sings 'The Power of Love' and I instantly recognise it as the song I heard at a Van Reenen petrol station years ago when I was fifteen and we were driving down from Joburg to make our life at KSB. I'd only heard a snippet of it, but it moved me then and it moves me now. Laura has my full attention. She sings about something I want so desperately. The kind of relationship I dream of – I want to be someone's lady and I want him to be my man. I want to learn about the power of love.

It's many years after this concert that a thought strikes me – was I on a date that night? I was so clueless back then that it might well have been. I would never have thought he could be interested in me, but I guess it's possible. I definitely fancied him, but would never have had the guts to give him a sign. So, Mike, if by some chance you're reading this – thank you for an eye-opening, amazing experience. I have never forgotten the yearning I felt while watching Laura Branigan on that stage. That's when I felt the first stirring of hope that maybe, someday, I could also feel – and be – that free.

Sometime after the concert, I meet a guy I think might be the one. Shelley has introduced me to her brother. He's really attractive. I can't quite believe that someone like him would want to hang out with someone like me, but when he asks me to go see a movie, I say yes. We date and it's all rather lovely. I can't quite believe my luck – this is definitely too good to be true. We kiss. And the more often we kiss, the more aroused I become. It's a familiar feeling, sure, but way more intense and a lot lovelier than before. I confide in him that I'm still a virgin. I feel no pressure at all from him. He's happy to take it slow and doesn't push me.

Some time passes and I decide, that's it, I'm going to lose my virginity and I'm going to have sex with this man. I'm going to hell anyway; I may as well enjoy the ride. It's not a straightforward decision to make. It feels as though by doing so I will definitely be sealing my fate. By staying pure, I have at least left the door open that God might still forgive me for turning my back on Him. I know that if I do this, I'm giving Him a very clear signal that I'm choosing evil over good. But eventually, after many nights of agonising over it, my mind is made up.

The lead-up to the act itself is utterly wonderful and I feel so, so good. But the moment we are naked, I feel frozen and panicked. It's awful. I knew there'd be pain, but not like this. It's not my lover's fault. I have become so good at pretending that he has no idea how I'm really feeling. I just don't get what the fuss is all about and why people willingly go to hell for this. But hey, I've come this far, I may as well carry on. The pattern repeats itself. Intense desire that suddenly, the moment I'm naked, disappears in an instant and I just leave my body until it's all over.

He senses something isn't right, but I insist it's all good, I'm loving this. But then, after time has passed, I ask him whether it's always going to hurt this much. He's instantly mortified. Who wouldn't be? I'm also mortified. I can't look at my own naked body, never mind his. I don't have the words to explain what happens to me, either. Gently, he suggests that he buy me a book about sex to read and learn more about it. My shame is intense. I feel so stupid, so inadequate. Sex is supposedly what defines me as a slut, a whore and a Delilah, and I can't even do that right.

Our relationship doesn't last that long. I don't blame him in the slightest. I am so desperate to be loved but so completely clueless about what love is. I also can't tell him what I'm feeling because, in any given moment, I don't know what I feel. My overwhelming feeling is always fear – which overrides everything else. And shame, I'm very familiar with shame. I now have a good reason to be ashamed: my hymen has been broken by a man who is not my husband. I am officially a whore.

35

RESTLESS

I think I've inherited my dad's nomadic gene; I'm feeling restless. As a kid, before KSB, we never lived anywhere for longer than three years. My dad always made a garden, and always planted the roses last. He never got to enjoy any of his roses. As for me, I went to six different schools. And now I've been in Pietermaritzburg for twenty-two months and it's time to move on. I look for jobs in Durban, so that I can move in with Chris. And we can be our own little family again.

The big city appeals to me – I'm not sure why. More distractions, more to do, perhaps? And I crave being near the ocean. Again, my lack of experience and qualifications hamper my job search. But hey, Gareth tells me about a company looking for people to sell timeshare. I go for the interview and get the job.

When I leave Pietermaritzburg in October 1994, I really leave it behind. It and everyone in it. I basically remove myself from everyone's life except for Iris. Shelley moves to Durban shortly after I do, and we reconnect. But for everyone else, I just disappear.

I'm not exactly sure why I do that, but I think I'm trying to remove myself from everything that shaped me. So many of the people I'm still in touch with knew me at KSB or know me as this timid, broken girl and I cannot recreate myself while they're in my life. I'm fooling myself, of course, because I carry those wounds inside me. The people in my life aren't the ones perpetuating my discontent, my pain, my anguish. I am.

I don't know this. I'm young and foolish, and it's easier to break off contact with them than it is to look inside myself and see what's going on in there. I hurt Jessie deeply. Of course I do. It is many years before the term ghosting becomes part of our lexicon, but that is what I do to her. How awful. She doesn't understand why I just disappear on her. And I don't explain – I don't have the words or the understanding. It's easier to promise myself that I'll call her tomorrow to chat. But tomorrow never comes. And then tomorrow turns into weeks, months and eventually years. By now, I'm too ashamed to pick up the phone and say, 'I'm sorry, I messed up. I love you and I miss you.' I'm floundering and trying to stay afloat and doing the best I can. But my best isn't good enough when I hurt people, and I'll never not regret doing that.

I last exactly three months selling timeshare before moving on – I do not enjoy the job at all. I have no clue what timeshare is and how it works, but after three months, I have a better idea. I definitely didn't enjoy asking people for money. But that job leads me to another job, one more suited to me, at Resort Condominiums International (RCI), where I become a local coordinator. Basically, I help people swap their timeshare for a different one somewhere else. I don't have to sell anything to anyone, just make sure that they have great holidays.

I like solving problems and I thrive in this environment. I make many new friends and life feels good for the first time. It's not long before they promote me to team coach.

Chris and I share a flat. Well, I move in with him. It's a one-bedroom flat with an enclosed balcony, so he moves to the balcony and gives me the room. That's the kind of brother I have. A kind one. He gets up really early – he's an engineer, building roads in rural areas – and he makes supper every night. Every night he asks me, 'Are you hungry, Erika? Want to have supper?'

Every night I respond, 'No, thanks. I ate lunch, so I'm not hungry.' Every night. My relationship with food is still completely messed up. I don't know when I'm hungry and I don't know when I'm not. I never feel hungry. I can easily go for two days without eating and not feel a thing. As much as I've divorced myself from my feelings, I've also divorced myself from my digestive system. But then, once he's cooked supper, it smells so good that I end up eating anyway. His food comforts me. But the portion I eat is the one he intended to take for lunch the next day. Every night. He eventually cottons on and starts making extra, never complaining.

I might be ambivalent about food, but I'm loving my drink. My new colleagues like to party, and I join them. How utterly lovely to escape all this turmoil inside me. With a few drinks under my belt, I can be the carefree, confident Erika I want to be. That's the only time I don't feel fear. Alcohol vanquishes my anxiety. I love it. It brings out the *kurkproppie* in me. I like who I am when I'm buzzing.

I steer completely clear of drugs and cigarettes, though. Cigarettes because I can't stand the smell, and the few times I've had a drag, I didn't like the resulting light-headedness. Drugs because KSB has done one thing right – it's given me a mortal fear of overdosing. And a recognition that drugs are an escape. I'm scared that if I take them, I'll never stop. I don't realise alcohol is my escape, my drug.

Chris isn't too happy about my partying ways and worries for my safety. 'Please,' he begs me, 'please never get into a car with someone you don't know. If you feel unsafe, call me and I'll come get you. It doesn't matter what time it is.'

And I do. There's one night, well, it's two o'clock in the morning when I suddenly feel very uncomfortable. I've been partying at a nightclub called Crowded House and I call my brother. 'Please come fetch me, Chris. I'm so sorry.' He does and never berates me for it. Friday nights become my big party nights. One day, Chris says to me, 'I don't get it, Erika. You spend every Saturday in bed with a horrible hangover. That's half your weekend gone. Why do you do this to yourself?'

I don't have the answer to that, but I know one thing for sure: my brother is a saint. I will always look at him through rose-tinted glasses because of the care and love that he lavishes on me, his little sister. I wanted to know what unconditional love is and here I have it. Chris loves me, he protects me, but even he cannot save me from myself.

36

MEN

Shortly after I move to Durban, I get my heart broken. I meet a guy, let's call him Peter, while still living in Pietermaritzburg and I like him immediately. Not that tall, blondish hair, handsome face, kind eyes. He asks me out and I say yes. In a panic, I call Gareth, who is still my go-to stylist.

'What am I going to wear?' I wail.

'Don't overthink it. Jeans and a white T-shirt. Classic and cute,' comes the verdict. Well, it does the trick, and soon Peter and I are dating. He lives in Queensburgh. I meet his mother and sister and really like them too. I'm head over heels. In my head, we're getting married, having kids, the whole shebang. Peter is going to save me, I'm sure of it.

Sex with Peter isn't painful. Our first time happens after we've been out drinking. The alcohol relaxes me, and I find it all mildly pleasant. I like the intimacy far more than the act itself. I still don't get what all the fuss is about. For me, the arousal I feel before we actually get down and dirty is greater by far than having him inside me.

Our relationship grows – or at least I think it does. But what do I know? I'm not sure how I find out, I think his sister lets something slip, but I realise that Peter has more than one girl. I don't know if I'm the main chick or the side chick, but that night I give him an ultimatum.

'If you want to be with me, you can be with only me, no one else.'

'I don't think I can do that,' he responds.

That's the first night I ever look someone in the eye and curse.

'Fuck you, Peter. And get the fuck out of my flat.'

I'm not proud of that. I don't like swearing at people. Words wound and these days I am careful what I say when I'm angry. I do like swearing, though. Growing up, even the word *gat* was forbidden. That's arse in English. In Afrikaans, a nectarine is known as a *kaalgat perske*, a bare-arsed peach. We weren't allowed to call it that. 'Damn' was the epitome of obscene words and I would have got a hiding had I ever said it. *Gat* and damn were the only swearwords I knew until my twenties.

Now, free of constraints, I revel in cursing. It's liberating. It takes me quite a while before I learn that some swearwords are more equal than others, and that some should not be said out loud in polite company. Oops.

There's a lot I don't know about this life, more than just the hierarchy of swearwords. One night, I'm at a bar in Florida Road with some friends. One guy has been paying me a lot of attention and buying me drinks. He's there with some buddies, and when my friends leave, I go over to them to say goodbye. He puts his arm around me and tells me that I'll break his heart if I leave now. So I stay.

Then he whispers, 'Want to come and have some coffee at my place?'

I'm not entirely stupid, I know he's not inviting me for coffee, but I say yes because he's a man. And he's been buying me drinks and I've accepted those drinks. And that makes me responsible for him wanting me. Besides, he might be the one, you know? He's not the first guy who picks me up in a bar and he won't be the last, but I learn something that night. As we leave, his one friend leans in and says to me: 'Now don't be silly, put a condom on his willy.'

It's the first time I get even the slightest inkling that I have some agency in what is about to transpire. I can insist that he wear a condom. I did not know this.

Here's the thing. Parents who think they are protecting their girl children by not teaching them about sex are actually leaving them wide open to exploitation. These parents, and they're mostly super-religious people, teach their daughter that purity is the ideal state. Her understanding of what purity entails will vary depending on what they allow her to know. They also teach their daughter that she is inferior to men. They may not think that this is what they're teaching her, but they are. Trust me on this.

She learns about her inferiority from watching her mother interact with her father. She learns it in their religious institution. She learns it from seeing how much more freedom boys have than girls. If she's Christian, she learns it when female characters from the Bible are decried from the pulpit. Chances are, she has no agency over her body, and she's not at liberty to decide what she wears.

Her purity is the prize. This is a message she hears repeatedly.

As long as she remains in their home with little or no access to the outside world and outside influences, her parents can probably keep her pure. Their aim is her purity and not her happiness, of course. They simply want to keep her pure until the day she marries.

What happens to her after she marries is not their concern – she's allowed to be defiled by her husband, after all. Because it's a union sanctioned by God, suddenly all the impurity is stripped from the act, and she'll have to get with the programme. But she still has no agency and must submit to him whenever he wants her. Consent is not a concept here.

Her purity is the prize. She has to keep it at all costs. And yet she'll constantly come up against men who want to take that prize from her. And men are her superiors, she has to give in to them in every other aspect in her life. Bow to their wisdom. Serve them first. Make sure they are happy. See the problem here?

Teaching young girls that they have agency over their own bodies is essential. And placing the onus on them to stay pure until marriage is just plain stupid. You cannot teach a girl that men are in control and also expect her to remain pure.

Because there are men who do not want her to remain pure, I can guarantee you that. And, unless you lock that young girl up until she gets married, how will you protect her?

You protect her by educating her. You protect her by enabling her to make the right choices. You protect her by giving her rights and teaching her that she owns those rights.

Yes, I chose to go home with that guy that night. And others on other nights. I am responsible for my actions. But I don't know any better. I don't know that I can say no. I feel responsible for his arousal because I allowed him to buy me drinks. I enjoyed all the attention. I was leading him on by going over to him and his friends. It is my duty to go home with him. I don't know that I can simply say, 'No thanks, good night, bye!' and make my way home to the safe space I share with my brother.

Educate your daughters. If you don't, you're throwing them to the wolves.

It's not all bad, of course. My ignorance and naivety lead me into many situations that will, in retrospect, provide my girlfriends and me with lots of laughs in years to come. Like the time John pushes my head down and I realise that this must be what they call a blow job. And so I take little John in my mouth and ... blow with all my might.

'What the hell?' John exclaims. 'What are you doing?'

Our relationship doesn't last long after that.

A few months later, never having ventured there again, I ask a girlfriend what the best way is to give a blow job.

'Just pretend it's a lollipop,' she says. 'And suck until you get to the sherbet.'

Suck? I'm supposed to suck? How was I supposed to know that? It's called a *blow* job, for heaven's sake! Life out here is seriously confusing.

37

THE BIG O

To get from our flat to work, I have to take two Mynah buses. It's somewhat tedious, but doable. I still don't have my licence – and obviously not a car. Chris also meets someone, and they decide to move in together. I'm the matchmaker; she works with me at RCI, and I really like her.

I find a great place to live. It's an old rectory-turned-digs called The Snicket, just off Florida Road and within walking distance of work. The house is enormous, with five bedrooms, and I immediately feel at home there.

I briefly date a genuinely good guy, let's call him Greg. Greg reminds me of my dad, and I fall for him. He introduces me to Celine Dion and buys me a CD of her singing French songs. Now I listen to Nana, Anne and Celine on repeat. With a bit of Laura thrown in, too. My musical repertoire is growing.

The problem with Greg is that when we meet, he's in the last stages of planning an overland trip up the east coast of Africa. And has no idea when he'll be back. So I know full well there's a time limit, but I can't help myself. I want to be with him, even if it's not for long. He meets all my friends, and they love him too.

I'm gutted when I say goodbye to him. He promises to write to me and he keeps his promise. I get a long letter written from the top of Mount Mulanje in Malawi, a postcard from Lake Victoria (in which he sweetly writes that it should be called Lake Erika), then Kenya, Zanzibar and Egypt, and finally Europe. I write to him, too, and post the letters *poste restante* to stops along the way. I still have all his postcards and letters; I'm sentimental that way. They live in the box where I keep my letters and cards from Chris and Janet.

Greg shows me it is possible to be with a man who treats me right, and for that I'll always be grateful.

A few weeks after Greg leaves on his trip, a friend tells me about a self-development course she's done. It's really helped her find herself, she tells me. And so I sign up. It takes place over five days in October 1995, and I'm blown away. For the first time, I question the validity of mission doctrine. It's always bothered me that everyone other than the few thousand mission adherents are going to hell. Perhaps they're not headed there after all.

I realise that I am not in control of my life, but that I could be.

It's on this course that I meet Samuel, which is not his real name. Samuel is a course facilitator, and he takes a shine to me, but there's a problem. He has long hair. I've been indoctrinated into believing that long hair on a man means he's a degenerate. And here's this caring dude who seems so lovely, but he has long hair. And he wears a bracelet or necklace sometimes. Men don't wear jewellery! Women don't either, for that matter, but definitely not men. I take a little while to get over my prejudices.

I have time. Samuel has undertaken that should he meet anyone he is interested in romantically while helping on the course, he will wait six weeks before getting intimate with them. I guess you could call it a cooling-off period.

These six weeks are exactly what I need. We get to know each other. We talk for hours and hours. And I grow to trust Samuel. Greg helped me to see that not all men just want to use me, and now here is Samuel, another guy who respects me and has the integrity to keep a promise, although no one except the two of us would know if he didn't.

One perk of working at RCI is that I get to visit some of these timeshares. When our six weeks are up, we hit the road to a resort called Castleburn in the Drakensberg for our first weekend away together. And it is here that I experience an orgasm for the very first time and finally understand what the fuss is all about.

What a revelation. I'm three weeks away from my three-year anniversary of leaving KSB, and for the first time I know I can do this.

38

REJUVENATION

Samuel is genuinely invested in my well-being and helps me tremendously by listening to me, questioning me and recommending books for me to read. It helps to shift my focus from what happened to me and what people did to me to trying to understand the decisions I made about myself and about other people as a result. My mother's neglect, for example, isn't as important as my decision that I wasn't worthy of love. I never talk about what Muzi did to me, but I start to understand that I decided I had no control over what happens to my body because of him and his roving hands and tongue.

I realise that I have become a spectator in my own life ever since I was a little girl. Everyone else has been deciding for me, and when I choose a course of action, no matter how small, I'm racked by doubt and only feel good about it when some-one else tells me that they think it was the right decision. I need to learn how to make autonomous decisions based on my inner principles, rather than hope for a stamp of approval from someone I regard as superior to me.

According to KSB, they are right and everyone else is wrong. For the first time, I question their intolerances and prejudices, all of which I've adopted. Men with long hair! People with tattoos! Girls who wear hot pants! I still condemn them in my head. And I want to stop doing that.

The yardstick by which I want to measure myself is how I treat other people. The security guard that lifts the boom gate for me every morning on my way to work – do I know his name? Do I acknowledge him with a greeting or a nod or a smile? Do I grant the beggar that comes to my car window (still on the passenger side, mind you) at a stop street dignity by meeting his gaze, whether I give him something or not? Do I give the head of a large corporation the smile I withhold from the couple in hippie clothing who walk barefoot past me on the street? Do I truly respect all people, or only those I deem worthy of respect? I examine the intolerant belief system I've adopted and make a conscious effort to accept others and their differences.

I ask myself: Have only the outward trappings of my life changed, or have I had the courage to examine and change the judgemental and limiting belief systems that KSB fosters?

Taking responsibility for my own life and truly respecting others only become possible once I acknowledge, accept and try to forgive myself for my participation in the abusive system of KSB. I hit little kids in my care. I cannot go back and undo that, not ever. I did not speak up when I saw others being abused. I can't go back and suddenly find my voice. And yes, had I spoken up, they would have punished me. But by not speaking up, I failed those who were being abused. If there are degrees of complicity, I am definitely low on the scale; I have no doubt about that. But I have been complicit, nonetheless.

My body does something strange just about every night these days. The more I recover memories and talk about my past, the more it happens. As I lie down in bed and relax, my body starts to tremble uncontrollably. You can hear my teeth chattering. These episodes last anywhere from five to fifteen minutes. I don't understand what is happening, but I also cannot fight it. When I tense up and stop the tremors, they simply return the moment I relax again. So I learn to just give in to them and let them pass. Samuel has learned that it is best to leave me to it, and so he potters around cleaning up the kitchen. He knows not to come to bed until I have been there for a little while. Because my tremors make the whole bed shake.

Sometimes, in trying to recount or revisit or get over anything, all I can do is weep – the pain is simply too much to express verbally. Healing is not an overnight process, but through it all, Samuel is there – and he never laughs at me about all the stupid things I'm scared of. Frogs terrify me – one night in that cold, dark corridor as a little girl, I came across a frog, blocking my way. Every time I moved, the frog jumped too, and I could not predict where it would land. The frog turned into a menacing monster about to pounce on me. I'm an adult now and I know this fear is irrational, as are so many of my other fears. What can a frog actually do to harm me? But when I see one, I freeze, paralysed by fear.

Samuel also doesn't condemn me for what I've done wrong. With his quiet strength, he helps me to recover.

In time, I come to understand that perhaps the truth of KwaSizabantu isn't the only truth and their way isn't the only way. It takes me a while, but I start to recognise that much of what happened to me was abuse, pure and simple. And what I witnessed other kids going through was abuse, and not God's way, as KSB professed.

As this understanding grows, my sense of responsibility increases. With knowledge comes responsibility, after all. I need to do something. I need to try to help the kids who are still trapped there. But how?

39

FIRST SHOTS FIRED

The next time I go back to KwaSizabantu is for a funeral. David Jaca was one of the co-workers who sang in Choir Number One, but he had always treated me with such kindness. I never felt condemned by him. Or judged. He had a beaming smile and generously bestowed its radiance on everyone he met. He always had a kind word for me. And yes, it's the same David who went to fetch the butcher's knife with which Jessie was threatened that day so long ago. Even so, I believed him to be a good person.

When I hear of his death in a car accident, I am devastated. And though I promised myself I would never go back there, I feel a burning need to go and pay my respects. To say thank you to him, thank you for being the one person who always smiled at me. I am so conflicted. He's dead, after all. But this will also give me the opportunity to see my family. My mother and sister. And my beloved nieces, who are growing up without me.

Samuel agrees to accompany me. As much as I want him there, his presence causes me great anxiety. He has long hair. He dresses in what KSB would call 'hippie clothing'. He wears jewellery. And he's my boyfriend. By going there with him, I am defiantly declaring my independence. My sinfulness. I want to do it, and I also definitely don't want to do it.

The church service comes first, as always. I get to say goodbye to David in my heart. After the service, as Samuel and I are walking down the road, a car pulls up next to us. The window rolls down and there is Dorothy Newlands, sitting in the passenger seat. She calls me over but doesn't get out of the car. I have to bend down to speak to her. I'm so used to these little power games, I hardly notice. Samuel is not and he does. He also notices how she blatantly ignores him.

'Erika! How are you?' The conversation is inane, and I don't tell her much. I don't trust this redhead. She has a veneer of cheer, but I find something deeply sinister about her. She's one of the handful of powerful women at KSB and as ruthless as any of the men, in my opinion. As the deputy principal of the school when I attended it, she witnessed the abuse of my fellow pupils.

Eventually, I've had enough. I straighten and start turning back to Samuel. Dorothy's hand snakes out of the window and she clutches my wrist tightly. I cannot pull away.

'You know, Erika, we have letters you wrote where you talk about how happy you are at the mission. We're not scared to use them.'

I instantly know why she is telling me this and where she got those letters.

'Good for you, Dorothy,' I respond, managing to pull free from her vice-like grip. Samuel glances at me quizzically; he senses something significant has just happened. When we're safely back inside the car, I explain how Dorothy just threatened me.

A few months earlier, I had heard of a French town whose residents were concerned about the proposed establishment of a branch of the Domino Servite School there. I don't recall how I heard about it, but I and one other former pupil contacted the town's residents and shared our own concerns about the way the school is run in South Africa. The *Sunday Tribune* picked up on the story and, on 31 March 1996, published an article titled 'Mission pupils help French'. After the article appeared, the newspaper was inundated with letters from people supporting KSB and from pupils who stated that our criticism was unfounded.

The next week, the *Tribune* printed a letter from a former head boy of the school who denied that beatings took place there. I can no longer recall whether the *Tribune* published my name or not – I seem to recall that they did. If so, it would have been with my permission. Either way, Dorothy and co knew it was me who had spoken out against them.

As for the letters, they would have been the ones I wrote to my mother on my travels in Europe. Back then, I used my many letters to her as a kind of diary. Before she'd disowned me, I'd asked to borrow them for a while so that I could make photocopies, as they were the only record I had of my time in Europe. I also wanted to get the return addresses of the families with whom I'd stayed so that I could write thank-you letters to all my hosts.

My mother had made some excuse about having got rid of them when she was clearing out. I'd thought that sounded odd. My mother wasn't the type to throw out letters. She still had notes I'd written when I was a little girl, when I could hardly write. It didn't ring true at the time, but a lifetime of not questioning my mother was a very difficult habit to break.

And now here is Dorothy, intimating that my letters are in her possession.

I swallow the feeling of betrayal – I need to see my mother now, and my sister and nieces. We drive down to the rondavels. A slight drizzle has started, but not enough to turn the road muddy. As we park, we see my sister and brother-in-law walking towards us. We get out of the car and I introduce everyone. The atmosphere is tense.

'Erika,' my brother-in-law looks at me. He is too short to look down on me, but his voice carries his disdain. 'God has given me a duty to protect my children from Satan,' he tells me. I start trembling and it's not because we're standing in the rain. I know what's coming.

'I am their father and must keep them safe from evil. And so I am here today to tell you that you may not have any contact with them ever again. Don't call them, don't try to see them.'

I have no words. Samuel is by my side, and he speaks, addressing my sister, not her husband.

'Hanna,' he says, his voice gentle. 'Can you really stand there and tell me that this loving, kind, warm woman who is your sister is evil and will harm your children?'

Hanna does not meet his eyes, and she does not look at me.

'I stand by my husband,' she says. They turn around and walk away.

And that is that. I'm not even allowed to say goodbye to my nieces. I've been cut from their lives, swiftly and decisively.

Shaken, I make my way down the slight slope to my mother's rondavel. I don't hold Samuel's hand out of respect for this place and its morals, though I badly need him to hold me. When we get there, she opens the door, but tells Samuel that he will have to return to the car and wait for me there. He's not welcome in her house.

I nod to him, it's okay, and follow my mother inside as he walks back up to the car park.

I don't spend much time with my mother. I cry as I share with her my despair at my brother-in-law's words. She tells me that she has nothing to say about it. He's their father, she says. He has the right to make decisions for his daughters.

I don't ask her about the letters. All I want to do now is get away and go somewhere safe, somewhere where I'm loved.

It takes a long time for my tears to stop flowing as we drive back to Durban. We're almost home when I ask Samuel what he thought of Uncle Erlo and the church service.

'You know who he reminded me of when he was preaching?'

'No, who?'

'Another demagogue I've only ever seen on tape: Hitler.'

40

LOSING MY RELIGION

Samuel is as restless as I am. I quite like living in the city, but he yearns for life surrounded by nature. He talks more and more about moving to a little town called Sedgefield on the Garden Route in the Western Cape. I've never been to the Garden Route, but it sounds lovely. Besides, Samuel has friends who live there – his art teacher from school and her three kids. And so we start making inquiries. But before we go, I know that I should get some kind of qualification. By now I've given up on a university degree – I simply don't have the energy. And I also lack the funds to keep enrolling in courses I don't finish.

So I sign up to do a certificate in reflexology, because I think that will guarantee me an income, as it's something I can do wherever I go. I thoroughly enjoy the course and the process, but I have to do ten case studies of ten treatments each, and I find that I only really like giving reflexology treatments to people I know, as I don't like touching strangers' feet. So this is probably not the best career path for me. All this 'New Age nonsense', as my mother calls it.

Anything KSB doesn't understand gets filed under 'New Age'. Meditation, yoga, reiki, reflexology. I remember being so scared at my uncle's house in Sweden when a friend of theirs came to visit and showed us some tai chi moves. I genuinely feared that I had become possessed by a demon that day. The only reason I hadn't gone to Uncle Erlo to have him pray for me to be released from whatever demonic presence I had invited in that day was that I'd fled KSB within three days of returning.

In February 1997, Samuel and I pack up our lives in Durban – everything we own fits into his Toyota Corolla and a hired trailer – and off we go down to Sedgefield to start a new life. I find a job there, thanks to my old boss at RCI in Durban. This time, it's a company that runs timeshare resorts and a timeshare points system. I'm the latest recruit in their client-services department.

An older woman handles the accounts at this company and she regularly invites me to attend church with her on Sundays. I always politely decline, but after a few months of this, I pluck up the courage to tell her that I appreciate the invite, but I won't ever be joining her.

'I'm not a Christian, you see,' I explain.

Her face is a study in surprise, mixed with a fair bit of horror.

'Nonsense,' she says. 'Of course you're a Christian! Look at you, you're such a good person, how can you not be?'

This is when I realise that Christians genuinely think being good is to be Christian. It's not, though. Being good is to be human. Kindness is a human trait. Charity and compassion are human traits, not Christian ones. Christianity encourages you to be good and kind and charitable. But just because I am all of these things doesn't mean that I am a Christian.

This has been bothering me for a while, I realise. It started back at KSB, when I simply couldn't get my head around the millions of people worldwide who were doomed to hell for not being in close enough proximity to KSB to hear the truth. When my brother questioned this, my mother told him that God would judge other people according to what they knew, but that anyone who heard the gospel according to KSB and turned their back on it, well, God would have no mercy on them.

From the pulpit, the message was clear. Only people who adhered to KSB's doctrines would have a place in heaven. They would rail against the World Council of Churches and those churches that espoused 'liberation theology' – anyone who supported anything that smelled faintly of communism was not Christian in their book. The idea of Catholics, Lutherans, Anglicans and others being able to set aside their differences and work together for the common good was anathema.

I was born and raised in a white Afrikaans family. An Afrikaans girl is a Christian girl. Had I been born in India, I might have been raised in the Hindu faith. Had I been born in the Middle East, Mohammed would likely have been my prophet and Allah my God. Had I been born in Italy, chances are I would have been a good Catholic girl, praying the rosary.

But no, I was born into the Christian faith. My parents were Protestants because their parents were Protestants. And they were Protestants because their parents were Protestants. And so we go all the way back to the French Huguenots, who came to South Africa because they were fleeing religious persecution at the hands of the Catholics. Somewhere, centuries ago, one (or more) of my ancestors made what was then a pretty brave choice. They chose to leave the Catholic Church and become Protestant. And so their offspring were Protestant, and their offspring's offspring, and so on until you get to me.

I had no choice – I was Protestant by default. And then, when my parents joined KwaSizabantu, I had even less choice. It was their way or the highway. Or that dusty road out of the compound, to be exact.

I realise that my big problem with religion is the lack of questioning. Until now, I have not interrogated why I believe what I believe. I have simply adopted the faith of my parents. I now realise there are elements of my birth faith I simply cannot endorse. I have way too many unanswered questions. And yes, the God of KwaSizabantu is a wrathful tyrant. I get that other Christians believe in his love, and that the KSB version of God is a particularly awful version of him. But still. Way too many questions. I simply cannot have blind faith in anything or anyone ever again.

I don't know what entity is out there – I don't know who or what it/he/she is.

Perhaps it's a collective consciousness? I'm okay with not knowing, however. I don't need to know, because I have control over how I live my life. How I treat people, how I treat myself, how I treat the world around me, how I treat animals and the environment – that's what's important.

I also don't know about the afterlife – if there is one. I can't imagine God or Allah or Yahweh saying, 'You didn't believe in me, so you are damned to hell for all eternity.' It simply doesn't make sense that an accident of birth determines whether I have a chance at salvation in the afterlife or not.

I have come to believe that it doesn't matter what I believe; what matters is how I live my life. And I want to live my life by doing good and being good. I won't always succeed, but it will just have to be enough. I don't need to know what comes next. I simply need to do what is right and what is good right now.

41

THE LIVING DEAD

In late 1997, my mother sends me a book she has written. We're still in touch sporadically. She calls maybe once or twice a year. I always call her on Mother's Day and her birthday. The book is titled *Die Stilgemaakte Hart* (*The Silenced Heart*), a slim treatise on widowhood as depicted in the Bible. She opens the book by writing about how bad she feels for the way she treated my dad, telling a story of how he ran inside from the garden one day to show her something and how she was more worried about the muddy footprints he was leaving on the floor than sharing in his delight.

She writes about how, after he died, she begged God to forgive her for how cruelly she treated him. And how God had mercy on her and forgave her. My mother is a good writer, and I find myself engaged in the book, despite my lack of enthusiasm for its subject matter. She takes various widows from the Bible and pontificates about their lives. It's basically a sermon, but in book form.

I don't get a mention, but my brother does. And it is so unkind that it slices through my heart and leaves a wound I don't think has ever healed. My mother writes about a widow in the Bible who loses two sons on the battlefield. She says she knows how that widow feels, because her own son is the living dead.

The living dead.

Chris. My brave, handsome, golden brother who has tried time and again to soften her heart towards us.

My mother compounds her cruelty by sending him a copy of the book. So that he can read what his mother thinks of him. So that he can know that she considers him the living dead and that she grieves for him as if he's no longer alive. She erases him just like that from her life. In one sentence.

It's easier for me to ignore all the ways she's hurt me, but I cannot let this go. I am appalled. Not so much at her description of him, because that's the way they all think over there, but that she could send her son a copy of the book, knowing that he will read the words she has written about him. I don't trust myself to speak to her, so I write her a letter instead and keep a copy for myself as a reminder, just in case I ever waver again and think KSB isn't as bad as all that. The letter is handwritten and in Afrikaans. Here's what it says:

Mamma,

I have just reread *Die Stilgemaakte Hart* and I have so many questions:

Will Esther also write two books about her daughter and son when it is too late? Will she also confess her guilt that she tried to push them into a mould, and then rejected them when they wouldn't fit? Will she write about the times her son and daughter pleaded with her to soften her heart, but that she was so blindly focused on her ideas of right and wrong that she forgot how to love?

Will she then write about how she trampled on the terms 'tolerance' and 'unconditional love' with her unyielding stubbornness? How she caused irreparable damage to her son, who loves her deeply, by viewing him as the living dead?

Will Esther then ask herself who gave her the right to make decisions about another's salvation – why she made herself God over her kids' lives?

Will she only then realise how deeply she hurt her two youngest children – so deeply that they lost all desire to see her?

Next follows the question, 'Where will Esther find a God to forgive her then?'

Erika

I post the letter, but never get a response. I cannot abide having that book in my home, but I also cannot imagine allowing anyone else to read it. I decide to follow KSB's example. They've shown me what to do with evil objects. The time has come for me to hold my own private fire service. Samuel helps me light a fire and I burn my mother's book, together with photographs of my time at KSB. I burn her reality of her children in those pages, and the emaciated, non-emancipated version of me in the pictures. I am no longer Erika, daughter of Esther. I will always be my dad's daughter and Chris's sister, but I cannot comprehend this cruelty, and I am finally starting to understand that I will never be able to heal the rift between us. Samuel holds me in a tight embrace as we stand watching the flames lick and consume my past.

42

'RETURN OF THE VIRGINS'

The weight of knowing what is going on back at KSB and not doing anything about it is crushing me. In early 1998, I spot an opportunity to unburden myself.

On page 54 of the January issue of *Cosmopolitan*, I see a face I recognise. Dorothy Newlands in *Cosmo*? The caption under her photograph reads 'PIONEER: Dorothy Newlands'.

What new fuckery is this? The article, titled 'Return of the virgins', is about True Love Waits, a campaign that originated in evangelical circles in the United States and that 'has attracted worldwide attention by loudly and proudly denouncing premarital sex as the root of all evil'. Not war or greed, no. The root of all evil is people shagging outside the confines of matrimony. The article talks about how Dorothy encourages teenagers and people in their twenties to sign a pledge that reads: 'I make a pledge to God, myself, my family and my future spouse to remain sexually pure until marriage, by the grace of God.'

She tells the journalist that advocating safe sex promotes promiscuity. 'Sex is like fire,' she is quoted as saying. 'If you take it out of the fireplace, it can burn down the home. Outside of marriage, sex is dangerous.'

She then goes on to say that the movement does not police people, and that they certainly do not conduct virginity tests.

Say what? Sure, you probably aren't conducting tests on the teenagers and students you manage to lure into signing your pledge, but we all know you allowed virginity testing on the black girls under your care. I remember how they were lined up after every school holiday to get checked. Even the underage ones.

I'm fuming. This. This is what anger feels like. The article is well written and presents a counterargument from Marlene Wasserman, the sex therapist known as Dr Eve. 'This virginity pledge is nonsense,' she says. 'It's naive to urge people to sign such an oath before God. And the religious undertones are harmful because they flavour the pact with guilt.'

The article ends with a case study: a couple who married at KSB, Coligny and Lizette Marloth. He says he was promiscuous in his student days, but then he met God and lost interest in girls and dedicated his life to purity. Lizette says she was racked by sin, 'such as lying and dirty thoughts', until she gave her life to God, and then she was no longer tempted by boys.

They met and decided to get married but abstained from all physical contact.

Well, duh. They're KSB congregants – they would not have been allowed to be alone together until their marriage, 'lest the devil get his finger in the matter', as Lizette so eloquently points out.

'Standing at the altar on our wedding day, it was wonderful to know I was marrying a virgin,' Coligny is quoted as saying. 'You don't want an orange that's already had the juices sucked out of it by someone else.'

I scribble furiously on my copy of the article. 'It's not the sex that harms self-esteem, but the guilt created by indoctrination,' I write. By the time I get to Coligny's comments, there isn't enough space in the margins for what I want to say, so I sit down and start typing. Then I email it to the magazine.

To my surprise, *Cosmo* agrees to publish it. My letter will appear in their April 1998 issue. (A few years later, the editor tells me it's the longest letter they've ever printed. It takes up a whole page.) They call me three times to make sure that I am actually, really, definitely, 100 per cent sure that I want my name published. 'We can give you a pseudonym,' they advise. 'We do it all the time.'

But no. I'm adamant. I want my name there and I want Dorothy and everyone else to see it. I am no longer that scared little girl. I am angry. They should not have tried to convince the youth of South Africa to fall for their doctrine.

Big mistake, Dorothy, big mistake. How dare you use a magazine you vilify in order to spread your message? The hypocrisy enrages me. They won't allow even a single copy of *Cosmopolitan* in the compound, but they're quite happy to use it for proselytising.

Well, I can proselytise, too:

Beware the missionary position
As a 26-year-old woman who spent much of her childhood living at the mission, from which Dorothy Newlands campaigns for celibacy until marriage (Return of the virgins, *Cosmo*, January '98), I would like to share my experience of the dark side of religion-induced chastity with your readers.

When I was a pupil at the KwaSizabantu mission school, Ms Newlands and the other leaders of the mission not only opposed sex education, but went as far as tearing out of our biology textbooks any chapters dealing with animal reproduction or human anatomy. Boys and girls were not permitted contact outside of the classroom and several were beaten or expelled for writing love letters.

We girls were not allowed to wear any jewellery or makeup and a strict dress code was enforced, so as not to 'tempt the men'. The few movies we were permitted to watch, such as *The Sound of Music* and *Chariots of Fire*, had all romantic scenes censored before they were shown.

It is from this kind of environment that most South African True Love Waits (TLW) counsellors come, spreading the message to our schools and universities. I fully agree with Marlene Wasserman, the therapist quoted in your article, that the celibacy pledge TLW members are asked to take is harmful because of the religious undertones and accompanying guilt.

I left the mission before 1994, when the pledge was introduced, so I never actually signed it. But I lived my childhood under those very same principles. It has taken me several years to undo the emotional and spiritual damage I suffered as a result. Because the mission so closely intertwines the concepts of God's wrath and sex, I have had to untwist my spiritual beliefs from my sexuality. Thanks to this process, sex with my partner in our loving relationship is now truly a spiritual experience. This is in sharp contrast to my first sexual experience. Because I had been convinced of the superiority of men and because I knew absolutely nothing about sex, I found myself in an extremely painful and humiliating encounter. I had never even seen a picture of a penis and was so indoctrinated about the 'dirtiness' of my own genitals that touching them was out of the question. I could have been spared a lot of unnecessary emotional pain and subsequent hang-ups had I been educated by a caring parent, or other older person.

In my experience, it is often people like myself, who grow up in conservative homes where any acknowledgement of sexuality is taboo, who later tend to do everything to excess.

TLW targets teenagers who are, by virtue of their youth, especially vulnerable to threats of eternal damnation. I can only imagine that it is out of fear that many take the vow of chastity – a vow that will disempower them to make informed and mature choices regarding their sexuality later in their lives.

Ms Newlands claims that sex outside of marriage is dangerous. I would argue that being completely ignorant about sex is also dangerous, leaving one vulnerable to mistakes and abuse. Education is crucial. Open and honest discussion with young people is what is needed. I do not condone promiscuity and I agree with Ms Newlands that the threat of sexually transmitted diseases is all too real. But ignorance is not the solution. It is the people who are well informed and have a good understanding of sex and its consequences who can make an informed choice as to how far they are willing to experiment.

To regard marriage as the certificate required to experience true love is ludicrous. This narrow-minded attitude rules out any loving long-term relationship that may culminate in marriage. Sex in a loving relationship where both partners communicate and share themselves is a wonderfully enriching experience. No marriage certificate can ensure that.

Lizette, one of the TLW counsellors you interviewed, was my friend until I chose to leave the mission (for which I was ostracised). She says that her first experience of sex with her husband Coligny was 'wonderful'. Could that not be because, while she was a virgin, he was a very experienced lover? The sexism and hypocrisy inherent in this doctrine is obvious and proudly borne out by Coligny's own comment: 'You don't want an orange that has already had the juices sucked out of it by someone else.' I wonder how any woman could accept this analogy from someone who, by his own admission, had done a fair amount of premarital 'sucking' himself? Sexually transmitted diseases being one of TLW's main trump cards, I wonder what regard Coligny showed for his virgin wife, in terms of his previous partners.

Sexual activity is the choice of each individual, but such a choice can be made properly only if that individual has the necessary facts. Unfortunately, Ms Newlands and her followers don't allow any room for informed decisions.

Erika Bornman, Sedgefield

43

DISCONNECTING

Writing that letter to *Cosmo* – and having them accept it for publication – opens a floodgate in me. I've been having all these internal monologues, trying to figure out how to live in this world. Hearing *Cosmo* say that they'll publish what I've written is the first time I realise I have a voice. I don't trust this voice, and I don't think it will achieve much, but I cannot remain silent. The kids growing up at KSB – my nieces included – haunt me. I know they're watching movies depicting the most savage sadism. I know they're being beaten for the slightest misdemeanour. I know they're being told that they're worthless.

I didn't want to be like an ex-colony, and it's time to let my old imperial rulers know that there's no Commonwealth as far as I'm concerned. They don't know what's coming in April. I want to catch them off-guard. I want to show them that I'm not that little girl any more.

I decide that I will never again call that man 'Uncle' Erlo. He continues to loom large in my consciousness, but he will no longer get the courtesy of an honorific title. He's not my uncle. And he was never a father figure to me, despite his promise on the day of my dad's funeral.

Over two days at the end of February, I write two letters:

Erlo Stegen
This letter serves to sever any remaining link between myself and you, your followers, and your dogmas.

I hold you personally accountable for usurping the place of God in my life and reject categorically all the derogatory condemning and demeaning statements you made to me, including:
- calling me a whore, a slut and a Delilah;
- placing God's curse on me;
- telling me that my future husband will mess around with other women;
- telling me that I will never be happy.

I also hold you responsible for your serious lack of discernment when I approached you for help with regards to my problem with Muzi Kunene. I was not guilty of any wrongdoing and yet stood accused by you and forbidden to discuss the matter with my own mother.

This is the earliest family photograph I have, taken in late 1971 or early 1972 in Malawi. From left to right: Chris, my mother, me and Hanna

Hanna, Chris and me at Lake Malawi, where we spent many an early childhood holiday. I wish we had never left – I would have loved to have grown up there. Instead, we returned to South Africa for good when I was four years old

The three of us always had our noses in a book. This was taken when we were still blissfully unaware of the existence of KwaSizabantu – little did we know how our lives were about to change

Patroon was a cross between a Maltese poodle and a spaniel, and the very best dog in the world. Here she's still a puppy and we're about to move across the country to be closer to KSB

We're all smiles, but my parents are about to abandon us at KwaSizabantu to pursue their dreams in France. They thought they were leaving us in safe hands – they were wrong

A recent aerial view of KSB. The four rows of rondavels are on the left of the development. The one where my dad had his heart attack was in the bottom row

Courtesy of Koos Greeff

Courtesy of Koos Greeff

Erlo Stegen leads the apartheid government's minister of law and order Adriaan Vlok on a tour in the late 1980s. A young Koos Greeff follows on the far right. Vlok's visits were always a big deal. We children would line the road as he drove past, waving our welcome

Trucks of people arriving were a familiar sight on Sundays. The big amphitheatre that can seat 10000 is still under construction in the background. Next to it is the striped tent where they had large gatherings. After the service, everyone would get a meal, then it was back on the trucks and back home

Thanks to some generous Americans, we got to spend Christmas 1982 with my parents in Albertville, France. It was magical and awesome, and a welcome reprieve from the horror of daily life back at KSB

My parents were in France to learn French, so my dad could be a missionary in French-speaking African countries. Here I am in their lab, hearing phrases and then repeating them. I fell in love with the musicality of the language, a love that has endured to this day

Music and books defined our days when not at KSB. Here my sister and I are in our lounge in Johannesburg, with a young visitor. Hanna, like my dad, loved making music and she's really good at it, too

My beloved dad, Daniel Marthinus Bornman. Born on 24 August 1943 in Kenya, died on 12 January 1987 en route to the hospital in Greytown, fifty kilometres away. Rest in peace, Pappa, I love you

Two friends and I (on the left) hold chocolates that Muzi brought back from one of his many overseas trips. He always brought us chocolates. Erlo and his co-workers made many proselytising trips to Europe

The only record I have of my stint teaching these gorgeous little five-year-olds is a copy of the badly printed Domino Servite School 1990 yearbook. I was only eighteen years old and fresh out of school, with no clue what I was doing. I remember them all with such fondness

It's 1992 and I'm high in the French Alps (chaperone in tow) wearing a skirt, because I had to wear a skirt or dress no matter what activity I engaged in. I will be forever thankful for those months in Europe and to those people who made my trip possible. It was here that I started to loosen the tendrils of captivity

In Pietermaritzburg with my darling aunt Iris, who gave me refuge, and Chris, who often drove up from Durban to visit his baby sister. I can tell from my dress and skinniness that this was taken shortly after leaving KSB in 1993

My guardian angels, in disguise as my uncle Chris, his wife Janet and my brother Chris, visit me in Sedgefield in the late 1990s. I can confidently state that I would not be here today if it were not for these three and Iris. They have my whole heart

A very special Christmas in Montagu on my uncle Herman's farm with my three nieces in 1998. These three girls are all adults now and I will never give up hope that they'll reach out for help to get away from KSB

Memories of this day by the pool have sustained me for more than two decades now. Apart from brief sentences spoken at two family funerals, these hours in 1998 would be the last I spent with my nieces, having been forbidden to have contact with them by their father

Whenever I find yellow flowers in the veld, I tuck one behind my ear in tribute to my dad, who planted a yellow daisy bush outside our many front doors

The summer I turned thirty in Greece was the first time I started feeling somewhat more comfortable in my skin, and the first time I wasn't self-conscious wearing a bikini. It helped that my tan made the scar on my tummy less noticeable

It was on an epic road trip through South Africa with my British boyfriend in 2003 that I decided it was time to take control of my life. We were at God's Window in Mpumalanga when I realised with absolute clarity that I needed to be in Cape Town. I asked him to take a photo of me to capture the moment forever

Deidré and Michelle were two colleagues from my first job in Cape Town who became lifelong friends. Here we are, fresh faced and young. We've been one another's cheerleaders ever since

In 2007, *Cosmo* sent me on a trip to Lake Malawi. It was the first time I'd been back to the country of my birth since the age of four and I loved every minute of it. It's the 'Warm Heart of Africa' indeed

Chris and I both love wine – my uncle Chris and Janet introduced us to its delights, as it was forbidden at KSB. Here we're celebrating Chris's birthday at Diemersfontein's Pinotage on Tap festival

Iris, my guiding light, how I miss you! The Midlands Meander will always remind me of the many special days we spent exploring its delights together

I am insanely scared of heights – even three steps up a ladder is too much for me. This excursion up India Venster proved it's possible to 'feel the fear and do it anyway'. I love hiking to the top of Table Mountain, but much prefer Skeleton Gorge or the gentler jeep track from Constantia Nek, thank you very much

My mother has long said that we'll meet at the cross or not at all. On a girls' trip to the Cederberg with Rose and Michelle, I said my goodbye to her here, at the Maltese Cross. Girlfriends are good for the soul

If I had to choose only one photograph to describe me, it would be this one by my friend Jean Collins. It captures that *kurkproppie* spirit my dad adored and that KSB didn't manage to extinguish

I'm at my happiest in the mountains and next to (or in) the water. Give me a dam in a mountain and add some Cap Classique, and I'm in heaven!

In December 2020, I travelled to KwaZulu-Natal to spend five days with Celimpilo and another dear friend from KSB days. We booked a cottage in the Midlands and laughed and cried and caught up. It was glorious

On our way back to the airport in Durban, we detoured past our old home. A few days earlier, there had been a protest against unfair labour practices at KSB. Here's the road sign that once had such significance in my life. A visceral reminder that change is possible

You can't buy love, but you can rescue it! Mornings at Casa Bornman – a loving space, full of purrs and cuddles. The moment Matilda and Troy realise I'm awake, they come to purr and love me

My life motto: 'When in doubt, be brave!'

I consider you and the fanaticism you preach and inspire in others the root of the cause for the breakdown of the Bornman family structure.

In creating for myself the successful, happy and spiritually fulfilling life I now lead, I found it necessary to rid myself of the harmful influence and destructive belief system impressed on me by your cult.

May peace and love prevail on Earth.

Erika Bornman

There's little point in writing to my mother; she still hasn't responded to my letter from last year. But I need Dorothy Newlands to hear from me that she has not intimidated me into silence:

Dorothy Newlands

Enclosed please find a copy of a recent letter to Erlo Stegen, the principles of which I feel are applicable to you as well.

I find the false sincerity you portray, and the veiled threat of the possession of letters detailing my supposed happiness at the mission, sickening in their sinister sweetness.

In my experience, your use of violence and fear to create order among children and young people is unacceptable and suppressive to the human spirit as well as being contrary to the principles you promote in the facade you project to the rest of society.

I hereby disconnect from you and your influence and would like you to know that I am prepared to publicly voice my experience of the negative undercurrents and occurrences of KwaSizabantu Mission.

Erika Bornman

I post the letters as registered mail, so I know they have arrived and someone has signed for them. I receive no acknowledgement from either Erlo or Dorothy, but I'm not expecting to hear from them. I just want them to know they failed. That they did not succeed in breaking me.

April comes and goes. I can only hope someone, somewhere, read my letter in a forbidden magazine and showed it to the KSB leadership. I've done what I can, I think to myself. Now I can get on with my life and leave the past in the past, where it belongs.

PART FOUR

THE WOUNDED
WHISTLEBLOWER

44

A CHRISTMAS TO REMEMBER

As I've mentioned before, my parents each have five siblings: my dad was the youngest, while my mother is the fourth in her family.

On my dad's side, I'm closest to Chris in Sweden and Iris in Pietermaritzburg. I love my other three aunts, but since moving to KSB, I've been mostly estranged from them. KSB does not encourage relationships with people outside of the fold. On my mother's side, I had fairly regular contact with most of her siblings and her mother (my only living grandparent), but since leaving KSB, it's been complicated. I don't seek to reconnect with them because they're my mother's family and she has disowned me. I'm pretty sure that they will all side with her, because why wouldn't they?

But then Samuel hears of a cycle race in Bonnievale. And that is right next to Montagu, which is where all three of my mother's brothers farm and where my grandmother lives in a cottage on the family farm that's been passed down to my mother's oldest brother. I haven't been to Montagu for many, many years. So I make a tentative phone call to the family farm. I tell my aunt that we're coming to do a cycle race, and could we perhaps visit? They welcome us with open arms.

While there, I ask for the number of one of my mother's younger brothers, Herman. He and his wife, Melanie, farm some kilometres away. I'm nervous to make the call. I have always loved them so much. They were also some of only a handful of people who visited us when we were kids at KwaSizabantu. Among those clothes the prefects tossed from my wardrobe all those years ago was a polka-dot dress Melanie had made for me – I felt its loss more keenly than any of the other items.

I make the call and they invite us round. They are so welcoming and, instantly, I have more family. Montagu, and their home in particular, becomes a place of refuge for me. Samuel and I visit often.

In December 1998, Melanie tells me that my mother is coming to visit for Christmas. My sister and her family will be there too.

And so Samuel and I decide to spend Christmas in Montagu as well. I crave contact with my nieces – I want to see that they're okay. My brother joins us, as does Samuel's sister. It's a proper big family affair with a long table set up under an enormous tree on the lawn.

With everyone there, Marius doesn't make a scene when I play with my nieces. He wouldn't dare – my uncles are big, burly men and he's … well, he's not. More than the physical disparities, though, is how important it is for KSBers to keep up appearances, so I'm secure in the knowledge that he won't say a word. My oldest niece and I have a joyous reunion; she's the only one who remembers me. The other two are so super cute, I instantly adore them too – I can't get enough of them.

'Aunty Erika, why don't you visit us any more?' my niece asks me, and my heart breaks. I know she won't have been told that I called every year on her birthday. When my sister answered the phone, she'd tell me that I knew she couldn't allow me to wish my niece happy birthday. Until the year before last, when I tried to argue with her. She wouldn't budge, and in frustration I said, 'Fuck you, Hanna!' and slammed the phone down. It's only the second time in my life I've said that to someone and it's not something I'm proud of. I never called again.

'Oh sweetheart, your daddy doesn't think it's a good idea for me to visit any more,' I tell her truthfully. 'I'm so sorry. I love you and I want you to know that I will always love you and I will always be here for you.'

She's so young, I don't know if she'll remember these words. I can only hope that one day I'll be able to help her and her sisters escape, the way my aunts and uncle helped me.

My mother and I exchange greetings and later the odd pleasantry around the table, but there is no actual conversation. My family know what's what by now and actively support me, so I'm never alone with her.

Samuel takes many photographs of my nieces, and of Chris and me playing with them. I treasure those photographs to this day – they have pride of place on my photo wall. I think Samuel has as much of a sense as I do that this is most likely the last time I will get to spend any quality time with them.

It's summer and we're in the Little Karoo. That means it's boiling hot. We spend most of the day in and around the pool. I can tell Marius is getting more and more frustrated, torn between policing his daughters in my presence and joining my sister and mother in conversation with my uncles and aunts. At one point, I'm alone at the pool with one of my nieces. I'm deliberately not saying which one, as I don't trust their father not to rain down retribution on them over two decades later. We're in the pool and she's got her legs wrapped around my waist and her arms around my neck and we're just kind of bobbing up and down and having a fantastic time.

Then I spot Marius stomping across the lawn towards us. My heart sinks; I know what's coming. My niece spots her father, and her arms tighten around my neck.

'I don't want to go to Daddy, I don't want to go to Daddy!' she whispers in my ear.

Marius stands at the edge of the pool. 'Erika, you know you're not allowed to be alone with my daughters,' he says, glaring at me. I can't tell him to go screw himself because I won't swear in front of my niece. And then he calls his daughter and tells her to come to him. Her arms tighten around my neck. I take her to the side of the pool and I hand her to her father.

45

FINDING MY VOICE

Life in Sedgefield is wonderful. I love living right by the lagoon and being so close to nature. One of my absolute favourite things is when the lagoon mouth is open and we get in further up the river and float down to the mouth. I spend many precious hours with Samuel's friends, who become my friends and eventually my second family. Sheila, the mother, is a renowned artist with a heart of gold. She opens her home and her heart to me – as do her kids.

I was at first nervous of meeting her daughter, Jean, as Samuel had made such a fuss about her being the most beautiful girl he'd ever met. And she is utterly gorgeous, it's true. But it's her lovely, generous nature that wins me over, and soon all thoughts of jealousy over her good looks wither away. My friendship with her will become one of the most enduring relationships of my life. Sheila's two sons are as warm and welcoming.

I'm not nearly as enthusiastic about athletic pursuits as Samuel, but I do cycle to work most days. I'm still skinny, but no longer anorexic. I love food now, though Samuel is very health conscious, so I rarely indulge in treats.

One day, I hear a little squeak outside and find a tiny field mouse in the grass. It's so young that its eyes haven't even opened yet. How did it get here? Something clearly happened to its mother, otherwise it wouldn't be abandoned on a patch of lawn. We rush to Sheila's house, and she gives me a syringe and a needle she uses for silk painting. We buy some baby formula and, for the next couple of days, we feed the little tyke every hour and a half – yes, even throughout the night. Everyone tells me he will not make it, but I'm determined. I name him Methuselah – he is going to live a long and fruitful life. Soon, he's simply Mafuzi, and I adore this little creature.

As he grows bigger, those distinctive stripes start showing. I just need to get him to a size where I can set him free, knowing he'll survive in the wild. He's probably ready to go before I am ready to let him, though, and when he escapes one night during a storm, I'm heartbroken. I lie awake many a night, wondering how he's doing, if he survived. I'd only taken care of this little field mouse for a few weeks, but my grief is enormous.

Samuel and I agree that we don't want children. I am too scared of turning into my mother. Of screwing up my kids despite my best intentions. With Mafuzi gone, I direct my maternal instincts at birds instead. Samuel and I feed some drongos and robins, and soon the drongos are comfortable enough to perch on our hands.

One little robin is my favourite, and my heart bursts with joy when she trusts me enough to hop onto my hand.

I don't enjoy work, though, that's the only fly in my ointment of contentment here on the Garden Route. A large part of my job is chasing people who owe money on their timeshare purchases. The vast majority of those I speak to about their debt no longer want what they bought, but the contract they signed is watertight. It distresses me that I earn a living by making people pay for something they no longer want or can afford. It goes against my grain, but I am trapped. Jobs are few and far between in this tiny village of ours. I could probably find work in a neighbouring town, but I still don't have my driver's licence, so how would I get there and back?

One day in May 1999, I'm idly paging through a copy of *Femina* when I see an advert for a feature-writing competition. Submit your story and you could win R15 000! Ever since *Cosmopolitan* published my letter pretty much word for word the way I wrote it, I've been dreaming about writing.

It feels as though someone has designed this competition especially for me. I *have* a story to tell. It's one I want to tell – one I need to tell. As far as I know, nothing has changed back at KSB, the place where my nieces are growing up. The knowledge that they're being raised in a community that believes in breaking the spirit of a child unsettles me.

The deadline for the 1500 words is 31 August. I sit on it. Through June, then July, and by the time August rolls around, I realise I've missed my chance. My procrastination means that now I'll never know if I'm a good enough writer to be published in a magazine. After a sleepless night, I arrive at work on Tuesday 31 August, and go straight to my boss. I ask him if I can please have a few hours to write something important. It's something I absolutely have to do, I say. He has no problem with it, so I sit behind my desk and type furiously. I've been mulling over what I want to say, and now the words just flow straight out:

> We had witnessed such beatings before. We were gathered in what they called 'The Upper Room'. She lay whimpering on the carpet, her body and legs pinned down by two elders as their colleague explained to his audience that their 16-year-old friend had sinned and would now receive God's just punishment. Her whimpers became louder as he led us in the customary prayer before punishment. Soon she was screaming her repentance as the piece of hosepipe hit her body again and again and again. I didn't count the blows that landed on her back, buttocks and thighs. They beat her until she was silent – her spirit broken. A prayer followed that God might forgive her the sin of writing a letter to a boy in her class. We obediently 'Amen-ed' at the close of the prayer and waited for the sermon.

That's how I open what I hope will become a published article. I write about my descent into the mire of mind control and how it began when I was nine years old.

126

How fear was my constant companion for the next thirteen years. What KSB taught me about being female:

Male supremacy was an unquestioned fact of mission life. A woman's life revolved around pleasing and placating the males in the community. A woman is a temptress. Full stop. Jewellery, make-up and beautiful clothes were prohibited so as not to lure the men into lustful thoughts. We wore loose-fitting, below-the-knee dresses with sleeves and high necklines. No pants were allowed because somewhere in Deuteronomy it states that women shouldn't wear men's clothing. Any attempt to look pretty was met with censure.

I never saw a boy being beaten publicly; that seemed reserved for girls. Female inferiority was affirmed in countless ways. Virginity checks were customary when the boarding schoolgirls returned from holiday. Female characters from the Bible were decried as evil – everything designed to teach the woman her place. No contact between the sexes was allowed unless the couple was married. Televisions, radios and any music with a beat in it were prohibited.

I detail my painful rehabilitation into life in the outside world, when I didn't know how to act. How I struggled to make sense of the world. How Erlo and my mother denounced me, but how the kindness of family, friends and Samuel helped me recover.

Muzi only gets a small mention, a single phrase in a longer sentence: 'the kisses my married counsellor bestowed upon me'. I don't know that I'll ever be ready to talk about what he did to me.

As I write, I realise that I've actually come quite far along this road of healing already:

I finally began to remember when I first decided I was a worthless person and so regained my self-esteem. I recognised where I had given up my willpower, and so regained my ability to make decisions. I saw how warped my idea of God was, and opened up to the love and compassion in the universe. I observed how I had allowed others to manipulate me, and started asserting myself. I examined the intolerant belief system I had adopted, and made a conscious effort to accept others and their differences.

Writing takes up most of my day. Just before three o'clock in the afternoon and 1638 words later, I decide I'm done. I email the document titled 'Running from insanity' to the magazine.

I do not know how big this bombshell I've just unleashed will be.

46

A DREAM COME TRUE

After an anxious three months of waiting, an email from *Femina* lands in my inbox in early December. I didn't win the competition. Damn. But I am a runner-up, and they will publish my article in the February 2000 issue!

The magazine will be on the shelf at the end of January. I'm nervous and excited. They need a photograph of me, they say, and would like to set up a shoot. Samuel is a photographer, so we follow their directions (they want me to wear white, for instance) and send them a selection.

I deliberately didn't name KwaSizabantu in my article, as I suspected there would be serious legal repercussions. *Femina*'s lawyers agree that it's a good idea not to name the mission, and they also advise me to change my own name. I can remain Erika, but I need a different surname. And so the article will appear under Erika Joubert. Joubert is my mother's maiden name; I feel it is at least part of me.

My primary purpose for writing the article has been to chronicle my growth as a person since leaving KSB. I hope other women will identify with the processes I went through in finding myself regardless of their specific circumstances. I want it to strike a chord in those who have never even set foot in the mission.

I also hope to elicit some response from KSB, as well as other survivors. I tell *Femina* that if the article can bring about even a small measure of change in the mission's modus operandi or help in the healing of even one person who has left, I will be happy.

The editorial team leave my article largely untouched, but they ask me to add something about the state of my relationship with my mother. I write a brief paragraph stating that we haven't spoken in at least a year. My mother's bottom line is that I'm a disobedient child living in sin. It's my refusal to obey her and follow 'God's will' for my life that makes it impossible for her to accept me as her daughter.

I make excuses for my mother's behaviour. I write that having lived at the mission myself, I know that it's not really her talking. It would make life very difficult for her if I kept going back to visit, and I don't expect her to leave the security of KSB or risk being ostracised. I can't offer her the financial support she would need to make a life for herself in the outside world.

Finally, I say that 'although I still hold her responsible for her actions, I know there is immense pressure on her to disown me in order for her to remain a valued group member. She is well loved there and, although I don't believe she is truly happy, she wants to live there.'

I don't really know much about responsible journalism and the right to reply and all that. But *Femina* does, and they need to do their due diligence before publishing anything. Their bureau chief in KwaZulu-Natal reaches out to KSB and Domino Servite, and the editorial staff write an addendum to my article. It's too good not to share – especially as KSB will have to eat some of these words in years to come:

THE OTHER SIDE

The mission school featured here is known to *Femina*. When contacted for a response, a senior pastor and teacher said it had 500 children of all denominations. He denied that there had ever been public beatings there, 'even at the time when corporal punishment was still allowed and widely practised, and it's been illegal for some time'. He also denied that the school did virginity tests, although he noted that the practice was being revived – and that some Zulu parents requested it. The mission viewed virginity testing as a traditional matter, he said, not a Christian one and would not get involved.

CONTACT BEING FORBIDDEN BETWEEN SEXES?

As to allegations of all contact being forbidden between the sexes, the pastor said this would be impossible as school classes were mixed. He said that he had taught Erika Joubert matric English when she was there some 12 years ago, and added that she had 'a particular history of grievances', which he believed were linked to her 'total rejection of Christianity', after being 'very enthusiastic about the whole mission at one time'. Visitors were welcome, and could speak to teachers and pupils and judge for themselves, he said.

TOO FRIGHTENED

Erika Joubert responded that this man had never taught her, and that staff and pupils at the mission were 'too frightened to reveal what really goes on there'. She substantiated her allegations with a copy of an email sent to a member of the mission in February last year by a Scottish evangelist and theologian who she said had had close ties to the mission since its inception. In the email he expresses concern at 'developments (there) in recent years,' adding, 'this is not hurtful criticism. I love the people and the work of God at that place and pray for it constantly.' His worries are that 'ancient Zulu customs could have influenced the present (mission) policy on courtship and marriage ... My plea is that extra-biblical demands may be recognised as such, that they do not supersede and eclipse biblical principles.' He worries too that 'so many of the folk at the mission have the same look about them – of resignation and submission, of crushed obedience ... they seem to have lost the ability to think independently

... they seem governed by the fear of getting into trouble with those above them.' And he adds that he has had 'letters from people who have been terribly hurt by their association with the mission. They left years ago but they are still struggling with the dreadful aftermath.' In an addendum the evangelist lists 'with deep concern' the four elements of mind control – control of behaviour, thought, emotion and information. 'I merely inform you of these,' he concludes, 'and leave you to apply them to anything in the situation at (the mission) and assess how far, if at all, it has progressed along this pathway ... If there are issues to consider then definite steps need to be taken to halt any further movement towards cultic mind control.' At the time of going to press, *Femina* had emailed the evangelist for further comment and was awaiting his response.

I will later learn that I got one thing wrong. For now, though, I anxiously await publication day.

47

'MISSION OF MALICE'

January 2000. The start of a new millennium, a new century and a new decade. And the end of my peaceful, anonymous life. *Femina*'s February issue hits the shelves towards the end of January. It's a surreal moment, looking at the magazine rack in the supermarket. There's Jennifer Aniston's face and, next to her green eyes, on the top right, a cover line: 'How I escaped a Durban cult'.

The response is immediate. The *Natal Witness* reports that my article 'has opened a hornet's nest, with stories emerging of split families, alleged physical and psychological abuse, excommunications and suggestions of sinister business dealings'.

In another article, the newspaper says someone else has come forward:

The woman [...] related how the mission leader would regularly arrive at the school to shout at the pupils. 'He would tell us, forcefully and charismatically, that we were from the devil. It was limb-freezing stuff,' she said in a telephonic interview with the *Witness*. She described how children were held down by their hands and feet if they screamed during beatings in the hall, while fellow pupils were forced to show no emotion.

There are many more reports in the *Witness*. And what does KwaSizabantu do? They double down and deny, this time with caveats because, thanks to all the people who have come forward, I'm suddenly no longer a lone voice. Many others confirm the beatings, and so KSB has to change their tune in order to retain any credibility. But first, they have to contend with many more secrets coming to light – stuff I knew nothing about.

A journalist at the *Sunday Tribune* contacts me. She'd like to investigate, and so we exchange a number of phone calls and emails. In one email, I tell her that I can sum up my experience at the mission, and I believe that of many others, in one word: fear. That is why people have remained silent about the place. I have decided to speak out, not because I have conquered my fear, but in spite of it. I tell her that I wanted my article to be one of hope and encouragement for people still stuck in the destructive behaviour patterns and belief systems imposed on them as children. I felt compelled to speak out – and hopefully something I wrote will help others in similar pain. I know that I was very isolated and unsupported those first few years after leaving the mission, and an article like mine would have been of great encouragement to me back then.

'Mission of malice' shouts the headline on the front page of the *Sunday Tribune* on 6 February 2000. It stretches across the page, huge, bold and impactful. Below the subheading ('Allegations of military spies in the confessional and of child abuse'), the lead talks of 'startling allegations linking a controversial Christian mission station with the shady activities of apartheid's military intelligence structure'.

I had no idea about any of this, but suddenly, those visits from Adriaan Vlok, the then minister of police, start making sense. He'd swoop in by plane – I remember it was an ugly brownish colour, but I guess official military transports aren't known for their elegance. We would line up to wave at him from the side of the road. There was always proper fanfare when he paid us a visit; we all knew it was an honour to be in this VIP's presence.

The article goes on to say that KSB 'allegedly doubled as an anti-liberation agency for military intelligence and the security branch in the '80s and early '90s. Well-placed sources told the *Tribune* this week that a sophisticated system of information gathering within the KwaSizabantu mission near Greytown is claimed to have led to the kidnapping and arrest of United Democratic Front and ANC activists in northern KwaZulu-Natal. This has been denied by the mission.'

What a can of worms. 'Information was secretly gathered during "confessions" – a cornerstone of the mission's religious practice – and allegedly passed on via daily calls on "scramble phones" to Colonel Tobie Vermaak – who worked in military intelligence – and a security branch captain in Greytown, whose identity is known to the *Tribune*.'

(Vermaak is still at KSB today, by the way. He's now their head of security. It's quite fitting that an apartheid security branch operative is still in charge of safe-guarding their secrets.)

I'm on more familiar territory on page three of the newspaper. 'My mission life of fear' is the heading, and there's a short synopsis of my story. This time I'm Erika Bornman; I no longer need to be a Joubert.

'Ex-pupils who contacted the *Tribune* this week claimed there were cases of excessive violence, in which they were beaten by mission staff until they were bleeding,' the article continues. Remember, KSB told *Femina* only a few weeks ago that there had never been public beatings. Now, they concede, a little:

> They [KSB] said pupils had been exposed to corporal punishment up until 1994, but this had only been the standard 'six cuts with a cane'. They confirmed 'hidings in the upper room' in which plastic pipes were used on pupils, but this had been carried out by parents, not staff.
>
> They were 'aware' that a boy had died after being beaten by his parents on their premises, but they had no specific details. They confirmed virginity testing was carried out at the mission, but only by Zulu parents who wished it.

They admitted excommunication was performed, but denied ever evicting anyone.

Had someone beaten their child to death on my watch, I would absolutely have the specifics. How come they don't? To listen to KSB tell it, it's the parents who are doing the beating and the virginity testing – not the school and not the mission.

This is a perfect example of the diabolical semantics KwaSizabantu employs. Yes, the people – mostly but not solely men – who beat the kids are parents in that they have biological children at the school, but they are not the parents of the kids who are beaten. They are school-board members, co-workers at the mission and teachers. Let's take Michael Ngubane, one of the main perpetrators of the abuse I witnessed. Is Michael a parent? Absolutely. But the public beatings were of children in his care and not his own. Other men I saw beating my fellow pupils were also parents in that they had children themselves. They were, however, not the parents of the pupils they beat.

To claim that it is parents, and not staff, who are abusing these children is not only a gross misrepresentation of the truth, but also an outright lie. Surely, I think to myself, they can't get away with this.

48

AN OVERWHELMING RESPONSE

I am inundated with emails and phone calls. Samuel is super supportive, but the time I am spending at my laptop is placing our relationship under strain. I become immersed in the stories people tell me. And the overarching message is clear: people are happy that I spoke out. Many are from overseas. I have great support in South Africa, but not as much as you'd think, considering how many South Africans have left the confines of the mission compound.

A missive from New York: 'Man, I have to tell you, I sometimes have to struggle not to hate those people because of all that. I think sometime somebody should write a book, I think all of us could fill many, many books. As I read your first lines, where you wrote about beating, I nearly cried because I know how it was. What can I say – I am so glad you had the courage to write this.'

Here's one from the Netherlands, from a young woman my age: 'Dear Erika, I don't really know how to express what I feel. I just want you to know I stand with you. The things you describe are exactly the things I am going through at the moment. Once back in "the normal world" you feel alienated, strange. Having to learn to live a normal life all over again. I am in the same process at the moment, at university, at work. It feels as if I only start living now [...] Thank you so much for writing the article. It put to words what I couldn't express but what I feel in my heart.'

There's lots of support from Germany, too. All affirming me and thanking me. 'If we start a webpage here in Germany, I would like to put your article up – it is the truth,' one guy writes. Another writes to *Femina* that 130 people have left KSB in Germany since June 1999. 'KSB is a sect, which abuses people spiritually, mentally and physically,' he tells the magazine. 'Its leaders seem to be very friendly – but behind the curtain they are absolutely dictatorial, brutal and unscrupulous.'

One email in particular warms my heart immensely. It's from my long-ago friend Celimpilo, and she writes: 'I see you did it! Excellent stuff! You look so angelic in that book. I envy you for your courage [...] I spoke to Laura [from *Femina*] and she told me the magazine has had a tremendous response. She was wondering how many people have had the same experience as yours. I told her a little about myself. One last thing: You are very gutsy.'

In April, *Femina* publishes a follow-up article and includes Celimpilo's account as well as that of another ally, Monika Greeff, and many others who choose to remain anonymous.

Erlo would often preach from the pulpit that it's okay to lie if you're lying to protect God's work. What he means, of course, is that it's okay to lie if you're lying to protect Erlo and KwaSizabantu. Because what kind of God needs human beings to lie to protect him? Seriously, an omniscient, omnipotent being who wants people to lie for him? If your God needs you to lie, you should take another look at your God. The day after the 'Mission of malice' article, I get an email from a young guy whose letter was published way back in 1996, after the *Sunday Tribune* got wind of me helping the French. At the time, he stated that my criticisms were unfounded, and he denied that public beatings took place, instead painting a rosy picture of justly applied corporal punishment.

In this email, he tells me that he has left KSB and asks for my forgiveness. He also attaches a retraction he has sent to the *Sunday Tribune*. I can't remember whether his letter is ever published, but it means the world to me. He writes that he wants to apologise for and clarify the lies in his previous letter. He 'defended them to the hilt; as a result of the youth there being rallied together and greatly pressured to bombard the newspapers with letters'. He goes on to say:

> The simple truth of the matter, with regards to my previous letter, is that beatings did take place. I witnessed them many a time. Not canings but beatings of the sort that I find no words to describe them with. I wrote what I did, believing in the system [...] Being convinced that lying to defend 'The Work' was perfectly acceptable, I obeyed a leader's instruction to include in my writing the statement that 'I was at DSS for nine years and never received corporal punishment.' On telling the leader that this was not true, as I had in fact been caned (thank goodness though, never personally publicly beaten) I was told something to the effect of: 'But that was nothing and was so long ago.' [...] I am absolutely appalled at the mission's ability to categorically deny they ever happened. I am shocked at and take exception to the fact that the mission invariably either blatantly denies true accusations levelled against them or resorts to character assassination of the individual concerned.

It is validation from an unexpected source.

Not everyone is happy with me, however. Many of the South African contingent of former members feel that the secular media should not be drawn into matters of the church, that my article has harmed God's work. I'm not always privy to these emails, but my new-found German friends copy me in on their responses, and they have my back. They disagree with these naysayers, pointing out that in all the decades, nothing has changed. One young South African guy writes that he hasn't yet decided whether or not he should speak out: 'I do know that if I were to go the route of exposing KSB to the media, I would have to go all the way, because any "half baked" attempt would simply be swept under the carpet as so many previous articles have. There is obviously a lot of information which I could give and which I could substantiate if refuted. I have experienced, seen and heard things at KSB which would make Erica's [sic] article look like a picnic on the beach.'

These emails affect me deeply. Again, this guy didn't copy me in, but the Germans do when they respond and ask what is stopping him from having a big braai on the beach and inviting everyone. I am perplexed by the 'so many previous articles' to which he refers. As far as I know, during my association with the place, I was the first to speak out in the secular media.

Later, I learn that over the past three decades, as many as thirty men and women, including congregants, co-workers, family members, pastors and even three of his siblings as well as his brother-in-law, have confronted Erlo with serious issues and grievances, and attempted to address concerns about hypocrisy, authoritarianism, extremism, violent abuse, fraud, misappropriation of money and an absence of accountability. The KSB response has been to excommunicate all critics and circumvent attempts from the outside Christian community to resolve matters.

I discover that in 1977, the international leadership of Youth With A Mission was asked to mediate between some of these people and KSB, but nothing changed as a result of that intervention. When I was still at the mission, I'd hear about people who'd turned to Satan and left. Now I learn that KSB targeted and retaliated against those who disagreed with them and wouldn't leave quietly. These people would be viciously slandered and cut off from their families. In some extreme cases, KSB actively worked to financially ruin or enact lawsuits against critics, including members of Erlo's own family.

I start to understand that KSB has an astonishing ability to silence and neutralise internal critics and to quarantine its members from them. I certainly never knew any of this when I lived there. What I cannot comprehend, though, is that not one of them, as far as I know, went to the authorities to report what was happening in the compound. Whether through a lack of evidence, ignorance or an unwillingness to take matters external, I'll never know. I, for one, don't share anyone's qualms about speaking about 'church business' in public. At least now the abuse is out in the open. KSB can't put this genie back in the bottle.

As always, my brother has my back. The *Natal Witness* publishes this letter – he wants the world to know he stands by me:

The ex-members of KwaSizabantu who had the courage to make their stories public need to be commended. Erika Bornman is my sister and I wish to publicly state my support for her and confirm the truth of her article published in the *Femina* and the *Witness*. As a male I was spared a lot of the humiliation and restrictions placed on the women. We were treated in a different manner and I will no longer let my sister stand alone. The ordeal of going to school at Domino Servite was also not in my experience. I hope other male ex-members will stand and be counted among the courageous women who came forward. The magnitude of the response to her article has given me hope that the mission will be forced to address all the questions raised.

One of the cornerstones of their teaching is to confess your sins and to make restitution. The confession is not done only between you and God, but with a counsellor present. One of the reasons for this is to prevent you from committing the same sin over and over again. The embarrassment of doing so should cause one to think twice about committing the same sin. This trust placed in the counsellor should be sacrosanct. If the allegations are true that information was forwarded to the intelligence services, then the following questions have to be answered:

1. Was the individual notified of the information's destination?
2. What kind of pressure was exerted on the individual to confess to the security forces?
3. Was immunity from prosecution guaranteed, and by whom?
4. If the info was illegally given to the security forces, what reward(s) did the mission and individuals receive?
5. Was anybody killed, maimed, jailed or punished as a result of this info?
6. Have the individuals concerned applied for amnesty if point 5 is true?
7. What justification was made to support the previous government?
8. How will they adhere to the teaching of confession and restitution if these allegations are proved to be true?
9. Are records of any confession kept, and is the info ever used against any individual named during the confession?

As far as I am concerned the mission has done a lot of good over the years. It is also true that many individuals and families will have to deal with the damage caused by their teaching. How they deal with correcting these faults will be the acid test for their religion. Will the hypocrisy, lies, arrogance, deceit, malice, etc. be confessed as I had to do as a kid, or will the status quo be maintained?

Prove to me that your religion is real and you practise what you preach. I might just listen to you again.

Chris asks some hard-hitting questions. Will we get the answers?

49

'NO GRAVE DEEP ENOUGH'

I will only learn the true horror of what my black friends experienced in the years to come. I always knew they were treated differently, but I had no clue just how bad it was for them.

My friends also set me straight on another matter: boys were definitely beaten in public, and often. I got that completely wrong. To this day, I still don't recall witnessing a boy being beaten, but I now know that I definitely would have. How is it that I can't remember specific incidents? I only remember a few public beatings clearly – I must have dissociated the other times. Also, the white kids were often instructed to leave, or were simply not called to a meeting.

I am incredibly grateful to everyone who has spoken out, especially Celimpilo and Monika. What becomes clear to me as I speak to people and read what they've written is that, as a white girl, I was sheltered from so much of the abuse. A guy named Khulekani Mathe writes about his experiences and titles it 'No grave deep enough to bury the truth'. It's an eye-opening read.

We shared a similar timeline at KwaSizabantu, but our paths would seldom have crossed, if ever, even though he was there from 1986 to 1995 and I ran away in January 1993. Today, Khulekani is an executive in the banking industry and an entrepreneur. He has carved out an illustrious career, one that includes policy-making in government and in the private sector. He has also graciously given me permission to quote from his 5 500-word missive, which he wrote in February 2000. Brace yourself. It's ugly.

When I first joined KwaSizabantu mission, fourteen years ago, as a young and zealous Christian, I never thought that KwaSizabantu mission was capable of so much evil. All I had heard of the mission were praises from people who had received help in various ways from the mission. Fourteen years later, I have to say that I doubt that the authorities of the mission, ever thought then that their evil would come out. It is indeed true that *no grave is deep enough to bury the truth*. This article is an account of my experiences over the nine years I spent at the mission.

The place which was supposed to bring the souls of people closer to Christ, proved the opposite for many people. While I can summarise my experiences at the mission as taste of hell on earth, I did not realise this right away. Anybody who has only visited the mission for a short time – a weekend perhaps – will disagree with the sentiments expressed in this article, as the mission made sure that short-term visitors are given the best possible treatment, especially if they were VIPs of sorts. Ask anybody who has spent a considerable amount of time as a student, general worker or ever part of the leadership at the mission, they will tell you about the evil that went on in the name of God.

During my short stay at the mission – considering that some people have spent over 20 years at the mission – I experienced discrimination practised in the name of God.

He explains the hierarchy of the mission, and how the grading of followers facilitated giving people the treatment they 'deserved' depending on how far advanced they were spiritually. 'While people who belonged to the leadership structure down to members of the second choir were given good and fresh food, those of us under, were given leftovers and at times food that had gone off,' Khulekani writes. 'Care was taken to ensure that the visitors were given good food, especially if they were white, and more so if they were from Europe, as they were potential sources of income for the mission.' He speaks of the appalling conditions of the workers' accommodation: 'Accommodation at the "*place of God*" was worse off than in hostels and compounds, but only for poor black people.'

Remuneration was also highly discriminatory. Many people at the mission were there as volunteers, but the workers who were there to earn salaries for themselves and to support their families didn't earn much:

I started as a general poultry farm worker, my first salary and that of most of my colleagues at that level was R30 [a month]. That was in 1986. In 1995 when I left the mission, my salary was R250, and the highest paid person received R300 with the exception of school teachers whose salary did not exceed R1 000. While people's salaries were a top secret, and we never got to know how much those high up the ladder were getting, we knew how much our peers earned. I am not convinced that a place like KwaSizabantu which had so many money-making projects and received considerable amounts of money from overseas sources was justified to pay us so little.

I know what he's talking about. In 1991, I was given R150 a month for teaching at the school. I was doing God's work, after all, and besides, they were feeding me and giving me a roof over my head.

We worked very long hours on these projects as we were assured that God will reward us one day. If we dared to complain about our salaries, we were told that we were being used by the devil against 'God's' work and had to apologise or face expulsion. I must admit, I never knew how much our white counterparts were paid, but I do know one thing, they received better treatment in all respects. At the point when I had grown to be the manager of the poultry farm as well doing a range of other things, my white counterparts who managed vegetable, dairy, kiwi fruit farms, drove around in mission vehicles, a luxury I never enjoyed.

Khulekani also writes about the beatings, revealing that it wasn't just the pupils of Domino Servite School who were subjected to such inhumane treatment:

The beatings that went on at the mission are now in the public domain in the sense that so much has been reported on them in the different newspapers. I do however feel it is necessary to confirm some of these and add my knowledge of it. It is true that the children who went to school at Domino lived in constant fear as they were often beaten for such little things as clapping hands during a play performance, dancing to a song, listening to music with a beat, rejoicing over defeating a netball team of elders, speaking to a girl or a boy, and many more [...]

These beatings did not only happen to school kids it happened to most people at the mission. It was a known thing at the mission that punishment for any wrong-doing in the eyes of the authorities was either beating or expulsion and in some cases both. Just about everybody who lived at the mission participated in this brutality by either reporting an incident to the authorities or physically beating someone.

In the case of other people other than the school kids, we had to show our disapproval of what our peers may have done by disowning them; stopping to communicate with them and in some cases beat him/her jointly [...] Strange as it may sound, as late as 1995, a married woman with three kids and a husband who is also a preacher at the mission was publicly beaten by her fellow members of the first choir. This cannot be right, not in a civilised country and certainly not in a supposedly Christian institution.

I finally learn the name of the teenager who was beaten to death. His name was Nkosi. Later, I'll learn that his uncle had allegedly killed him. May you rest in peace, young man; I'm so sorry for what happened to you.

While I do not wish to suggest that the mission condoned this, they may have reported it to the police, but I just wonder what kind of statement was given to the police as no one was prosecuted. We can never be sure since it is a known fact that the mission has a long-standing relationship with the Kranskop police. Surely this calls for an inquiry; a person cannot just disappear? [...]

People in authority, not necessarily Rev. Erlo Stegen, but his co-workers, could just about do anything to punish a person who was perceived to have broken the rules of the mission. Someone known to me was in fact locked up in a deep freezer as a form of punishment. Although this incident I am told happened over 20 years ago, I feel it is relevant to mention.

As a result of not only the beatings but all forms of punishment that we were subjected to, we lived in fear and could not trust the people we shared the rooms with. A person you shared a room with was a potential informer of the authorities, and in fact, during the confessions we were encouraged to tell on our colleagues. A term used for telling on other people was 'helping them'. It was meant that if you reported someone, you were helping them from the devil that was using them against God's work.

Khulekani goes into great detail about KwaSizabantu's apparent involvement with the apartheid government and military intelligence. It is a riveting read. You can find the full document on ksb-alert.com. Those German guys really came through for us. They started the website in 2000, documenting people's testimonies. Kudos to them. Now when someone leaves, they can find support online. For one man, it came at great personal cost. He registered the domain name kwasizabantu.com, but KSB sued him. He offered to settle out of court, but they refused, vindictive bastards that they are. He ended up having to pay thousands of Deutschemarks in damages. Thank you, Benjamin, we all owe you a huge debt of gratitude (not to mention money) for what you did. Today, the website is still maintained by brave volunteers and has current as well as historic content in English, German, French and Dutch.

Do go and read Khulekani's entire testimony – he talks about how KSB denies people the right to an education, despite boasting that they have one of the best schools in the country; how they deny access to information; and how they violate the privacy of their followers. I'm going to end here, though, with some of his final words:

This is not a script for an American horror movie production, it is the truth. Many people out there know more, and I only hope that they find the time, energy and courage to either write what they know or tell it to someone [...]

On the final note, I love the people of KwaSizabantu; I spent the most precious time of my life – my youth – at KwaSizabantu. I love Rev. Erlo Stegen and some of his workers, but I hate the things that go on there. I am writing this article not so much for me as I have moved on with my life, but I care about the many people who are literally slaves and live in fear as we speak. Many people have been touched by the work of KwaSizabantu in many ways, there is some good that happens at KwaSizabantu, and it would be a pity if the evil triumphs over the good. May God have mercy on KwaSizabantu.

May God have mercy on them indeed. For me, the ones most in need of mercy are the defenceless kids growing up there. The adults at least have some level of agency, the kids have none. This book is for them. And the ones who are as yet unborn.

50

AN ICE-COLD
BLAST FROM THE PAST

There's one rat who sees KwaSizabantu as a sinking ship and decides to show himself on deck in the hope of saving himself. Muzi left the mission of his own volition a number of years ago. In the *Femina* article, I merely refer to the kisses bestowed on me by a counsellor, but I bet he's been agonising over whether or not I'm going to publicly name and shame him. One morning, I log in to my email and find a nasty little surprise waiting for me.

From: Muziwendoda Sikhona Kunene
To: Erika Bornman
Sent: Tuesday, March 07, 2000 1:44 AM
Subject: My Apology

Dear Erika

I was happy to find your e-mail address from Ex-KSB-ecircles. Please forgive me for using it without your permission to convey this message to you.

Since I left KSB in 1995, I have been longing to talk to you. I have asked around from many people to try and get your contact details in order to address this matter with you.

I would like to apologise for everything that happened to you and the wrong I did against you. It was all a big mistake on my part, I should have known better. My own marital frustrations and the fact that I was forced to marry a woman I did not love should not have led me to hurt you. I should have dealt with my frustrations differently. I apologise humbly for all that happened.

We have now divorced with [name redacted], [name redacted] decided to stay with me. He always asks for you. The other two stayed at the Mission and am sometimes barred from seeing them, they do however phone me occasionally. They are well. I have never been able to thank you for all you did for my children before I hurt you. Thank you very much for that, they will never forget.

Please forgive me. If you can allow me I would like to see you sometime, and apologise in person. I am sorry to revive the wounds, but I have to apologise for what happened. Recently I met one journalist who told me she had spoken to you about the Mission, She wanted to hear more from me about their involvement with the SA intelligence. I then asked her to convey my greetings to you. I am sorry if that hurt you as well. I was hoping I might be able to contact you to address this issue. I am sorry for that and hope I did not add to the hurt. If I did, I beg for your forgiveness.

Thank you.

Muzi Kunene

I know the journalist he mentions. She conveyed Muzi's greetings to me at the time and I told her I didn't want any messages from him until he had the guts to come clean about what he did to me. She must have passed that on to him.

I am at work already by the time I read this and pass the rest of the day in a daze. How dare he, and what kind of an apology is this anyway? You were my father figure, Muzi. I trusted you. You violated me, even when I asked you to stop. You forever tainted my relationship with my body, with my sexuality. You taught me arousal is shameful, forbidden, wrong. 'It was all a big mistake.' A mistake?

I see what's happening. You're scared that I'm going to name you in the media. That's what this is really about. A pitiful attempt to stop me from saying: 'My abuser was Muzi Kunene.'

I'm not going to name you, you idiot, for the simple reason that I cannot speak of what you did to me. My shame is too intense, and I still blame myself for not resisting your advances. The shame is all yours, though, and, while I'm starting to understand that, I carry *your* shame inside *me* still. Even Samuel doesn't really know what you did to me. I can't get myself to talk about it, not even with the man I trust more than anything.

I forward the email to my brother, adding: 'Our hero has suddenly found the guts to apologise in a very non-incriminating way! What a guy!' That night, the mysterious tremors are back, for the first time in years. They don't last as long as before, but they unsettle me further. I mull over my answer for two days, then respond.

From: Erika Bornman
To: Muziwendoda Sikhona Kunene
Subject: Re: My Apology
Date: Wednesday, March 08, 2000 6:22 PM

Muzi,

No, I am not prepared to accept your pathetic, insipid and cowardly attempt at an apology. What is 'I would like to apologise for everything that happened to you and the wrong I did against you' and 'I apologise humbly for all that happened'?

What did you do to me, Muzi? Go on – try and be a man and admit what you did. Don't give me those bullshit little phrases – you don't fool me. I don't believe for a moment that you have changed your spots – you are still as manipulative and conniving as you have ever been. Oh, and I also know that I was not the only girl that you took your sexual 'frustrations' out on – I have news for you – it is not frustration, it is perversion. Tell me, have you been for counselling to help you with your sexual perversions and have you come to terms with the terror and grief you have caused by your selfishness? I want that psychologist's report. And if you don't have it, then you have not acknowledged that you have a problem and I want nothing to do with you. So go for therapy, coward, and take responsibility for your perversion and the effect it has had. Go and study and read up on the results of sexual abuse – have you done that? Have you lost even a moment of sleep? I think not.

So here's the deal: unless you radically change the way in which you 'apologise', leave me alone. Surprise, surprise – I have grown up and have a mind of my own now and I DO NOT ACCEPT YOUR APOLOGY.

Any forgiveness will be for my sake and my sake only and not to appease your measly excuse of a warped conscience.

Erika

Muzi and I never speak or correspond again. Karma will catch up with him eventually, but he will first murder a woman and try to kill his son before he lands in the prison where he belongs.

51

MORE MEN OF GOD

In my imaginary book *Starting a Cult for Dummies*, there's a chapter called 'Prep for persecution'. It's essential reading for anyone in need of a road map to hoodwink their flock. I know, because I learned from the best in the business. Here's what it says:

> You have to prepare your followers for persecution, because at some point someone is going to go, 'Wait a minute. This is not right.' Get ready for that day. If the Bible is your go-to, you'll find plenty of verses to support this idea. There's 'Blessed are those who are persecuted for righteousness' sake, for theirs is the kingdom of heaven', and also 'Indeed, all who desire to live a godly life in Christ Jesus will be persecuted.' Or this one that combines persecution with the end-times message in the previous chapter: 'And you will be hated by all for my name's sake. But the one who endures to the end will be saved.' Don't worry about context, just repeat it often enough and it will become the truth (see chapter 'Create your own truth').
>
> Right off the bat, teach your followers that there is an 'us' and a 'them'. As the 'us', we are the only ones with the truth; everyone else is being deceived by Satan. If he's your chosen adversary, that is – you can tailor your message to whomever you choose. This serves several purposes:
> 1. It helps your followers feel special and gives them a sense of belonging.
> 2. It cements you as the only purveyor of truth.
> 3. It creates suspicion of anyone who questions you. They are being deceived by [insert chosen adversary – Satan, big tech, vaccinators, liberals, feminists, atheists, communists – it's probably just easier to make it all of the above].

Then, when 'they' start holding you to account (see chapter 'Accountability is for arseholes'), you have an easy way out to stop your followers from questioning anything you've either done or told them is the truth.

It is absolutely essential to attack those who question you. Do not give into the temptation of introspection. Turn the tables on them: their motives are questionable. Why are they attacking 'us'? What's in it for 'them'? For more on this, read the chapter 'Who is the real victim here?'

By the time my article appears, there has already been quite an exodus of people from KwaSizabantu. Not everyone was kicked out. Many left voluntarily, having decided they simply could not reconcile with the teachings of the mission any more.

I find out that a group of ex-KSB leaders, members and former friends of the mission have been communicating among themselves about rising controversies in KSB branches in South Africa and Europe. After my article appears, they convene to discuss the situation and then write an open letter to KSB and the broader Christian church community. In it, they outline their concerns. As a result of this letter, Reverend Martin Frische, the executive director of Trans World Radio in South Africa, contacts the group and then communicates their concerns to The Evangelical Alliance of South Africa (TEASA), whose ecumenical leaders decide to investigate.

In March, some twenty former KSB members, myself included, meet with a TEASA panel at Hilton College in KwaZulu-Natal. I don't remember much from that day, but I know I tell my truth, truthfully. It isn't easy – after my past experiences with men of God, I'm deeply sceptical, but I also recognise that if Erlo is going to listen to anyone, it will be these men. I can't – and don't – speak about theology. I tell them about my experience and then go back home to the Garden Route. I'm still dealing with daily emails and calls from fellow survivors and often find myself wishing I had the tools to help them. Instead, all I can offer is my shoulder, my ear and what has worked for me.

A few months later, I get an email from Dr Michael Cassidy, one of South Africa's most respected Christian leaders. I'm moved by his words. He tells me, 'Hearing your testimony when we were out there at Hilton College was very moving and memorable for all of us. Your sincerity, lack of bitterness, and gracious manner impressed each of us who heard you.'

The TEASA panel has been trying unsuccessfully to get an audience with the KSB leadership, he says. KSB considers them to be part of a conspiracy to do damage to the mission. He tells me that they'll be releasing a statement soon, 'untempered by any response or defence from [KSB]' by way of information and caution. So TEASA is part of the 'them' now too. Welcome to the club!

KSB particularly doesn't like that the panel spoke to me and the handful of others who went to the media. TEASA sends them their report in June, but KSB decides not to address the panel directly. Instead, they publish a response on their new website in August 2000. It's called 'Response to various documents about KwaSizabantu', and in it they state their reasons for not cooperating with the panel; they also refute the criticism they've faced:

> KwaSizabantu has often been mentioned negatively in the press. In contradiction to the Scriptures, people have resorted to the world to discuss church matters. This has caused much damage and makes KSB feel that true reconciliation is not being sought, rather it would seem that the panel is being used as

a means to pressurise KSB into submitting to ex-KSB members and others' demands.

Yeah, right. Fifteen respected church leaders are going to be led by the nose by a few 'disgruntled' ex-members. The statement is classic cult: deny and attack. Remember how they first flatly denied public beatings, then admitted to the standard 'six cuts with a cane' and blamed the parents? Well, they've had a bit more time to reflect by now and their story has changed yet again:

> There were aberrations and excesses of corporal correction, which were dealt with by Church discipline and teaching. As we have said in the past, we say again: If there are still any outstanding issues regarding corporal correction, the individuals concerned should please come forward so that reconciliation can be facilitated.

In whose universe would we want to 'reconcile' with those who abused us? And why is that reconciliation up to us, anyway? They have a list of all the pupils who attended their school in those years. But of course, the hundreds of beatings were 'aberrations' and so they can neatly wash their hands of the whole affair. You're hurt? Come talk to us, we'll stick a band-aid on it as long as you don't 'resort to the world' to hold us accountable.

Celimpilo heeds their call, for her own sake and healing. In her meeting with them, they acknowledge that she was wrongfully expelled and apologise to her. She asks them to please tell her father, hoping it might help heal the rift that still exists between them. No, they say, your father has left the KSB fold and we're not talking to him. When she tells me this, I know for sure that the mission's idea of reconciliation is one that silences survivors – they have no interest in making things right. I'll be damned if I indulge them. (Celimpilo's parents die before she is fully able to repair her relationship with them. And I believe that is on KSB.)

In a follow-up letter to KSB, the panel of ecumenical leaders note that they confined the distribution of their report and were hesitant to allow people to publish it online because 'we wanted to limit the access the secular world had to these church concerns, particularly because the KwaSizabantu leadership had heavily emphasized this concern'. However, now that KSB has decided to publish their response online, it's 'important that those who have read KSB's response can also read our report to which KSB was referring. Thus we have released our report into the public domain.' The letter continues:

> The question we put forward to you, the KSB leadership, as well as the wider Body of Christ is 'who is telling the truth and who is not telling the truth?' Our interactions with those who testified, and the consistency of their reports still stand as valid in our opinions, despite the rebuttals of KSB's 'Response.' It

is for these reasons that we feel we do not have sufficient reason to believe that in your response you have been successful in your efforts to 'examine and prove' yourselves.

TEASA's statement and report are available online at ksb-alert.com. The report is long and its signatories read like a veritable who's who of ecumenism in South Africa in the year 2000. There's Dr Cassidy, of course, and Reverend Moss Ntlha. Reverend Martin Frische is there too. There is also a professor, a bishop emeritus of the Anglican church and at least ten other church leaders.

The 'evidence brought before us in the past few months has led us to believe that KSB is not in totality what it might claim or might appear to be at face value to the Christian public', the panel notes in their report. 'Extensive testimony points to the existence of a questionable system "within" KwaSizabantu; a system which seems to revolve inappropriately around the personalities of KSB leadership and its exclusive beliefs.'

The panel 'has been profoundly alarmed and deeply concerned at hearing these repeated stories of excessive reverence of man, apparent authoritarianism and abuse, psychological manipulation, the breaking of confidentiality, and serious family and relational disruption'.

They further conclude that the overwhelming evidence 'leads us to believe that KwaSizabantu is in danger of developing a cult-like behaviour, in seeing itself as an exclusive way, in seeking control over people by misusing authority, and manipulating people through confession and other questionable practices which has created an environment of unquestioning submission to the KSB leadership.'

What would my life be like had Dr Cassidy been my pastor? I'll never know. I can well imagine that I would have believed in God's goodness and grace and that I would still consider myself a Christian. Of course, a true 'man of God' would never be in charge of a place like KSB, so it's a bit of a moot point.

I have enormous respect for this group of church leaders and am grateful for their efforts on our behalf, and for trying to effect change for the benefit of those still living there. To this day, KwaSizabantu is completely independent and operates with no oversight. They are not accountable to anyone, and that is why they can treat these holy men, their efforts and their subsequent report with such contempt.

52

ANOTHER ESCAPE

My relationship with Samuel has become quite unhappy in many respects. We care deeply about each other, but we are so different and we don't have the tools to help our love grow. Instead, we are smothering it in our insecurities. He doesn't have the wherewithal to help me heal my childhood wounds. How can he when he doesn't even know what those wounds are? I don't understand them myself yet. And I don't have the tools to help him heal his childhood wounds. How can I when I don't even recognise the depths of my own?

Samuel didn't feel heard as a young boy, and so for him today, it is so important to talk about things, to discuss issues, and to speak about feelings and get it all out in the open. I can't talk about my feelings. For the most part because I don't know what I'm feeling at any given moment, but also because I can't trust myself to really let someone see how much I despair, and how often. I have a sense that if I let him see everything that's inside me, he won't want me, because there's something not right with me. I should be ecstatically happy, but I'm not. There *is* something wrong with me.

He gets frustrated because I won't talk to him about what's going on with me. Understandably. His frustration pushes me to retreat even more. Also understandable. Who knows what might have happened had we the maturity, the understanding and the means to seek help and go for couples counselling? Or individual therapy?

What I do know is that I'm overwhelmed and feel unable to cope with life right now. All the media attention and exposure and emails and phone calls – it all gets too much for me. I had no idea that telling my story would garner such a response and I hate how people now think they know me just because they read my article, especially since I shared so very little of what I actually experienced. I don't even know myself, so how can these strangers think they know me?

Chris and Janet recognise my growing sense of despair and invite me to spend a few months with them in Sweden. I resign from my job and leave Samuel to fend for himself. He won't find it easy – we've been surviving on my salary for a long time, as he hasn't managed to get his photography career to a place where it earns an income. I'll be back in three months, but right now, I need to get away and reflect and make decisions about my future.

Chris and Janet spoil me. There is no other word for it. They lavish me with love and encourage me to keep learning. I take a French refresher course at the university in Lund where they both teach. They introduce me to the delights of good wine. They've done that before – the very first wine I ever remember drinking was a German gewürztraminer, which was the perfect choice for a starter wine. This time it's a proper education. Janet also teaches me to cook. Our first lesson is making custard. Our second, basil pesto. I learn about beauty on this visit. After my dad's death, I'd forgotten about beauty. He used to point it out often. And here I am, thirteen years later, rediscovering it. I find it in food, in wine, in nature, in art, in libraries, in music. In clothing, too. My wardrobe was so restricted back at KSB. I delight in dressing well now and clothes are important to me.

They introduce me to something else that is magical and beautiful. I've always loved classical music, but the only opera I'm familiar with are the rousing choruses and famous arias most people know. We go to every opera in Malmö and Copenhagen while I'm there. It's a revelation and the start of a whole new love affair. Janet also takes me to one of Nana Mouskouri's last concerts in Copenhagen. Seeing her live is absolutely magical.

I have time to breathe. Time to reflect. Time to heal. The three months are over much too soon, and Janet helps me extend my visa by another two. All this introspection leads me to try to figure out what's happening. One morning on a walk from the university down to the town library, I realise how I hold pain at bay by not looking people in the eye. Am I scared I'll see my own anguish reflected in theirs? I've become a nameless face in an anonymous crowd with a zipped-up soul, choked with unshed tears and stifled screams.

I start wondering about this all-pervasive fear that sits in my solar plexus and won't let go. Is fear a human condition that I should simply get used to and deal with, or is it something more individual? Also, what is the best way to deal with the fear, seeing as it is so universal and yet so personal? On the universal level, I'm not sure, but on the personal level I guess I know what I need to do: express the feelings around the fear and go back to earlier incidents when I felt fear.

I remember this one semi-tame blue crane at the mission that was really quite vicious. One day, it stormed towards me. I was so scared, and yet the adults around me simply laughed. No one came to my rescue and chased it away. It actually nipped my hand, but no one did anything. Now, as I lie in bed at night, I remember that blue crane. And the frog. Odd how it's the natural world that is still so sinister to me and not the people in it.

I recall another incident – one of the few times we went swimming at KSB as kids. Someone held my head underwater and I was terrified that I would drown. Shouldn't this have taught me that I can survive being held down? Instead, I developed a fear of putting my head under water. What is it within me that one bad incident can cause lifelong avoidance? I wonder about my deep-seated belief that I am fragile and easily broken. That's something I remember my dad telling my brother when I was a little girl and I ran to him for protection: 'She's just a girl,

Chris, she's fragile.' Why does that stick in my mind? I am not fragile, I am start-ing to realise that now, and yet I think many of my fears are based on that shadow belief. What puzzles me most is that these incidents, and others, should have taught me that I can survive, whereas the lesson I took from them was that the world is not a safe place for me.

Here in Sweden, where I can walk alone whenever and wherever I want without the danger of being attacked, I start thinking that perhaps South Africa isn't the right place for me. I'm scared all the time and I wonder whether the threat of violence is part of what's holding me back. And so I start applying for jobs else-where. I'm hoping that if Samuel and I decide to stay together, he'll come with me. Though I'm starting to see a future without him. There's a job at a hotel in the Maldives. A summer job in Greece as an activities coach, whatever that might be. Anything that doesn't require a university degree and that looks mildly interesting or is in a beautiful place appeals to me.

I hate the saying 'all good things must come to an end'. I want to rage against it. No! Why should they? But not liking something doesn't make it any less true. My sojourn in Sweden comes to an end and I return to the Garden Route. Back to Samuel and no job.

PART FIVE

THE RESOLUTE RUNAWAY

53

FACE TO FACE

I'm wearing a pretty pink top the day I come face to face with my mother on national television. Janet gave me this top for Christmas just a few weeks earlier and it helps to think that she's with me in some way. It's early 2001 and I've just returned from Sweden, unsure of what to do with my life. Samuel and I have to decide if we want to be together. I need to find a job and potentially a place to stay if we break up. I'm almost a hundred per cent sure that we should break up, and I'm both terrified and exhilarated at the thought of facing life alone.

The very day I arrive back in South Africa, I get a phone call from Rian van Heerden, a well-known Afrikaans talk-show host, asking me to come and talk to him about my experiences. That Thursday, I watch his show, *Voorblad*. I have a good feeling about him and so I say yes. I tell him that I want it to be a story of hope, not despair. The producers agree, and then tell me that a representative from the mission will be there as well. Gulp. But what better way to exorcise my demons than by facing them?

The show's producers arrange for me to stay in a guesthouse in Johannesburg the night before. I'm really nervous about speaking Afrikaans on national television – it's been years since I spoke it every day and Miss Perfectionist over here doesn't want to mess up.

I'm on my way to the airport when a producer phones to tell me that KSB is sending my mother as their representative. I want to cancel it all; I'm not a fan of US talk-show host Jerry Springer and the way he airs the dirty laundry of families in public. But first I call Chris and we chat about it as Samuel's car takes me closer and closer to the airport. Chris is working in Bloemfontein now, 400 kilometres from the recording studio. He tells me that he'll take the following day off work and make sure that he's there in time for the taping, then drive back again that night. I've said it before and I'll say it again: my brother is my hero.

The producers are very kind and arrange for my mother to wait in a different room. Then we enter the studio, where we join the audience that sits in a circle in two rows. I immediately spot some KSB members dotted about, including Waldemar Engelbrecht, the leader of the Joburg contingent. I tell a producer and point them out – the way they're not sitting together immediately arouses my suspicions. I'm pretty sure that they're probably going to try to pretend they're just 'normal' spectators. The men are tricky to spot, the women easier – they're not wearing any jewellery or make-up and their dress code is pretty uniform.

Rian interviews a young man who had been a high priest as a Satanist, and then a mother, a piano teacher who speaks of her battle to wrestle her son from the clutches of a cult. Then it's my turn. I'm alone next to Rian – an empty chair ominously reminds me that it's not going to stay that way. He asks me when last I was at KwaSizabantu.

'I left in 1992 and haven't been [back] there since 1996,' I respond.

'Are things still the same?'

'I don't know,' I reply.

'Let's talk about these "things", the problems,' Rian says, inviting me to give a short synopsis. He's a good interviewer and I grow more at ease with every minute that goes by. We chat a bit about what I experienced, the beatings, the movies, my mother disowning me, Erlo cursing me. We laugh about how I'm transgressing their dress code by wearing a pair of black trousers, and then Rian says, 'Your mother is here,' and he invites her to join us on stage.

'She is representing KwaSizabantu today,' he announces as my mother walks up and hands him a pamphlet. 'And there are a number of other people here from KwaSizabantu.' He asks the audience, 'Who else is here from KwaSizabantu?'

Waldemar puts up his hand. One of the only ones, from what I remember. Rian establishes Waldemar's credentials, then reads two excerpts from the TEASA report and addresses Waldemar, who now holds a microphone. When Rian gets to the part about how KSB is dangerously close to becoming a cult, Waldemar starts laughing. His smile fades as Rian continues, however.

'The report basically says you're a cult, sir,' Rian says to Waldemar when he's done reading.

'Well, I'm happy to hear what a cult is,' Waldemar retorts. The laugh is back. 'The only command I ever got from my boss, Erlo Stegen, was "Don't tell people what to do." Our teaching, if I can call it that, is that someone must come to God, have an experience with God and then he must do what the Lord tells him to do—'

'And if he doesn't do it, is that when the hosepipe comes out?'

I've liked Rian from the start – he was kind and compassionate when we spoke off camera, and as I've watched him interview the others, my respect for him has grown. At this moment, he gains a lifelong fan.

Waldemar prevaricates a bit and then says, 'It would be good if there was an investigation.'

'So, you don't hit people there if they transgress?' Rian asks. 'Nobody? Ever?'

'Never,' says Waldemar. 'Never hit anybody.' I note the lack of pronouns in his response.

'Erika, is he lying?'

'Yes,' I say. 'Yes.'

I look Waldemar in the eye, and I'm also smiling. I know for sure now that I have an ally in Rian; I'm not alone on this platform.

'So, is Erika lying? Who is lying? One of you is lying. Who could it be?'

'She says, you asked if I've hit people,' Waldemar protests. 'I say no. She says I'm lying. I've never hit anyone.'

Rian sets him straight. We are not referring to him specifically, but KSB in general.

'You asked if I did it.' Waldemar won't let it go.

'No, that was going to be my second question.'

Hello, hero! I have feared Waldemar and his ilk for so many years, and here's this man standing up for me, for all of us, on national TV!

'No, I've never been present during a beating,' Waldemar concedes. 'I've never seen it and I've never experienced it.'

Rian now turns to my mother.

'Esther, have you been brainwashed?'

'No,' she also laughs. It's a regular laugh a minute here.

'Your daughter is shaking her head.'

Now my mother tells him about me and how I've lost my gratitude. Rian hears her out and then asks her what I've done to make me so evil that she's decided I am not her daughter.

'That's also not true,' my mother says. 'That's also an untruth.'

She forgets my brother is here, sitting in the audience, listening to her.

'I was there,' Chris says. 'I heard it too.'

'Yes, but not in so many words,' my mother counters. But neither Chris nor I are going to let her deny she disowned us. Eventually my mother capitulates. Yes, she says, and she stands by what she said then, because our standards are now different. I flash my brother a smile; I'm so grateful he's here.

'Erika got angry with me,' she continues, but Rian interrupts her, pointing out that she's just changed her story.

'I'll get back to that. Erika was angry with me because she was living with a man and I didn't want to accept that,' she continues. 'That's not how I raised her. And that time Chris and Erika came to see me was in 1994, I remember it well. I asked you, "Children, how can you speak like that of a man of God, don't you fear God?" because I knew what you were saying were lies. And that is why I said, if you continue like this, you cannot be my children any more, because then our paths part ways. You choose your path and I have already chosen mine.'

For the record, Samuel and I only moved in together in 1996. He's the first man I ever lived with 'in sin', but not the last. I can't be too upset with her for getting the date wrong, though; I only know the details of dates and conversations because I've kept journals over the years.

My brother tells our mother that a man of God who treated his sister that way is not worthy of the title. My mother asks him if he's referring to Uncle Erlo, and he confirms that he is.

'What did he do to your sister?' she asks him, as if I'm not sitting right there next to her.

This programme is nothing like *The Jerry Springer Show*, I needn't have worried. But it's still awful. I haven't allowed myself to cry, but all I want to do is run away, curl into a little ball and pretend none of this is happening. It will only be many years later, when I order the DVD of the episode and watch it again, that I consider how awful that day must have been for my mother, too. And I wonder whether it really had been her choice to appear on national TV with her children or whether they'd coerced her into doing it, though I imagine she didn't for one minute think my brother would be there, backing me.

I didn't want this for Chris, this confrontation with my mother. He's here to support me. I've brought this on us, I need to deal with it. Also, I know Chris won't speak of what Muzi did to me and how Erlo covered for him – I've only just told my brother some of what happened, and he knows I won't want it in the public domain.

'Please,' I interject, 'it's becoming a family affair. And I think that's the reason my mother came today, to reduce everything from an organisational, human-rights point of view back down to a plain family thing.'

'Sure,' Rian agrees, 'but I do want us to finish this,' and he gestures towards Chris.

Chris tells of how Erlo got us together on the day of our dad's funeral and told us he would be our father now. The camera pans to me as I lose my battle to not cry at the mention of my dad.

Chris concedes that KSB has done a lot for our family and that Erlo is head of a big organisation. 'But when I see what happened to my sister ... She was three-quarters the weight she is now. I cannot reconcile those two things,' he says.

'So they mistreated your sister,' Rian confirms.

'I don't know,' Chris says. 'I didn't witness it myself. I'm not talking physically here. Emotionally ... it happened to all of us.'

The camera now shows my mother as she looks from Chris to me. I don't detect any visible emotion.

I tell Rian about the day my father died and what transpired.

'The point is,' Rian says, looking at my mother, 'your two children are emotional wrecks. Look at them. Look at your children. You can't tell me that place is normal, that there isn't something wrong with it.'

'Is there not something wrong with my children, sir?' my mother asks as tears roll down my cheeks.

'The bottom line is that you don't tell someone that, what we've just heard. You don't say that to someone,' Rian tries to reason with her. I could have told him there's no reasoning with KSB people, but I love him for trying.

'But you're listening to children—'

'They are not children!' Rian exclaims.

'Uncle Erlo has never in his life placed God's curse on anyone,' my mother continues. 'Never in his life! And what's happening now is that two children whose lives are not one with the Lord—'

And then all three of us are talking at the same time. And Waldemar throws in a 'It's totally against our policy!' He's referring to the curse, of course. Years later, a woman from Europe will tell me Erlo placed God's curse on her life, too. I wonder how many of us there are, walking around with this curse.

'… their problem is with Jesus Christ,' my mother finishes.

'My point' – Rian takes control of the conversation and raises the report he's holding – 'is that it's here in black and white. Something is wrong at that place.'

It's time to draw the interview to a close.

'Do you consider these two to be your children?' asks Rian.

'They are my children. I pray for them often, but the lifestyle they've chosen is not up to my standard. And that is why our paths have diverged.'

A man, a KSB adherent, sitting behind my brother starts applauding. What the actual fuck? Waldemar joins him, as does the woman in a red top sitting next to him. Way to go, KSB. Applaud the breaking up of families, why don't you? Clap your hands at our pain. Show the world your true colours.

My mother confirms that she's told me that we either meet at the cross or not at all.

My brother says that it is possible to overcome and to get out.

I can't cope with the Afrikaans any more, I'm too emotional, so I switch to English. I tell Rian that what helped me was not so much trying to make sense of what happened to me, but rather examining the decisions I made about myself and the world as a result.

'And boy, I hated myself when I left there,' I say. 'It's a warped society that creates warped people.'

And that's a wrap. I remember nothing of what happens next. On the recording, I'm sitting next to my brother again for the last segment. My next memory is the flight back to George. This is early 2001, pre-9/11, and I get invited to sit in the cockpit with the pilot and co-pilot. I eat peanuts as they tell me how dangerous it can be to land at George airport if there's a certain combination of wind and cloud cover because of the proximity of the mountain to the landing strip. That mountain has seen its share of casualties, but on this day we land safely. I've faced down my mother on national television. I'm ready for whatever comes next.

54

TAKING BACK MY TUMMY

You'd think with all the allegations in the press and the furore my article causes, the media houses would continue to investigate, right? You'd think the authorities might even step in, right? The Truth and Reconciliation Commission is still going at this stage. You'd think the allegations of collusion with the apartheid government would be of concern, right?

You'd be wrong. KwaSizabantu has always had powerful friends, and they are brilliant at pivoting. During apartheid, they pivoted from being under suspicion as a multiracial compound to one that allegedly supported the regime.

Then came the late 1980s and early 1990s, when they were outspoken and virulent in their anti-ANC rhetoric. Forgotten are the days when they preached against Joe Slovo and Nelson Mandela. Forgotten is the time they bussed hundreds of men, women and children up to the Kempton Park World Trade Centre to launch a mass protest on behalf of 'South Africa's eighty per cent Christian community' against the negotiation process. Most had no idea what they were protesting against, except that the ANC equalled communism and must therefore be evil and there should be no negotiation.

Khulekani remembers this time. Here's what he wrote back in 2000:

I remember during the 1994 elections when the mission embarked on what was called voter education, which was in actual fact semi-IFP [Inkatha Freedom Party] election campaign. Only bad things were said about the ANC and only good said about the IFP. Those who have been following developments at the mission will know that only the leader of the IFP was invited on several occasions to address meetings at the mission other than apartheid bosses. The only explanation given for affording the IFP and NP [National Party] an opportunity to address large audiences at the mission was that the leader of the IFP, Inkosi Mangosuthu Buthelezi was a professing Christian, and that Adriaan Vlok and others in the case of the NP, were also publicly professing Christians. At one stage in 1993/94 when there was pressure from the people who visited the mission that the mission should demonstrate its impartiality by inviting leaders from other parties, they invited the Honourable Jacob Zuma – now Deputy President of South Africa – to a secret meeting which only involved a few of the leadership. He was not given an opportunity to address a large audience of over five thousand people as was the case with the NP and IFP leaders.

KSB has again pivoted and are now seemingly friends with the very political party they so vehemently opposed. The mission has become a huge commercial enterprise, exporting avocados to the UK and Europe, and their new water-bottling plant, aQuellé, is really taking off. In my opinion, they probably need the government to like them and not question their dodgy past.

I feel disheartened and overwhelmed. I don't regret writing the article, and I don't regret it being published; not at all. I still think that if it helps anyone heal, great. If it helps bring about some changes at KSB, great (although I'm starting to doubt that that will ever happen). But I simply don't understand how the uproar can all just fizzle out. I guess it's partly because KSB have once again corralled their followers into writing reams of letters praising the place. Also, as every South African knows, people can be bought to turn a blind eye and do nothing. Because that's exactly what happens: nothing. KSB denies the misconduct and abuse, and the world swallows their stories.

I do running away quite well. And I have to get away – again. My relationship with Samuel is over, we both agree. We're not good for each other any more. And so, once the paperwork is sorted, I pack my bags and disappear to Greece for their summer. My birthday is in August. I'm about to turn thirty and I'll be damned if I do it in the rain. I want sunshine.

On the last night of my twenties, I set my alarm for five o'clock. As I lie in bed that night, it feels as though all those years of hurting have turned into compressed blocks of pain inside me; densely packed and pounded down every day, impossible to work loose. I'm so tired of all this pain I carry around. I don't understand why I can't just let it go. What do I have to do to forget? How do I move on? Alcohol provides only a temporary relief; I still wake up as me the next morning. What do I have to do to be happy? What is wrong with me that I can't just embrace life?

On my birthday, I get up before the sun rises and make my way to the beach. I like the Mediterranean; there are no real waves to speak of, so I'm not that scared of the water – I can control whether I dip my head under or not. I'm in the ocean as I watch the sky change colour and the sun rise.

'Garrakachok, I'll find my den,' I vow to myself. Somehow, I will find my way to happiness. Find my way back to the *kurkproppie* I know I am, deep down. Find a way to not tap into this vein of sadness that runs through me. I can do it. I know I can.

It's summer in Greece and I'm young and tanned and toned and basically living in a bikini. The more tanned I get, the less visible my scar becomes. I hate this scar on my stomach, running from my navel to my pubic bone. I'm ashamed and embarrassed every time I look at myself. Every time I look at my tummy, I'm reminded of hell.

I meet two guys who will help me do something about it. The first is a young guy from Oxford, Chris. We instantly bond over our love of reading. He introduces me to *The Lord of the Rings*, which I've never read. Of course I haven't, they don't allow books like that back at KSB. It's the first time I read Tolkien and I'm transfixed by his world.

Then I meet Tamir from Israel, who's on holiday here with a friend. Tamir is hands down the most handsome, beautiful man I've ever seen in my entire life. He's also a pretty good artist. One of his artworks is on display on his bicep. It's a naked angel.

I've been brought up to hate tattoos, and definitely to hate any depiction of nakedness. A tattoo of a naked angel? That's pretty much the ultimate blasphemy. But I'm mesmerised, because this angel is unbelievably beautiful. On an unbelievably beautiful bicep of an unbelievably beautiful man.

It's during the week that Tamir is here that Chris and I decide to get tattoos, referencing the book we now both love. After seeing that magnificent angel tattoo, I've decided I know how to take back my tummy. I'm going to get a tattoo right next to my scar. I'm not quite brave or imaginative enough to think about turning the scar into a tattoo – it is too long and takes up too much real estate for that to even cross my mind.

I show Tamir the list of runes in the back of the book. Together, we figure out which symbols would depict my name. One day, as we're relaxing on the beach, Tamir takes those symbols and designs a monogram for me in my journal. It is beautiful.

Shortly after my thirtieth birthday, Chris and I and a handful of friends head to a tattoo parlour in town. Chris's tattoo is also inspired by *The Lord of the Rings*, but it's not the same as mine. He goes first and gets it on his bicep. Then it's my turn. My tattoo goes next to my scar. I've taken back my tummy. And I'm busy taking back my life. I still don't know what I want to do. Actually, I do know what I want to do. I want to write, but I just don't know how to make that happen.

55

LONDON CALLING

I have nothing waiting for me at home, so I procrastinate some more. I like to think that if I were an animal, I'd be a lion (I'm a Leo and a cat lover and I'm from Africa). Fierce and proud, protective of her young, and also playful. The reality is that I'm probably more like an ostrich. All that burying my head in the sand – if I hide from reality, is it really reality?

After three months in Greece, I head to London to stay as long as my money lasts, which I know will only be a week or two. I'll book my flight home from there.

London is a revelation. The city seduces me. A good friend from my Durban days gives me a place to stay and I decide to explore London and what it has to offer – I'm here after all, so why not? I find a job in a bar for a while. I have nothing to return to back home; I'm lost, and I just want to live a little.

I find a place of my own to stay, a loft room on the top floor of a house in Herne Hill. I consciously steer clear of the large contingent of Saffas in London. I'm older than most of them – who takes a gap year at the age of thirty? And also, I want to experience the world, not my own culture upended into a different city.

I go to every single opera and ballet production I can. Except for Wagner operas. I make the mistake of going to one, *Tristan and Isolde*, and I hate it so much, I leave during the first interval. It's not the music – I recognise that much of it is great – it's the man behind the music. Richard Wagner was a virulent anti-Semite, and his views turn my stomach. I am unable to appreciate his music, as his bigotry puts me off completely. Despite that one fail, the Royal Albert Hall becomes my favourite place. I scour the newspapers – if I act quickly, the moment ticket sales open, I get a cheap seat. And then there are the classical music concerts held in St Martin-in-the-Fields – it's a church, sure, and not my usual hangout, but the music is sublime. Plus, their midday dress rehearsals are free – anyone may enter and listen.

Bookstores are another favourite refuge. Books are relatively inexpensive here compared to back home. I'm a voracious reader. For me, reading is an escape and a way to learn about the world. Also, it's a way to understand myself better. I soon amass a huge library in my little loft.

I discover Jack Reacher, Lee Child's fictional character. Jack is everything I want to be, except I don't really want to be quite that tall or quite that male. He stands up for what he believes in. He champions the underdog. And he does what he feels is right, which is not always necessarily legal. He's the absolute antithesis of the toxic masculinity I encountered at the mission. Jack does more to redeem men for me than any living man. Not counting my dad and my brother – they're family, and more like Jack Reacher than you'd think.

I binge on Jack Reacher books, one after the other. I'm blown away. This man is everything I need in my life. You know how some people walk around with bracelets that say 'WWJD' (What would Jesus do)? Well, I don't have a bracelet, but I find myself thinking, 'What would Jack Reacher do?'

It's Jack who crystallises what becomes my motto for life: When in doubt, be brave. It's a motto I stick to, to this day. With one caveat added much later: Except when in doubt about marrying someone. But we'll get to that.

I fall in love with many other fictional men – Myron Bolitar and Inspector Rebus and Kurt Wallander, among others. But it's Jack Reacher who has my heart. He's a drifter who does good and rescues people. He's much more than that, of course, but that's who Jack is for me, right now. An ethical man who makes the hard decisions. A man who helps the underdog.

Books save me. Books have always saved me. I also start writing a lot more while I'm in London. The laptop Janet gave me many years ago died an unfortunate death after a particularly awful power surge back in Sedgefield. In London, I get myself an IBM ThinkPad. I'm still a fan of writing by hand, though, and I always have a journal next to my bed. Here's an undated journal entry from that time:

Phone call
Only one person says my name like that: My mother. When I answered the phone this afternoon and heard her voice, my heart stood still. She said my name with such hesitancy and tenderness that my heart broke for all the pain-stained years between us. Hearing her say my name has undone me.

I cannot recall if my mother called me when I was in London or whether this is me remembering a phone call from the 1990s, when we still spoke once or twice a year. I have many journal entries like this. Random paragraphs, often only a sentence or two, sometimes five pages long. (Many of them are woven into the narrative of this book.) I know that I want to write my story, that I need to write it. I like to imagine that my book will be a help to someone the way other books have helped me. I devour books written by survivors of abuse. They give me hope that there is hope. I need to keep going, keep at it.

A common refrain from my childhood was my mother's admonishment: '*Erika, jou mond gaan jou nog baie ellende bring.*' (Erika, your mouth will bring you much misery.) She silenced me then, and her voice in my head continues to silence me now. My article in *Femina* skirted so many painful issues. I didn't have the wherewithal to share them then, and I still don't. I am doing the best I can, but years from now I'll look at this time and realise how deep my unknowingness of my own trauma is, how little I understand despite the decade of distance from the mission.

I meet many men, mostly at the bar where I work, mostly nice guys. I go on many dates. It's a great, hedonistic time when I'm not alone in my loft, furiously trying to write my way to happiness. And then I meet a lovely guy who adores me. I'll call him Philip. I don't really know what to do with Philip's adoration. When I'm really down and think about the way I love, I come to the conclusion that it's destructive. Will my love turn him into a traitor, too?

I cannot tell anyone about how my love was too pure for Muzi, who soiled it with his adult desires, who taught me innocence is an ambush, trust a weakness and love a tool in the game of power. Run, I want to say to Philip, run away while you can. I don't know how to love, don't know how to give it, don't know how to take it. Please, I want to beg him, please just leave me be. But, of course, I don't say any of this. I go with the flow, the way I always do when it comes to men.

I needed this time in London. I've had time to think. I've had time to regroup and ask myself: If there was nothing standing in my way, what would I want to be doing? The answer is absolutely clear: I want to make magazines. And if there was nothing standing in my way, where would I want to live? That answer is equally clear: Cape Town.

I can't stay in London. I need to go home. And so I make my way back to South Africa, boyfriend in tow.

56

THE ACHE THAT
WON'T GO AWAY

We return to Sedgefield, to my second mother, Sheila. I don't really have anywhere else to go, but then something rather lovely happens. My aunt and uncle in Montagu loan us a car to do a road trip around South Africa. Philip and I head up the East Coast, camping overnight in various spots, making our way to Durban to catch up with old friends of mine, and then on to Pietermaritzburg to see Iris and her partner, Linda.

It's a joyous reunion. Iris is one of the most beautiful people you could ever hope to meet. She's warm and gentle, compassionate and non-judgemental. Iris is also a Buddhist – you will never find a better advertisement for any religion. I would be married to a man I didn't love, stuck in a place I thought of as hell, trapped in a world that reduced me to nothing had it not been for Iris. And in the years since leaving KSB, her wise counsel has carried me through many, many tough times.

It's not easy being back in KwaZulu-Natal. I don't feel comfortable here. KwaSizabantu is too close for me to let down my guard. I love it, though, and never more so than when I'm with Iris. The four of us meander through the Midlands, and then Philip and I head to the Kruger National Park via the Drakensberg. Before we leave Pietermaritzburg, we attend a concert at the City Hall. It's a South American artist, I forget his name, playing classical guitar. One of the pieces he plays is 'Recuerdos de la Alhambra'. It hits me right in the gut. That's my sister's music. The sister who right now is probably getting ready to go to bed, 120 kilometres away from here, blissfully ignorant that her wayward younger sister is nearby and missing her.

I have a piece of music for every family member. The Hanna I know is incredibly accomplished. She aced every test and exam at school. She inherited all my dad's musical genes: music just pours from her. She taught herself to play the guitar, and she loved Tárrega's classical piece in particular. To this day, I cannot listen to it without thinking of her sitting on our couch in Joburg, her dark hair falling over her face as she looks down at her fingers plucking the strings. My heart aches for her. She had a coffee-table book filled with beautiful black-and-white images of conductors at work: Herbert von Karajan was a particular hero of hers.

My sister wanted to become a conductor, and she could have. She wanted to conduct orchestras. Instead, she married an inadequate man. Diminished by his score, she has to move to his music, her gentle cadence lost in his staccato rhythm. This beautiful sister of mine, who wanted to live with abandon, now conducts herself with restraint. When I see her, she's composed and stoic, her eyes discordant symphonies of forsaken dreams as her music dies.

Or maybe I'm just projecting.

My mother is 'Morning Mood' from Grieg's *Peer Gynt*, op. 23. Melancholic and haunting, telling a tale that I will never know or fully understand.

My dad is 'Ombra mai fù', also known as 'Largo from Xerxes', from Handel's opera *Serse*. It is stunningly beautiful, and my dad loved it. He played it on the piano often – it's the soundtrack to my childhood.

My brother is trickier. His music has changed over the years, because how do you pin one tune onto a hero that's still part of your life? For a while he is 'The Charge of the Light Brigade', and those trumpets are him coming to my rescue – he has come to my rescue a lot. And then, one day, I'm listening to the third movement of Mendelssohn's Violin Concerto in E minor, one of my favourites, when I realise, that's it! That's my *boet*. The only way Chris differs from a violin is in stature: it is a small instrument, and he's nice and tall. They're both handsome, and both contain great depths from which stunning beauty arises. The more you get to know them, the more you love them. I love the violin above all the instruments of the orchestra. Of course Chris is a violin concerto, duh.

I find beauty and sorrow inextricably linked – perhaps that is why I love classical music so much: the one perfectly expressed by the other. Sunset and autumn strike a much deeper chord in me than sunrise and spring. I tap into a deep well of sadness within me when I'm surrounded by beauty. In my darker moments, I think it is because I see myself as an observer of beauty, an outsider allowed a glimpse of what she can't have.

As for me? I'm either the Andante from Mozart's Piano Concerto no. 21 or Beethoven's 'Emperor Concerto'. Some days I'm the 'Flower Duet' from Delibes's *Lakmé*. On other days, I'm Leonard Cohen's entire body of work.

Most days, I'm a complete mess. It's Philip who one day tells me that I should really move on with my life and let go of the past, resulting in the letter you read in Chapter 9. Even though I opened myself up to the whole nation in the *Femina* article and the *Voorblad* interview, there is so much of my story that I didn't share. I still feel so much shame, and guilt, because I know I had it easy compared to others. I hate myself for not being able to let it go. I am ashamed that I can't just get over it. And then Philip goes and sticks his fingers into my gaping wound.

I was never raped. I was never beaten in public. I was clothed and had a roof over my head. If I went hungry, it was by choice. I was educated – not adequately, but I have a matric certificate with a university exemption that I failed to translate into a degree.

I feel my failure in my bones. My shame and impotence are amplified every time someone tells me to let it go, get over it. Because I don't know how to do that. How am I supposed to let go when I don't feel that I really have anything to let go of? Other people have suffered so much more than me. Who am I to say that I am traumatised? I *should* be able to just move on and be happy and make a life for myself.

What would Jack Reacher do? Jack would get on a bus to Cape Town, dammit. And that's exactly what I do. Philip returns to England, his heart broken, and I make my way to the Mother City.

57

MAKING HONEY

I'm thirty-one years old. I need to stop drifting. I need to find a job, preferably one I like. I need to find a place to stay. One of the two people I know in Cape Town, Lindsey, offers me a room in the house she shares with her boyfriend while I find my feet. It is an enormous gift and I'm so grateful. They live in St James. I still don't have my licence, and I still don't have a car, so I ride the train. It's a new experience for me, taking a train in South Africa. My best friend in the world, Jean from Sedgefield, also moves down to Cape Town around this time, and she never complains about having to drive whenever we spend time together. I will always be grateful to her for that, too.

How do you go about making magazines when you're me? I realise it's a tall order, and so I also apply for jobs that I'm confident I can get. I'm offered a job as a receptionist at a five-star hotel near the V&A Waterfront, probably because I speak French and German. I'm a people's person, so it's a good fit. As I read the job offer, Lindsey shows me an ad in the *Sunday Times*. Struik Publishers are looking for an editor for their travel and tourism division. Making books? Actual, proper books? That's not something I've even considered a possibility. Lindsey knows the head of the division and puts in a kind word for me.

I send in my CV with a covering letter asking them to please ignore my attached CV, as it contains none of their stated requirements. I tell them that other candidates will be better qualified and more experienced than me, but that they will find no one who has more passion for the written word and its ability to change lives. The letter – coupled with, I'm sure, Lindsey's intervention – affords me an interview. The interview results in an afternoon of rigorous testing: writing, editing, psychometrics. And then, miracle of miracles, Struik offers me a job as an editor. I am going to make books!

The very first book I edit appears on the shelves in mid-April 2004. It's a small collection of road trips through the Western Cape. As I look down at the book in my hands, it fills me with such deep gratitude. A year ago, I was showing Philip around South Africa, desperately scared that I wouldn't find my place in the world. I always felt in my gut that I could excel at something, I just didn't know what. Now I do. And oh, how badly I want to own the happiness I hope is heading my way!

Struik presents me with another three gifts, the most precious of all: three life-long friends in Michelle, Deidré and Sean. There are others, but these three are still constants in my life, almost two decades later. A colleague introduces me to her boyfriend's brother, who is looking for a housemate. We meet, we click, and I move in. He's quite a few years younger than me, but very sweet and funny, and he has a fantastic, tight-knit family. Before long, we're an item, and oh my God, that's all I've ever wanted. To just belong and be part of a family. They welcome me into their hearts. Soon, we're engaged. We're going to get married and have kids.

This forces me to confront my biggest fear: driving. I can't have a baby and not be able to drive to the doctor or a hospital if something goes wrong. My first few lessons involve me sobbing behind the wheel, literally shaking with fear. But I'm not doing this for me, I'm doing it for my future child. I'm thirty-five years old when I get my licence. Then my fiancé's job requires him to move to Port Elizabeth. It soon becomes apparent that I love my new job more than I love him. There's no way I'm leaving Cape Town, so we split up.

My new job is making magazines. I stayed at Struik for two years and loved editing books, but the siren call of the magazine world was still strong. I spotted an ad for a sub-editor at *Cosmopolitan* and applied using pretty much the same covering letter as before. This time, at least, I could add book editing to my CV. My letter got me an interview. The interview got me an afternoon of more tests. And then I got the job.

Imagine. The misfit working at *Cosmo* – the epitome of cool, and the magazine that seven years earlier ignited the idea that I could make a living with words. It's now thirteen years since I ran away from the mission, and although I haven't found lasting love, it feels as though my past no longer affects me all that much. Besides, I can recognise it wasn't all bad. My experiences have made me compassionate. They have given me the ability to spot an outsider in a group and to do what I can to help them feel at ease. I also grasp that stories have two sides, because I know that there is so much more to people than what meets the eye. And sure, there is that undercurrent of sadness I tap into easily, but I don't think I wallow in it any more. With each year that passes, that undercurrent gets gentler.

There's a fantastic poem by Spanish poet Antonio Machado that strikes a chord: 'Last night as I was sleeping, I dreamt – marvellous error! – that I had a beehive here inside my heart. And the golden bees were making white combs and sweet honey from my old failures.' Never mind failures, in my life the bees also make honey from disappointment, pain and loss. And I absolutely love that image of bees working away in my heart, making honey.

My underlying wounds – I can't even name them – surface one night when I join my friend Deborah to watch *Jesus Christ Superstar* at the Theatre on the Bay. I've heard some of the music before and I think I'm in for a fantastic night out. A fun-filled excursion to the theatre.

One movie we watched regularly back at KSB was *The Redeemer*, which depicts in graphic detail the last days of Jesus. As a little girl, I found the crucifixion scenes particularly harrowing.

I don't have fun at the theatre. I'm a sobbing wreck by the time Deborah gets me home. I cannot even articulate my distress. Fifteen years from now, I will read a book called *The Body Keeps the Score* by Bessel van der Kolk, and I will gain a better understanding of how my trauma has nestled itself in my body. And how watching a crucifixion, even a tame, Andrew Lloyd Webber–stylised version, would be re-traumatising.

So no, I haven't left the past behind. But I am doing my level best to convince myself that I have.

58

RECLAIMING CENTRE STAGE

One day, Deborah stops me mid-sentence.

'Erika, do you realise how often you use the word "bad" when you talk about yourself? "I was bad." "What I did was bad." "This writing is bad." "Sorry, this dish is bad. It didn't come out the way I wanted."'

Wow. I hadn't even noticed. I'm so used to condemning myself in my mind: *I'm worthless. I don't know what I'm doing. I can't do this.* I hadn't realised it was coming through in my speech as well, in the me I projected to the world.

After Deborah points this out, I hear just how often I use 'bad' when talking about myself. I try to stop, but it's difficult. This is how I've thought of myself for the past two-and-a-half decades.

Deborah echoes what Jean has been saying to me for years: 'Erika, I wish you could see yourself the way others see you, the way I see you.'

How do you go about rewriting the narrative in your head? Answer: therapy. Deborah introduces me to her therapist, an amazing woman I'm going to call Jenny, though that's not her real name. I'm in my mid-thirties, but if I could go back to my twenty-something self, I would tell her to find a good therapist, and to stick with therapy for a while.

I found a good one in London, but only saw him three times. I don't remember his name or what he looked like. I remember the entrance to his rooms and one clear lesson. We were discussing relationships, and I said something to the effect of, 'But my boyfriend should know that.' And my therapist asked, 'How? How would he know that? Do you expect him to read your mind?'

And then we had a discussion in which I understood so clearly that by expecting my partner to 'know' what I needed or what I was feeling, I was basically making myself a child and him the parent. Because the child trusts the parent to recognise its needs and to respond appropriately. That's the parent–child relationship. I was bringing that energy into my relationships by expecting my partner to just 'know' what I needed. It's a lesson I've never forgotten.

After the first session with Jenny, I know that this woman will be able to help me. In our sessions, we discuss how I'm struggling to know who I am. I'm still that scared little girl battling to control the all-abiding fear of doing something wrong. The girl who can't make decisions, who is powerless in the face of abuse. The girl who is easy to neglect, easy to abandon, easy to not love. And yet I know

I am also the person other people now meet – the bubbly, outgoing, confident woman.

After a few sessions with Jenny, I tell her that I feel I haven't achieved anything in my life, that I feel useless and unaccomplished, that I should be so much further along by now. Jenny instructs me to ask five close friends to write me a letter in which they describe how they see me and how they feel about our friendship. I'm aghast. I can't do that! That's basically asking people to praise me, surely? 'Still,' she says, 'bring them with you next time.'

So I do it. My heart is in my throat. I'm apologetic. 'I'm so sorry about this, but my therapist has told me I must ...' The five letters I am given move me beyond words. Four of them are from friends, and the other is from Iris. I present them to Jenny, tears streaming down my face. She asks me to read them out loud to her.

'You remind me of a circle of yellow poppies in a field – bright, sunny, upright, beautiful – a splash of colour in a dreary landscape. There they stand making a statement to the whole world,' Iris writes. Every one of my friends describes me as the person I've always aspired to be. Wow. What a revelation. Somewhere along the line, I've become 'her' without even knowing it. This is what Oprah would call a lightbulb moment.

Jenny explains to me the power of the problem stories from our past, and how they tend to take centre stage in how we view ourselves. They sideline our other, more positive experiences. I have been shining the spotlight on that terrified little girl for so long now. This, in spite of living a life that demonstrates strength, confidence and fearlessness. Therapy helps me to gently start letting go of that sad little girl, allowing me to be the me that I want to be. The resilient, cheerful *kurkproppie*.

To this day, I have much to learn about myself. Recovering from abuse and trauma is like peeling an onion. It's one layer after the other. And you only get to the deeper layers by dealing with the more superficial ones first.

Don't stop peeling. Keep at it, but do take breaks when you need to. Also remember, it's an onion. Stock up on tissues.

59

A STRANGER AT THE TABLE

Fast-forward two years to early 2009. My mother still sends me the odd message now and then. One day she tells me that she's making my favourite chicken dish and wishes I lived closer so I could come and enjoy it. Mostly, the texts say she's praying for me. One tells me that God's mercy is going to run out on me.

Her messages are random. Sometimes weeks go by, sometimes months, before I hear from her again. I don't respond to most of them. We still chat on the phone sometimes, perhaps once every three years or so. I see her at a beloved uncle's funeral. The day before the funeral, we speak on the phone, and she reiterates that we reconcile at the cross or not at all. She also says something that cuts me deeply. She says it's good my dad isn't around to see what has become of me.

Out of the blue, one week in March, I get a barrage of texts. My mother is in Montagu, visiting her brothers and mother. She wants me to come and see her there. I check with Chris. He's also been getting more texts than usual. So I sit down and write her a letter on the Friday afternoon. It's long, but here are some extracts:

Dear Mother

[...] I'm really happy that you're having such a great visit in Montagu. But I find myself wondering why you would want to see me. The last time we had any kind of real conversation [...] you told me in no uncertain terms on the phone that we would meet at the cross or not at all.

From where I'm standing, nothing has changed in either of our lives. I believe that it matters not what you believe in, what matters is how you live and how you treat yourself, others and the world around you. You have always stood firm that your way is the right way and that I am not worthy of being called your daughter for as long as I reject that way. [...]

My question to you is this. If I were to come and visit, would you accept me for who I am or would I have to skirt around what my life is really like to keep the very fragile peace? I am a woman now, I haven't been your child for a very long time. [...]

My father would have been proud of the person I've become, despite what you told me to the contrary on the phone that day. This I know for sure. If you knew me, allowed yourself to see past the fact that I don't follow your God, you would be honoured to have this woman as your daughter. [...]

Has anything changed for you? If I come to visit, will you accept me for who I am? Or will I be faced with yet another rejection? I have faced and handled your outright rejections from when I was 21 and left the mission, and the more subtle rejections from before that. I am being blunt in this letter, spelling everything out, but I want you to understand that I am not prepared to keep hoping for a reconciliation of sorts between us, only to be rejected the first time I voice any kind of disagreement with you. [...]

What I want is a mother who accepts, even loves, me for the person I am. The non-church-going person yes. But also the compassionate, loving, full-of-life, happy person I am. If you are not able to be that mother who loves her daughter unconditionally, then please do not ask me to visit you when you come down to the Cape. I'm not asking you to approve of everything I do, but to accept me regardless.

Finally, in case we don't get to talk again, I would like you to know that I have forgiven you for all the rejection, for all the hurt you caused me and all the neglect. I am not angry at you and I ask for nothing but your acceptance of me.

Love

Erika

I don't hear from her. I phone Chris and then Iris. I'm so conflicted. Should I go or not? I check in with my aunt Melanie and we decide I'll join them for Sunday lunch. Montagu is only about 200 kilometres from my home. When I arrive, I spend most of the morning avoiding my mother by swimming and hanging out with my cousin.

But I didn't drive here for the day to make small talk. I'm here for a serious discussion, one that will have to wait till after lunch. I sit at the table across from this woman who gave birth to me, and I am looking at a stranger. I don't recognise her at all. I search her features for something familiar, but I find nothing. There is nothing familiar about her eyes, her smile, her voice. I search inside myself for a flicker of something. Some feeling. Love, anger, fear even. Nothing. I look at my mother and feel nothing. Except shame at feeling nothing. And dread. Dread at having to face up to her. And I almost get in my car and leave, because I have nothing in common with this woman, and the things I want to say, I don't want to say to a stranger.

But I can't leave. I have to try to talk to her. As much as I'm resigned to not having her in my life, what is it that everyone keeps telling me? 'She is your mother, after all.'

'Mamma, can we talk?' We're in the lounge now and everyone else disappears in two minutes flat. A nap after lunch is a Sunday tradition on the farm. Melanie, bless her, potters around for a while, and it is so comforting to know that she's right there if I need her. I smile at her, I'm okay.

My mother must have read my letter. She must be prepared for what I have to say, on some level at least. Except I don't know how to say what I came to say.

'Mamma, I spoke to Chris last night and we're both a bit puzzled by the SMSes you're sending us, the phone calls, the wanting to see us. Why are you contacting us?'

'No reason, really,' she replies.

Whew, this is *so* difficult. She is contained, her voice measured, as though she's talking to a child. Inflection at the end of every sentence. And then I start feeling. Boy, do I start feeling.

I ask her whether anything's changed, because the last I remember, she had disowned me. She says she never disowned me.

What?

I won't let that remark go. We back-and-forth for about an hour. She maintains she does not remember disowning me. I am gobsmacked that she can gloss over something so significant. We are getting nowhere. She's sitting there, contained and still. I'm sitting here, tightly wound and shaking. This issue goes to the root of the problem between us.

My mother denies having anything to do with our estrangement. I don't believe her, not for a second. Lies are acceptable at the mission if they protect 'God's work' – I simply don't believe that she doesn't remember.

I whip out my phone and call my brother. 'I am sitting here with our mother, and she says she never disowned either of us. Do you remember that time we went to visit her? Do you remember her saying, "Don't call me your mother?"'

Chris remembers, all right. He remembers her saying those words out loud a few times, and later in several different guises. 'Why don't you ask God why you can't be my daughter? His mercy is going to run out soon,' she'd told me when I'd phoned her the day after my twenty-fifth birthday to ask her, in tears, why she hadn't called.

'So, Mother, if it didn't happen the way Chris and I remember it, how did it happen? How did we become strangers?' I ask her now.

'You rejected me when you rejected Christ.'

'That is simply not true. I tried so many times. Visited you so many times. Tried to reason with you so many times.'

'I don't remember you visiting me often. I'm the one who visited you. Once in Pietermaritzburg. Remember? You were nasty to me that day.'

I don't recall this visit. But if it's true, I doubt I was nasty to her.

Inside, I do battle with myself. I recognise that I'm angry because I'm actually in pain. I need to allow myself to feel the pain, because anger will get me nowhere in this conversation. I need to show her my pain, but I'm not one to show people when they've hurt me. Except now I have to, even if it requires opening myself up to getting hurt again.

Then, at last allowing myself to cry, to feel, to show my pain, I ask: 'Tell me, Mamma, how do you lose two children? How?'

And just like that, she softens. She crumples. She allows herself to cry, too. She has no tissues, but I came prepared; I have a pocket full. I walk across the lounge, hand her a tissue and sit down next to her on the couch.

'If both you and Chris are so sure that's what happened, then that must be what happened,' she sobs. 'I am so sorry. Please, please, please forgive me. Tell me what I did wrong.'

We sit on the couch and cry. I tell her about the dark, dark days when I was ten and they abandoned us at the mission to go to France for a year. I tell her for the first time that I started wetting my bed and that they made me wash my sheets by hand. I tell her how I protected her and my dad from the knowledge of what happened to me, to us, in that year because I thought they would never forgive themselves if they knew.

I tell her about those months after my dad died and how it felt to lose my mother, too. I ask her if she remembers having any meals with me in those years. She doesn't. She lost herself in her work and forgot about her daughter. I tell her how I lay awake every night until after midnight and only went to sleep when she got home. How I imagined every night that she had slipped and fallen and that I should get up and go and look for her and how I couldn't because I was too scared that I would find her lying dead somewhere.

I tell her how I ate half a slice of bread every second day because my despair made me lose my appetite – for food, for life. I ask her if she remembers how thin I was. She remembers. I ask her if she knew that I weighed forty-four kilograms when I was nineteen years old. I tell her that the doctor in France, the one who attended to me when my lung collapsed, said I would die within a few months if I didn't start eating.

And then I ask my mother why she never asked me if anything was wrong. How she could have neglected me so horribly. It is the hardest conversation of my life, to sit and tell my mother what she has done. I wish I could have spared her this. I wish things were different.

We talk about Muzi, too. About a time, many years ago, when Samuel and I drove to see her so we could talk. That was when Muzi was still at the mission. She scolded me for speaking about a man of God like that. How dare I slander his name? She said she simply could not and would not believe he would do such a thing.

Well, things have changed and Muzi is no longer the golden boy of KSB. He is on trial for murder, at this very moment. Now she tells me that she's sorry she didn't believe me. I can't help the flash of anger. Because he stands accused of murdering someone, now she's prepared to believe me?

My mother then tells me that she loves me. She says when she talks about me, she tells people that I'm the child closest to her heart. I never knew that – not even when I was a little girl. She tells them that I'm the child who pays attention to the little things. How she would come home and find her duvet turned down, a little note on her pillow. A tea bag in a mug, the kettle filled. She remembers how I spent my very first paycheque on fixing her engagement ring. And then she says she realises now that it was her neglect that drove me away from her.

We cry and cry and cry. She tells me about things that happened in her childhood.

How she has only now, in her sixties, realised things about herself and how she keeps people at arm's length. How she regrets hurting Chris and me.

And then, suddenly, I want to hug her. But I can't. I simply can't. I tell her that I don't know where we go from here. That it doesn't seem possible to undo twenty years in one afternoon. But that I'm glad we spoke.

I decide to leave, but first I wake Melanie so that my mother has someone to talk to. It must be horrible to be confronted with the pain you caused your child. But to get through to her, I don't know how I could have done it differently.

Back home in Cape Town, I call Chris. His reaction is one of total and utter disbelief. Understandably so.

'She's manipulating you,' he says.

'No, this was real.'

'Not possible. When is she going to change back again?'

'I don't think she's going to change again. I think this is for real. Welcome to the mindfuck that was my day. I'm passing this mindfuck on to you now. She's going to contact you to ask for your forgiveness too.'

By now I'm sharing a flat with Jean and she's cooked my favourite chicken dish. I have a bath, all the while talking to her, so light and relieved. We open a bottle of red wine and eat supper, talking all the time. Before I go to bed, I call Iris to tell her how it went. That night I dream that I'm back at the mission, getting married. Go figure.

The next morning, I write my girlfriends a long email, telling them in detail about the encounter. 'It seems I have acquired a mother. What am I supposed to do with her now?' I ask them.

Chris sends me a text message: 'I'm still in shock. Has anything changed overnight?'

Sadly, no. Nothing has changed. It will be many, many months before I hear from my mother again, and then it will be the usual 'save your soul from eternal damnation' messages. The more things change, the more they stay the same.

60

PRIMED FOR FAILURE

My therapy sessions with Jenny help me tremendously. An exclamation I often hear from people who find out that I am estranged from my mother is: 'But she's your *mother!*' Followed by: 'Of course she loves you' or 'Of course you love her' or something along those lines. I tell Jenny it makes me feel ashamed, because how do you explain to someone that your life is better without your mother in it?

Jenny asks me whether I think these people would say the same thing had my mother put me in hospital with a broken arm, for instance. Or burned me with cigarettes. Something visible and physical.

'No, of course not!' I exclaim.

'Well, then?' Jenny is so wise and so lovely.

And so, finally, my need for self-love outweighs my need for my mother's love. Miraculously, my shame around the disintegration of our relationship vanishes, just like that. Now, when someone expresses their disbelief about how things are between me and my mother, I can say with absolute honesty, 'Aren't you lucky? It's a credit to your mother that you don't understand my situation.'

I have several huge realisations in quick succession in therapy, the biggest being the one about the woman I am. I tell Jenny that I think I need to take a brief break, to really allow it to sink in, but that I'll be back. I need to talk to her about my relationship with men, and my relationship with money. These are two areas of my life where I really need help.

But dammit. I allow the short break to turn into months, and before I know it, it's been a year or three. When I finally realise, after yet another failed relationship, that I need to see Jenny, she's retired. She offers to refer me to someone else, but I demur. I can't imagine anyone else helping me in quite the same way. It's a decision I will come to rue.

But then one night I meet a man in a bar in Main Road, Green Point, and everything turns rosy, and I forget all about therapy.

It's been three years since my engagement ended and I've gone from one relationship to the next. One lasts almost a year, some a few months, others a few weeks or even days. I'm never not dating. I don't understand when my friend Michelle asks if I don't just want to be by myself for a while.

I'm not really that attracted to many of the guys I date. I pretty much just go for (or succumb to) the man who is the most persistent at the time. It's almost as if, by virtue of him choosing me, I agree to love him. And isn't that a terrible personal indictment? That I value myself so little that I go to the 'highest bidder', so to speak. And that I string them along, whether I'm aware of it or not.

It is, of course, not as clear-cut as that, and my feelings are also genuine. But I silence my intuition often. Too often. I talk myself into staying with someone; I tell myself that I'm falling in love and persuade myself that it's a good idea. And maybe that's why I get over the guys so quickly after we break up, because I was never really that into them.

He wants me? Oh, okay. He can have me. By now I've gone freelance and one of my gigs is writing a relationship advice column for a men's magazine, for heaven's sake. I know in theory what a good relationship looks like. Can I put it into practice, though? Hell, no.

There's a huge payoff for me too, however. It feels safe, because they really, really like me. And if they're big in stature, so much the better. I feel safe with a big guy. You'd think that I'd understand by now that just because a man can potentially protect me from physical danger doesn't mean I'm emotionally safe with him. But no.

There have been two notable exceptions. But with each I identified from the start that we only had one month together – and what glorious months those were. (One turns into a lifelong friendship across the many air miles that separate us.) It seems that I relax my rule about not dating guys I'm really into when there's a time limit. There was a third guy, in Cape Town, who was more than ten years my junior. I fell for him. Head over heels. But it was doomed, of course. I wanted to put down roots, he wanted to go and explore the world. As he should! As he did.

The guy in the bar is big and burly and Afrikaans. I've never seriously dated an Afrikaner; I've always thought they'd be too conservative for me. He's also about nine years younger than me. Our relationship progresses quickly; we have ups and downs, but I think there are more ups than downs. There are some serious red flags, one of which is his alcohol consumption, but I ignore them because it's easier to ignore them than to listen to them.

After a lifetime of silencing my intuition when it comes to men, I've grown really good at ignoring red flags. I don't realise it, of course. I like to think that I've become more enlightened, but the indoctrination I got at KwaSizabantu – that women are inferior to men, that we have to guard against leading men astray, that we're whores, sluts and Delilahs – left an indelible impression. This despite the fact that, intellectually, I've known for years that their ideas of gender roles are totally unsound.

My big, burly Afrikaner and I move in together, then we buy a house, and then we get engaged. By the time we move into the property we've bought, I've relocated thirty-two times since leaving the mission. Garrakachok, I've found my den. This is it, I decide. I'm sick of drifting, I'm sick of moving. If I never unpack another box in my life, it will be too soon.

But we are not meant to be. And it happens again. After every serious relationship that ends, I feel this intense relief. It's as if I can breathe again. As if I can stand up straight and stretch.

'I shrink myself to fit with them,' I tell Michelle, trying to analyse where I'm going wrong. 'I become less me.' It's amazing to have such self-awareness and still be so stupid. Because it's a pattern I repeat over and over and over again.

I'm lucky, though. With only two exceptions, for the most part they have all been good men. For a while, they're good-for-me men. But it never lasts.

'It's like one day I wake up and suddenly I can't stand the way he breathes,' I lament to another friend. 'What is wrong with me?'

What's wrong with me is that I didn't stick it out in therapy. I didn't persist until I understood that KwaSizabantu and Muzi's ministrations have obliterated my personal boundaries. That I have only a nebulous understanding of personal boundaries is another red flag I completely ignore. I leave therapy before I learn how toxic my belief is that I can make a relationship better if only I do better. My belief that he mustn't change, but that I must mould myself to suit him. That if there's something wrong, it's because I'm wrong. And so I keep floundering.

'This man is my saviour,' shouts my subconscious every time a new guy appears on the horizon. 'He's going to save me.' If only I'd stuck it out in therapy. I might have learned that no man is going to save me. That I don't, in fact, need saving by any man. I will learn that lesson, but it will cost me dearly.

PART SIX

THE AWAKENED ACTIVIST

61

A TINDER LOVE STORY
IN 940 DAYS

On 25 January 2017, I meet a British guy for a date at a Thai restaurant down the road from me. We met on Tinder a few days earlier. We clicked online and we click in real life. I really like him – he's big and kind and funny and chatty. We get serious real quick. In those first few months, he hands me many red flags, gift-wrapped in perfectly good explanations that I eagerly accept. I'm going to call him Percy, though that's not his actual name. Percy love-bombs me. He's met no one like me. I'm his soulmate; this he knows within days of meeting me. I'm different to anyone he's ever met. He wants to know everything about me, and I happily oblige. It's so unusual to have a guy ask me so many questions about my life and background. The mission, Muzi, my past relationships, my mother, my dad – the whole bang shoot. He wants to read stuff I've written. He seems perfect. Everything I've always wanted in a man (minus the smoking and the snoring).

On 19 October 2017, Percy proposes to me at that very restaurant. I say yes, despite the way he treats me and the many times he's broken up with me, only to beg me to take him back. Without knowing it, I have handed him the road map to my psyche by openly sharing and answering his every question, even the really intrusive ones about my past relationships and sex life. I have given him all the tools he needs to verbally and emotionally break me down and then build me up time and again. I will later learn that this is textbook trauma bonding: an emotional attachment forged from a repeated cycle of positive reinforcement and kindness, followed by abuse and devaluation, followed by expressions of love. My need to belong is so strong, it overrides all my misgivings. He *says* he loves me, and that's good enough for me. If he says it, it must be true, right? Anything bad I feel is on me, not him. He's a great guy. He has some issues, but don't we all? Who am I to judge him?

On 10 August 2018, we get married in the UK with only a handful of his family and a couple of friends in attendance. The next morning, I'm overcome by such a wave of despair, I make my excuses and don't join the family as they go for a long walk in the countryside. The despair is partly because I feel in my bones that I've screwed up, that I shouldn't have pledged my life to this man. And partly because my beloved Aunt Iris is seriously ill and in hospital. When I get back to South Africa,

I go and visit her. Percy pays for my flight. He's very generous when it comes to spending his British pounds on me.

On 30 September 2018, on my brother's birthday, we celebrate our marriage with friends and family at our favourite getaway spot two hours from Cape Town. That morning, I lie in a bubble bath and weep. 'I can do this,' I tell myself. As Percy keeps telling me, I just need to love him more, love him better. I'm also sad because Iris is too ill to travel to the wedding. My two cousins arrive just after I get out of the bath and see my tears. I tell them it's because I thought I'd misplaced our rings (also true). I put on my game face, and it turns out to be a beautiful day. Chris and his wife and baby son have come from Mexico, where he's working. Janet has come from Australia, where she and Chris are now living. Percy's family from the UK is here. And many of my friends – I have the best friends in the history of friendships, that I know for sure. It's a joyous occasion, and then it's over. Everyone goes home and we go on honeymoon.

On 6 October 2018, Iris passes away. Grief overwhelms me. 'This is our honeymoon. It's supposed to be the best time of our lives! And look at you,' Percy berates me daily. I try, I really do. And I keep trying. Just like I did with Muzi all those years ago, I protect Percy and his image by not telling anyone what actually goes on behind closed doors. He's charming in public, this man I married. But increasingly after our marriage, all pretence ends the moment it's just the two of us. He becomes distant, unloving, angry. I'm to blame – he's merely reacting to me being unloving, hateful, unkind, bitter, secretive. He *wants* to be loving; that's what he's all about, after all. It's just that I make it impossible for him to be who he is.

He tells me that my past has damaged me so badly, it's creating issues for us. It's easy for me to take the blame, to buy into his narrative that all I need to do is love him better. I do stand up for myself, though. I'm not a total pushover. I tell him that he seems to be married to his idea of me rather than to the real me. Whenever I assert myself, we end up having a huge fight. One that sometimes lasts for weeks, until I apologise.

On 5 August 2019, five days before our first wedding anniversary and one day before we're supposed to leave on an epic safari with my aunt and uncle, our marriage is over. We didn't even make it to a year. It's not the first time our marriage has ended. Percy told me that our marriage was over four months into it, and then again three months after that. Twice he told me that he was done with me. Twice he begged me to take him back. Twice I forgave him. The second time I insisted that he attend therapy, but he only went a handful of times and decided it didn't help him at all. This time, though, when he says the words, 'It's over,' I look at him and say, 'Yes. Yes, it's over.'

On 23 August 2019, a friend sends me screenshots from Tinder. There's my husband. Already trawling for the next love of his life, his next soulmate. He took two of his three profile pictures on my uncle's farm, the place where he found refuge after their niece kicked his heart-broken arse to the kerb. He's good at playing the victim and they fall for it hook, line and sinker. I don't blame them. I know better than anyone how good he is at making people believe exactly what he wants them to believe. If only Tinder bios told the whole truth ...

Percy, 50
I am Tall, good sense of humour, loving, affectionate and just want to meet a like minded caring woman who loves life and cares ... x

62

MY OWN PRIVATE CULT

My friend Michelle saves me from killing myself when she doesn't even know I'm suicidal. Let's backtrack four months to April 2019. I've just taken my husband back for the second time in the seven months we've been married. When we met, Percy was on an extended contract to work in Cape Town. That changed, and now he's working in the UK while I continue to live in the Mother City. We'd always said we'd live here, in South Africa, but now he wants me over there and persuades me that it will be safer for me there.

I'm walking with Michelle next to the Milnerton lagoon when I break down. 'I fear I'm sentencing myself to a life of misery if I go over there,' I sob. I haven't told her much of what Percy does and says to me, but she knows enough. She also knows me well enough to see that there's something seriously wrong. Michelle urges me to contact her therapist – and in doing so, saves my life.

What Michelle doesn't know is that I am in such a deep place of despair that I lie awake every night thinking of how I can kill myself with the least amount of trauma for the people I love. I have saved up enough sleeping pills, but thoughts of my brother (I know he'll blame himself), my cats (who will love them as much as I do?) and whoever finds my body (what an awful thing) stop me from acting on this suicidal ideation of mine.

It's not that I want to die. I simply don't know how to live any more. I'm hearing on an almost daily basis that I'm unloving, I'm bitter, I'm twisted, I'm filled with hate – and I'm starting to believe it. This echoes what I've thought of myself since the age of nine. Percy is simply confirming what I've always known: I'm worthless and I am basically bad (sorry, Deborah).

By the time I go for therapy, I have no more defences. I'm ground down to the bone. And here is this incredibly wise woman who holds me so gently and listens to me and counsels me. Slowly but surely, I start feeling like Erika again.

One day in July 2019, I ask her: 'How did I lose myself to such an extent that I no longer wanted to live? How did I go from someone I liked to someone I didn't want to be any more?'

As we discuss this, I realise with absolute clarity what I've done. I have recreated KwaSizabantu inside my home. I have brought in an authoritarian male figure, who has to know at all times where I am, who I am talking to, what I'm wearing, every mundane detail of my life. Someone who tells me what to do, where to be

and who to be (and not be). A male who continuously berates me for my misde-
meanours, for my unacceptable behaviour, for not being good enough, for not
treating him properly. I've given him complete control over me. Percy vetoes work
that comes my way because he's concerned that I'm having an affair with whomever is offering it. I've stopped seeing my male friends. My friendship group has
shrunk to a handful of girlfriends. I am desperately unhappy, yet I smile and pretend
all is good. Just like I did at the mission.

At this stage, in July, I still think I'm safe with this man – I still think he's loving
and kind. Sure, he's controlling, but he'd never hurt me. Then, a few days later, Percy
and I have a chat. Our marriage is at breaking point. I tell him that he's going to
lose me if he continues to treat me the way he does, that he has to temper his anger
when addressing me. Then I raise the day I told him that I wanted to kill myself.

It was back in March, a month before Michelle's unwitting intervention, and
I'd been spiralling deeper and deeper into depression. I didn't understand it. I was
newly married; I should have been dancing with joy. So I finally confided in my
husband that I was suicidal and that there were days when I felt unable to even
get out of bed.

'Thoughts of suicide consume me,' I told him over the phone. 'I have amassed
seventy-six sleeping tablets and I know they're more than enough to do it. But I
haven't taken them yet because I don't think I want to die. I just don't know how
to live any more.'

'I know how you feel,' he responded. 'I've been there myself.' And that was the
last we spoke of it.

'How did you not send a message to even one person?' I ask him now. 'You
have all my friends' contact details, and those of my brother, my aunts, my cousins.
There's Michelle, who lives five minutes down the road from me, and you have
her contact details, too. How could you not send a message to say, "Hey, won't you
check up on Erika? I'm worried about her. I don't think she's doing too well." Why
did you never again ask me how I'm doing? How could you just carry on pretending
that everything's okay?'

His response? 'The thought never occurred to me.'

Your wife tells you she's suicidal when you are thousands of kilometres away
and it doesn't occur to you to ask her loved ones to check up on her? This is the man
I married – despite my many misgivings. That is on me. And that's when I realise
I'm not safe with him.

Four days later, after another big fight the night before, Percy tells me it's over,
and I agree. In the weeks and months to come, I realise that my husband held up
a mirror for me and said: 'This is what you believe about yourself, Erika. I'm
just here to confirm that you think you are worthless and unlovable and easy to
abandon and basically not really worth anything.' With this realisation, his spell
over me shatters. I no longer need my husband to hold up this mirror, I no longer
need this mirror, and I definitely no longer need my husband.

My friends rally around me the moment I tell them that my marriage is over, and why. No one knew how bad it was because I didn't tell anyone. My brother, as always, is immensely supportive.

'I have only one question for you,' he tells me when I confide in him. 'How will you stop this from happening to you again?'

I tell him that I will pay attention to red flags. I will listen to my intuition and not silence it just because I'm so desperate to belong. I will continue to go to therapy to gain a better understanding of myself and the world. I will pay attention to a man's actions and not listen to his words when the two don't match.

I don't regret my marriage. It was soul-destroying, and I almost succumbed to the lure of oblivion. But I didn't. I survived and I came out of that relationship with a much better understanding of myself. It also made me realise, properly realise, just how badly KSB messed me up. For thirty years, I pretended that I had dealt with things, but my psychic wounds ran so deep that I could not detect them without the help of a very experienced therapist. If they screwed me up this bad, I wonder, how are the kids faring who had it so much worse than me? And how can I sit back and allow them to continue destroying lives? If it has been this hard for me to break free from the lessons they taught me, how can I simply carry on with my life and pretend nothing is wrong in that compound in the lush green hills of KwaZulu-Natal?

By now, all three of my nieces are young adults in their twenties. The youngest matriculated in 2015. Back then, I read in the newspapers that she got seven distinctions. She was in the top one per cent of achievers in six of her subjects. And then, the devastating blow: '[She] plans to begin a computer science degree via distance education next year while she pursues voluntary work in her home town.' Neither of her sisters escaped, and it looks like not even her superior academic performance will get her a pass to go to an actual university. Nothing has changed at the place I once called home.

63

PICKING UP THE FIGHT AGAIN

Three strangers have had an ongoing and lasting effect on my life: my nieces. To me, they represent every child who has grown up at KSB. Over the years, I've worried about them: defenceless, isolated, alone and, unlike me, without the benefit of having known the outside world even for a short while. They have grown up in that repressive environment knowing absolutely nothing else. I am powerless when it comes to helping them. They've been taught to be deeply suspicious of me, and I'm not allowed to have contact with them. I've met them at two family funerals in the last fifteen years, and our interactions were closely monitored. I tried speaking to one and my mother kept interrupting us. My sister spotted me talking to another and immediately joined us.

I simply have to trust that should one of them want to leave, she will reach out to my brother – he has more frequent contact with them and they adore him. We'd be there in a flash and move heaven and earth to help. All three have a home with me in Cape Town, and one with Chris overseas.

For the sake of my mental health, I've not been able to dwell on them or their fate too often. As much as I can, I've put thoughts of them, behind me, tried to still the ache I feel whenever I think of them. In therapy, I'm learning so much about myself and about the way I react to the world, the way I perceive myself, the way I conduct myself in relationships, in friendships. It feels like I'm one of those old-fashioned bicycle combination locks – the ones where the lock opens when all the correct numbers are aligned. I feel as though I'm getting the right numbers in the right places – finally. Things are clicking into place.

I'm still married to Percy when I get a WhatsApp from Koos Greeff in May 2019. Koos left KSB in the 1990s and, unbeknown to me, had been working with others to effect change there. When that failed, he began helping people who wanted to leave and those who managed to break free. His message shakes me to the core.

Apparently, KSB may expel six young women tomorrow because a prophetess says they're Satanists. We can arrange for someone to pick them up, but they'll need accommodation. Rumour has it one of your nieces is in that group. Would you be able to help if necessary?

My heart drops and leaps at the same time, if that's possible. And I respond, of course, my house is her house and I'll do anything I can to help her. What is going on? And he tells me someone's had a vision, and there's a list of names of people who have been identified in this vision as Satanists. My niece is one of them and she's allegedly being kept in a hospital onsite. She's allowed out, I'm told, for meals and to go to church (of course!) and to the teacher's training college I now hear she's attending.

I know that 'hospital' where they're apparently keeping her. As a child, I was terrified of that place and the women who stayed there. What I understood back then was that they were possessed by demons. I now think that they were probably suffering from mental illnesses that were not acknowledged or treated in any way other than with prayer. Or perhaps they were just being punished for not toeing the line. That's a scary thought, that they could have been perfectly sane and being locked up as punishment. And now that's happening to my niece?

How is someone who has grown up in that cloistered environment ever going to be a Satanist? Can we just get real here, please? I'd always feared demons and being possessed by demons while I was at KSB, and I was led to believe they often cast demons from people. But Satanists?

I do some research on ksb-alert.com and find the testimony of a woman who looked after the hostel girls. I've spoken to her since, and the stories are simply unbelievable. In 2010, a fourteen-year-old girl who had supposedly been a 'top Satanist' converted and moved to KSB. According to the former hostel worker:

> Because of her background she was able to identify certain children as Satanists, as she recognised them from 'encounters under the sea', we were told. [... The leadership] hung on her every word [...] Even in the night some girls were roused from their sleep and accused of 'Satanism'. None of the children were allowed to breathe a word of this to the parents. Some children were trauma-tised by the tremendous psychological pressure, fear and confusion [...] When I told my counsellor [...] about this he said that Westerners find it very difficult to understand the African way of doing things.

In 2017, another eyewitness reported:

> During these 'devotions', a certain teenage girl who had claimed to be a Satanist (and who 'ran away' afterwards), was given free reign [sic] by the KSB leader-ship to intimidate, threaten, accuse, and verbally as well as spiritually abuse the people [...] Some of those present were also falsely accused by this Satanist of having been under the sea together with demons, taking part in satanic rituals, doing astral traveling, and such like ...
>
> After each of these meetings, attendants were in a state of shock and confu-sion. Some of them never recovered from the trauma inflicted on them, and eventually left KSB.

And, weirdest of all, there's this excerpt from a 2005 KSB newsletter, translated from German:

> Recently a young girl was vexed by evil spirits and went through physical and mental suffering. This was supposedly caused by worship of the ancestral spirits and contact with supposed Satanists. She sought help from an *inyanga* (medicine-man) and tried various magic potions consisting of snakeskin and tortoise fat. Out of curiosity she went to KwaSizabantu and confessed her sins. After a prayer various live animals appeared out of her body, such as snakes, a tortoise, a frog, a locust; but also such objects as safety-pins, needles and a bent teaspoon.

I'm glad I wasn't there; I'm not a fan of frogs.

But in all seriousness, I'm really worried now, especially after discovering that being identified as a so-called Satanist is an actual thing at KSB. When I tell my therapist about my niece in my next therapy session, those mysterious tremors return and take over my entire body. She makes me lie down and talks me through some breathing exercises, and gradually the trembling subsides. They're known as neurogenic tremors, she explains to me, and they're the body's response to trauma. Think of an impala that has just escaped a lion attack. Its entire body trembles for a while, and then the impala moves on. It literally shakes off the traumatic event. As humans, we've developed ways to control the trembling, but sometimes the trauma is so overwhelming that it, well, overwhelms us. And so, my therapist tells me, this trembling is actually a good thing, because it's releasing trauma. Just thinking about how my niece might be feeling traumatises me all over again, and it feels as if I'm back there, trapped and alone.

The aunt of one of the other girls being kept at the hospital tells me that her niece has a cellphone. I speak to this young woman – I can hear how scared and unhappy she is. I tell her there's an entire world outside, with support, if she leaves. I beg her to get a message to my niece, but she isn't able to do so before she gets away. Where is Jack Reacher when you need him? I won't be allowed to set foot there to help her, I'm *persona non grata*. And my niece is an adult, so I can't exactly call child protection services for help.

Chris also doesn't manage to get hold of her. It's a delicate situation – we know that if we make too much fuss, we could further endanger her, if indeed she is in danger. We have never felt the lack of information flowing from that place more keenly than now. This episode leads to renewed contact with not only Koos, but also others who have left. I find out that a group approached the South African Human Rights Commission but got no joy there.

They also suspect the mission of the fraudulent disposal of more than R130 million (public benefit organisations in South Africa must abide by strict rules and, if true, this is a clear violation) and have asked the Directorate for Priority Crime

Investigation – or the Hawks, as we all know them – to investigate, but so far they've had no joy there either. A restorative justice lawyer is speaking to some survivors, seeking damages for them, but no lawsuit has yet been filed. I join a group of women on WhatsApp who are actively working to help survivors. It feels good to reconnect, especially with people who are trying to make a difference.

Then Koos tells me that he met with someone from the National Prosecuting Authority, who advised him to get the media involved. This person has been equally frustrated with the lack of progress in the investigations, and says that if this story is made public, the authorities will have no option but to act. KSB will not be able to keep sweeping everything under the carpet. No matter who its friends are (my addendum).

Towards the end of 2019, some articles appear in the Afrikaans press, but they don't get much traction. Koos asks me to help, seeing as I work in publishing. I chat to my good friend Peter about it. Twenty years ago, I published an article in a women's magazine and nothing really happened, so I'm not sure that this is the right route to go, but it's where most of my contacts are. Peter suggests I talk to Adriaan Basson of News24.

'Dude, how am I going to get an audience with the editor-in-chief of News24?'

So Peter emails him.

64

THE GENESIS OF *EXODUS*

On 6 February 2020, I meet with Adriaan Basson and spark an intensive, seven-month investigation into KwaSizabantu by the News24 team. They're about to do a deep dive into depravity, and I'm not sure any of them know what they're getting themselves into. They eventually decide to call the exposé *Exodus* – it's a perfect title and evokes the Old Testament laws that KSB twists and manipulates to suit its needs.

At our first meeting, Adriaan asks me what I want to achieve. I tell him that I want the abuse to stop. It has to stop. They cannot continue to abuse children. Adults too, of course, but it's the kids who are defenceless and have no recourse.

I warn him that it won't be an easy investigation – no one wants to talk about their own abuse. It's not pleasant, but it is necessary. Because, if we do not speak up, nothing is going to change. And I'm starting to think that maybe I was put on this earth to have these experiences because I am eloquent and strong and brave enough to say: 'Enough!'

The team asks me what makes me think that there is still abuse going on at the mission. It has been twenty-seven years since I left, after all. My answer is straightforward: when I heard the allegation that they were keeping my niece captive, I realised nothing had changed. The men at the mission have absolute control over everyone, I tell News24. Women are nothing. (Most of them, anyway. People like Lidia and Dorothy wield a lot of power, but they're in the minority.) Children are nothing. As a twenty-one-year-old, I still had to obey my mother, and I would have had to obey her until the day I got married. And then I would have had to obey my husband.

Neither women nor children have a voice. And because there is a ban on sex education, children, especially girl-children, are not taught that when someone touches you inappropriately, you speak up. You know that something is wrong, but you don't know what exactly. And this is a man of God who is touching you inappropriately, but you're not one hundred per cent sure that he's touching you inappropriately, and how could he be touching you inappropriately when he's a man of God? So whatever is inappropriate here is obviously inside you. You are evil, you are bad, you are just the worst person on earth. Firstly, because you're a woman, and secondly, because this is a man of God. You are completely, totally, utterly vulnerable to abuse. You have no boundaries. You have no knowledge. You have no voice. That is how it has always been, and I firmly believe that that is how it still is.

I'm on a quest now to track down more witnesses, especially the Zulu kids who were at school with me, as they had it the worst. I'm hampered because I've distanced myself from everyone over the past two decades, though I have connected with some old schoolfriends on social media. Everyone in the group of ex-KSB members puts out a call to action to find people who might be willing to talk to News24 about what they experienced. Here's what I post on Facebook on 16 February 2020:

Calling everyone who grew up/went to school/lived at KSB: I know you'd rather forget what happened there. I know you'd prefer to make jokes and remember only the fun times. I know it's easier to pretend everything was okay.

I know. Believe me, I know.

But think about the children who are there now, through no choice of their own. Remember how helpless you felt? How irredeemably bad you believed yourself to be? Remember your despair? Your desperate loneliness? Remember how you had nobody you could go to for help?

It's not fun, this remembering malarkey, but I beg you. Set a timer for 60 seconds, close your eyes, go back there and remember.

Then think about the defenceless children there now who have no timer that releases them after 60 seconds. Who cannot get up from looking at this post and carry on with their lives. Think about the kids who are still getting beaten, still getting told that they're evil and going to hell, still getting broken down, never to be built up again. (And I believe, because a leopard does not change its spots, some kids are still getting [assaulted] Or perhaps, like me, simply still being kissed and fondled and molested by their pastoral counsellor. I use the word 'simply' when I should use the word 'horrendously'.)

All in the name of God.

Now ask yourself if you can stay silent should someone offer you a platform to use your voice. Can you carry on as if none of that happened to you? As if you didn't experience or witness horrific abuse?

We have a voice.

Let's use our voices to right some wrongs. Let's try and save some kids.

For me, it's not only what I witnessed. I was 18 years old and just out of high school myself (having fielded my first proposal of marriage) when they gave me a classroom, some crayons and scissors – and 45 little five-year-olds! I was told to teach them English. I was clueless and did the best I could. But I got overwhelmed sometimes and I gave the kids hidings, too. Gave. It's not a gift! Stupid phrase, so let me rephrase. I hit some kids who were in my care and I carry that shame with me still. If I hit one of you, let me know, I'd like to talk to you and apologise in person. I knew deep down what I was doing was wrong, it never felt right, but I didn't stand up to them and so I became complicit in the abuse. I'm sorry for that. So, so sorry. I know corporal punishment was still legal in SA at that time, but it was wrong then and it is wrong now and I'm sorry.

I believe that with knowledge comes responsibility. I spoke out 20 years ago and I'm going to speak out again. And I need your help. Please.

I was one of the white kids there. I had it so easy. Well, easy is a relative term, but you will know what I mean. I may have been beaten, but not to within an inch of my life. I never had to endure the shame of standing in that queue after a holiday to undergo virginity testing by the mamas. I was spared a lot. I still have a story to tell – and it's no less important, but it doesn't paint the whole picture.

Tell me your stories, please. You can remain anonymous if you like – your name will not be used unless you expressly consent to it being used, I promise you that. But use your voice, tell me – and if you're okay with it, allow me to tell the world.

You might remember the passion play in 1989. And laugh about it. It was funny, of course, when [name withheld] cross fell down, and he with it. But you know what wasn't funny? The aftermath. Remember how the little ones peed their pants because nobody was allowed to leave the hall for four hours? Remember that man of God, Michael, standing up there with the orange hosepipe in his hand? We all know what he did with that orange hosepipe – what they all did with all those hosepipes of different colours. Tell me about it, please.

Maybe you were expelled for writing a letter. Or maybe they didn't allow you or a sibling to go through to matric because they didn't think you/they were academically strong enough to matriculate and spoil their perfect record. I could carry on, you know I could …

My nieces have grown up there. And recently, one of them was subjected to horrific treatment because she was accused of being a Satanist. That mild, sweet child, a Satanist? Seriously?

I can stay silent no longer. I couldn't save my nieces. But they are going to have children. And they will have children who will have children. When will the abuse end?

Please email me at […] and please share this post on your timeline – or send it privately to people you think may want to read it (I've made it public so you can).

Talk to me – let's help one another heal. But, most importantly, let's do what we can to stop others from needing that healing in the first place. #metooKSB

Please. *Ngiyacela. Asseblief.*

I've since made this post private and deleted some comments to protect my friends' identities. But this is what one brave soul had to say in response:

Just reading this brought tears to my eyes. The abuse was horrendous, the sad part is people would not believe you if you talk about it. I was locked up in a toilet for six weeks during school holidays without seeing the sun. During Christmas and New Year's, I was there, still locked up. The mosquitoes had a feast on me. When my gran came for me, she cried bitter tears and she washed me herself. Out of all incidents that happened to me when I was there, this one stands out.

I was given a Bible to read, an exercise book and a pen. I read it from cover to cover and had to write all my sins and when [name withheld] brought me food, she would take my sins to Thofozi [Lidia] every day. She would not talk to me. Just put the food down and take my sins and lock up the door.

I was locked up in the toilet by choir number two. *Ngemuva kunobhayela* [behind me was a geyser] and the heat day and night. Just imagine being locked up without bathing and brushing your teeth for so many days.

One day, I wrote a letter to Thofozi and told her that my sins are finished. I have nothing to write. She said I should write down all my dreams.

I could go on and on. The Kranskop services where we were beaten to a pulp by [name withheld] and [name withheld] taking turns. The beatings when the school started. The horrific abuse. The list is endless.

I know that once you start talking about what actually happened there, they will start calling you names, a slut, or say you are delusional. They have spies here on FB, they know and they will start threatening us. This time around we are unstoppable. We will talk.

Amen, sister, amen.

65

LOCKDOWN

On Monday, 23 March 2020, President Cyril Ramaphosa announces a twenty-one-day lockdown in South Africa to contain the spread of the coronavirus, Covid-19. This does not deter the team at News24 – by now they've interviewed several people and they know they have a story that needs to be told. They decide that they will tell it through articles, a documentary and a podcast.

I spend the next few months in a daze. Some of it is spent with them, recording the podcast, being interviewed for the article and being filmed for the documentary. When I'm not doing that or working, I'm talking to people, fellow survivors of KSB. I spend hours on the phone. I don't pressure anyone to speak to News24. I ask, and if they demur, I leave it at that. I know how difficult a decision it is. (I strongly believe any survivor of any abuse gets to decide what they do with their experience: whether that's making it public or staying silent, going to the police or choosing not to.) Most of the time, we simply talk about what happened to us. For me, 2020 is the year of tears. I cry so, so much and so, so often. Our collective pain is palpable. There is no getting away from the trauma we all still carry in our bones.

The News24 team is amazing. There's Deon Wiggett, who's been hired to create the podcast. (If you haven't read his book *My Only Story*, do so – it is incredibly moving: part memoir, part true crime, part detective story of how he tracked down a serial paedophile. And it's essential reading for parents and anyone who has children in their care, with valuable lessons on how to spot a predator.) There's Tammy Petersen, who is writing most of the personal stories, and Azarrah Karrim, who is investigating the allegations of financial misconduct and the business affairs. I'll get to know the documentary's director, Aljoscha Kohlstock, well, as he does all the filming with me as well as the recording for the podcast. Then there's Nokuthula Manyathi, who is producing and narrating the podcast. Mpho Raborife and Sharlene Rood are also part of the team, and then there are others I don't get to meet, but who play an integral part in the investigation. And Adriaan, of course, leading the charge.

I tell the News24 team that while they're gathering witnesses, to please make sure that they're speaking to the Zulu children who went to school there. They had it worse than anyone. This proves tricky, until one day Celimpilo calls me to tell me that I've unleashed something with my Facebook post and call to action. Past pupils are now talking – and healing – among themselves, she tells me. She says she knows how cold and lonely the place I inhabit right now can be, and so she just wanted to reach out with a virtual hug. We haven't chatted in years, and while we're catching up, I ask her whether she'd be willing to speak to the team investigating the abuse at KSB. She says yes, and I put her in touch with Deon and Tammy. She agrees to feature alongside me in both the podcast and the documentary.

The documentary features a number of survivors, including Koos. It's not easy for any of us to share our stories, but revealing your pain on camera, that takes an extra dose of bravery.

It's lockdown, so we do my recordings in my home and turn my lounge into a studio for the documentary. For the podcast, we need the quietest room in the house, and that's my bedroom. We cover the windows and mirrors with blankets and basically create as much of a soundproof room as we can.

Every now and again, my cats interrupt – they're used to having the run of the place. I could not have done any of this without Troy and Matilda. Troy, in particular, follows me around when he senses I'm struggling, which is pretty much all the time. Lockdown is a pretty shitty time to be going through a shitty time – an online chat is no substitute for a hug from a friend. Troy gives me plenty of love, though. He comes to lie on top of me and purrs and purrs and purrs. And Matilda joins him often. They were both rescue kittens, only I'm no longer sure who rescued whom.

I'm not sleeping much, mainly because there's something I'm grappling with: do I name Muzi as the man who molested me or not? News24 puts no pressure on me, and for the first two recordings, I merely talk about 'that man'. I have kept his shameful secret for decades now. The vast majority of my friends, people I'm really close to, don't even know he exists. I battle with this for weeks. I'm not a psychologist and I don't fully understand the nuances between sociopaths, psychopaths and narcissists. Or people who are just bad apples. What I do know is that KSB fosters an environment where people like Muzi can thrive. Where they're above the law. And if they're a man, they're even further above the law. I was not Muzi's only victim. Their stories are not mine to tell, but perhaps in telling my story, and by actually naming him, I will help them achieve a measure of peace: it wasn't you, it was him.

I'm also genuinely scared of Muzi. He's in jail for murder. And when his own son turned state witness against him, Muzi tried to kill him. Luckily, the attempt failed. If a man can try to kill his own son, what is he going to do to me? Sure, he was given a life sentence, but we all know that a life sentence in South Africa doesn't mean you stay in jail for life. Muzi has been incarcerated for just over ten years, which means he could be let out at any time. What if he comes after me? And even if he remains in jail, he can still get to me.

But I have to speak up. And I decide that I have to name him. I am sick and tired of men hiding behind anonymity. If I'm going to tell my truth, I'm going to tell *all* my truth, the whole *boksemdaais*, as my dad would have said.

Here's another reason for naming Muzi: when he gets out of prison, I believe women need to know that they are not safe with him. And parents need to know that their daughters are not safe with him. He's the most charming fucker on the planet – don't fall for it. Please. Protect yourselves and protect your daughters.

66

DENOUNCED FROM THE PULPIT

I have always known, from that first meeting with Adriaan, that KwaSizabantu will at some point use my mother and sister to discredit me. And even though I expect it, it still hurts like hell when it happens. What is it about family bonds that they can be so powerful despite years of estrangement?

The first personal attack comes eleven days before News24 launches *Exodus*. In what the mission calls the evening devotional.

In July and again in August, News24 sends KwaSizabantu detailed lists of the allegations against them. KSB does not want to comment, except for a blanket statement that says that these are mainly family matters from very long ago. My mother also declines to comment. She tells News24 that journalists twisted her words twenty years ago, so she won't speak to them today. She has no such reservations about talking to the flock, though. In early September, my mother denounces me from the pulpit. The video is on YouTube for all to see.

My mother opens the sermon with a verse from Hebrews 12:15: 'See to it that no one falls short of the grace of God and that no bitter root grows up to cause trouble and defile many.'

I won't transcribe the entire sermon here, but she goes on a bit about how the characteristic of a bitter root is to defile. She cites the example of Korah, who led a rebellion against Moses. 'Bitterness changes a person's attitude,' she says, 'and bitterness changes your outlook.' Then she gets to the heart of her message. This bitterness is not only found in biblical Israel, she says:

> It can happen in a family, in a home. It happened in my home. I want to use my two daughters as an example tonight. The eldest daughter served God. And she is with her family – her husband and three children – still here at the mission, serving the Lord. But my youngest daughter, who grew up in the same home, who had the same mother and father, who came at the same time to KwaSizabantu Mission, she allowed a root of bitterness in her life that she did not deal with. And that root of bitterness grew. So that eventually she could not stay any longer in the home. She could not stay any longer at KwaSizabantu. So she left. And that bitterness in her grew.
>
> Now we have noticed that bitterness has the power of the lie within it. And then it paints all the happiness in different colours, not the true colour

any longer. And that happened in this youngest daughter's life. The bitterness, the lie, the power of the lie entered into this root of bitterness that had grown. And after some years, it burst open into the media. But now, it was so mixed with lies that one could see this bitterness has changed the perception of this daughter, it changed her so much that she became a victim in her own mind. So her mother was to blame. Others were to blame, because there was no responsibility that she had because of these circumstances. And in this victim mentality, because of the root of bitterness, lies were easily spoken. So she said that she was chased away from home. But that's not the truth. She left out of her own.

Let me set the record straight. I have never in my life said anyone chased me away. Never. Not once. They need to discredit me, however, and telling people I'm a liar is the easiest way. (KSB's lawyer will pick up this narrative in a few weeks' time.) My mother continues:

So everything was coloured with this bitterness. And she hasn't been home for the past twenty years. But my eldest daughter lived here at home. And she's still serving the Lord in great joy because we experience the life here at KwaSizabantu. There's no root of bitterness living in our hearts. No lie. So we see the people that are being so, so smeared because of bitterness in other people's lives.

There's a fair bit about Erlo and Lidia and how the glory of God is in their faces, etc. She talks some more about Korah and his rebellion – how his bitterness drove the fear of God from him and he touched Moses or something, but don't quote me on that. I should know, though, as the whole Korah affair is in *The Burning Hell*, after all.

And it is a terrible thing to have a child that has gone away from the blessing of God, from the life of God, from the people of God, because of a root of bitterness. And to see that the bitterness has driven the fear of God from that heart, who was taught from small to fear God.

But I think one of the most scary things of this root of bitterness that grows up that it becomes visible, is that the fear of God is so removed that Korah touched the anointed of God. He touched that which God declared holy. And that can happen and that happened also to this younger daughter of mine, this youngest daughter, when she left, and this bitterness grew and grew and grew. It doesn't matter now what comes from her mouth about this place of God. And that is what is such a fearful thing, that a person who could have experienced all the beauty, all the kindness, all the blessing, all the mercy of God here at the mission can leave and speak bitter words.

There's more, much more. Korah is now in hell. The earth just opened up and swallowed him, my mother says. He's been there all this time and will be for all eternity. The insinuation is clearly that her youngest daughter is heading to hell unless she repents, because, like Korah, she has gone too far. It's really the narrative of my childhood and teenage years playing out in one sermon. She has this to say just before the final prayer:

> If you happen to meet up with my youngest daughter, you can tell her her mother is still waiting at the foot of the cross. There is still time that the Redeemer can uproot that root of bitterness and save her life.

Then she prays and asks the Lord to have mercy on them. Her youngest daughter doesn't get an intercession.

It hurts to watch this video, to hear my mother's voice, to see how dispassionately she talks about me. Of course it does. I tell Chris about it, but I don't send him the link. He doesn't have to sit through all that. Their narrative hasn't changed in twenty years: I'm a bitter, disgruntled child. And who better to deliver that message than the child's mother?

But KSB doesn't seem to realise that I'm no longer the only one. How many 'bitter children' can one cult spawn? They're about to find out.

67

A THREESOME WITH ERLO

Who needs Jack Reacher when you have Adriaan Basson? That feels like blasphemy. Sorry, Jack. But I'm serious. I have been in the publishing industry for nearly two decades by the time I meet Adriaan and his team of investigative reporters who will dedicate the better part of a year to uncovering the nefarious shenanigans of Erlo and his cohort.

The News24 team treats me and all the other survivors they interview with so much care and gentleness. I remark on this during one of the podcast recordings and Deon responds: 'Isn't it telling that you're getting more care from a news organisation than you ever got from that religious institution?' Indeed, Deon, indeed.

It's a harrowing seven months. Most of it takes place during lockdown, increasing my sense of aloneness in my struggle, although the connections I'm making with old acquaintances – and new ones – are intense. My brother and close friends check in on me often, for which I'm grateful.

Celimpilo and I grow closer than ever. Deon weaves our stories together so beautifully and Nokuthula's narration takes it up a notch. (Do listen to it – it's on news24.com, search for *Exodus* under podcasts.) Deon conducts the interviews, and his empathy and understanding completely transform each recording into a kind of therapy session. Deon understands trauma, and he brings such wisdom and insight to these Zoom sessions, I look forward to them when I thought I'd be dreading them. Later, Deon will tell subscribers in a webinar: 'It's a real human story of two women surviving and flourishing against all odds. It's an incredible privilege to be able to tell that story and get everything from this perspective.'

It's a powerful four-episode podcast. As Celimpilo says: 'Deon has taken our pain and turned it into a work of art.' (In June 2021, the prestigious One World Media Awards, recognising the best media coverage of the global south, will agree with Celimpilo's assessment and awards *Exodus* best global podcast of the year. A well-deserved accolade!

And then, joy of joy, Jessie and I reconnect. Our first phone conversation in over twenty years lasts about three hours. I ask her to forgive me for ghosting her all those years ago, and she does – she did, long ago, she tells me. It's as though the intervening years fade away; we're instantly confiding in each other again. Thank you, Jessie, for your friendship and support.

Then, one day, Tammy tells me that she's going to be interviewing Muzi in prison

– telephonically, I'm glad to hear. I'm not sure how I feel about this; I have had no contact with him since his apology email back in 2000. But hey, everyone has the right of reply, including a convicted murderer.

I don't expect what happens next. Muzi denies knowing me beyond the odd casual conversation. He denies that he was my counsellor. When Tammy tells me this, I send her a photograph of my email to Muzi all those years ago.

When she speaks to Muzi again, he tells her it's a hoax email. He wants to see the one I claim he sent me, because he says he never wrote it (I don't send it, screw him). It's part of a conspiracy. And then he says to Tammy, 'I don't want to destroy her, I don't want to hurt her, but if she carries on, I think I will go nuclear as well.'

Muzi and I agree on one point only. He tells Tammy that a counsellor's role is 'leading the individual in a spiritual route, you are trying to make them reach certain levels of spirituality. That's what I am talking about. That is not what I was to Erika.'

Damn straight. He was trying to make me reach certain levels of depravity instead.

Tammy and the documentary crew decide not to publish any of Muzi's preposterous claims. But Deon and I chat, and we think there's a place for it in the podcast.

'He'll provide a much-needed moment of levity,' I tell Deon. Because, get this: according to Muzi, I was having sex with Lidia *and* with Erlo. In fact, he tells Tammy, one day they discovered us having a naked threesome.

But that's not all. Muzi claims the reason I spent so much time with his children was because I was working for Lidia. I was a 'slut' who would sleep with men to get information from them that Lidia would then pass on to her apartheid masters. And because Lidia suspected Muzi of working for the ANC, she tried to use me to lay a honey trap for him. He wasn't grooming me – I was the one trying to seduce him. He resisted all my advances, though, great guy that he is.

It gets worse. David Jaca, the man whose funeral I attended in 1996, supposedly told Muzi that he'd taken me to have three abortions. Muzi tells Tammy he doesn't want to hurt me, but if I'm adamant he was fondling me, then he's going to tell the truth about me. He's going to subpoena the men I slept with to testify against me in court.

Muzi is no stranger to hoax emails and conspiracy theories – his various criminal trials testify to that. But this is so beyond anything I've ever heard that, months later, I still don't know what to make of it. I don't regret saying his name, though; to me, it's clear that he's unhinged.

I do regret, deeply, that one of the villains in my story caused such irreparable damage to the family of the woman he murdered. Muzi took away my innocence, but he robbed them of a wife and mother, and he robbed her of life itself. I am sorry if naming him in my story has brought them more sorrow or opened fresh wounds. May she rest in peace, and may he stay behind bars, because that is exactly where he belongs.

68

'THE REAL VICTIM'

Two roads diverge in the lush green hills of KwaZulu-Natal. And KSB takes the road almost all abusers travel by, and that makes all the difference. Once again, KSB picks the Lane of Denial over the Avenue of Accountability. The Road of Remorse doesn't even make it onto their map.

On 19 September 2020, *Exodus: Uncovering a Cult in KwaZulu-Natal* is published. There are articles and the feature-length documentary, as well as the first episode of the podcast. The landing page of the special-projects website News24 has set up states: 'A 50-year-old Christian mission in KwaZulu-Natal stands accused of gross violations of human rights, turning a blind eye to sexual abuse, and money laundering spanning four decades.'

Two days later, Adriaan follows up with an editorial that gets much of South Africa talking: 'Want to stop a cult? Then don't buy aQuellé bottled water.'

Professor Luka David Mosoma, the chairperson of the Commission for the Promotion and Protection of the Rights of Cultural, Religious and Linguistic Communities (CRL Rights Commission), announces that they're launching an investigation into the claims against the church. He says that when there are claims against any religious organisation, the commission doesn't have to wait for a formal complaint to be lodged.

I feel intense relief when I hear this news. Finally, someone in authority is paying attention! The CRL Rights Commission is a constitutional body with a constitutional mandate to strengthen our constitutional democracy. The world cannot ignore them.

Major retailers also take note and say that they're demanding answers from KSB. Woolworths is the first to announce it has suspended buying produce from the mission. Spar follows shortly thereafter. That's got to hurt KSB – many of the leaders are Spar franchisees. Pick n Pay eventually follows suit. The Shoprite Group says it will only end its relationship with its supplier when there are 'legal findings' against it. Throughout this controversy, it is the only large retailer who, as far as I know, never stops buying aQuellé.

The KwaZulu-Natal Department of Social Development announces that they'll be following up on investigations. And the Hawks confirm to News24 that the Pietermaritzburg serious commercial crimes unit is investigating the allegations of fraud at KwaSizabantu. Also, at last, the South African Human Rights Commission says that they'll investigate. 'What is of concern for the commission are the human rights violations conducted in the name of religion,' their CEO, Advocate Tseliso Thipanyane, tells News24.

KSB does what they have always done: deny, deny, deny. It's so predictable, I almost feel sorry for them. Accountability is a four-letter word on the KSB compound. This is all a smear campaign, they proclaim. Press releases follow one after the other in quick succession. One from 22 September reads:

> The vicious attack on KwaSizabantu Mission is shocking. This media explosion aims to spread rumours and destroy the humanitarian and spiritual work of this Christian Mission [...]
>
> Those driving the current smear campaign have resorted to the low tactics of libel and defamation. It smacks of racism, misguided, out-of-context narratives presented by disgruntled members of society.
>
> People making such horrendous allegations against the Mission are free to follow the normal lawful procedures. Those who have been 'allegedly' violated against, should seek justice through the judicial system. The fact that these allegations have never been taken to the authorities begs the question: why not? Why have the so-called victims not done what the law requires? Why blame the Mission?

And so, the victim shaming starts – and continues to this day. Why did the rape victims not go to the police? Well, maybe because when they told Erlo someone had raped them, he supposedly made them apologise for causing a man of God to stumble, called them whores and swore them to silence?

KSB claims they were blindsided by the media reports. They're reeling from these unwarranted attacks. Blindsided has such a nice ring to it, doesn't it? It smacks of a conspiracy. But if they were blindsided, how do you explain my mother's sermon from Mount KwaSizabantu more than a week before the story broke?

Next, KSB and the company they own, Ekhamanzi Springs (Pty) Ltd, trading as aQuellé, announce in a letter to their customers that they have appointed an 'external panel' comprising 'legal, political, business and grassroots level individuals to investigate the allegations and publish their findings'. They call the allegations 'sensational, vicious and [of a] factually inaccurate nature'. I'm not sure what 'grassroots level individuals' are, but they sound impressive.

Another press release two days later, titled 'aQuellé – THE REAL VICTIM', tries to discredit those of us who have spoken out. They have this to say about me: 'She alleges that she was suspended and expelled from the Mission school when she was 16 and at the same time told by her mother to leave the house. The Mission and Erika's mother deny that Erika was suspended or expelled. It is also denied that Erika was "sent away" at any time by the Mission or her mother.'

In the documentary, I clearly say I was threatened with expulsion, I never say I was expelled. Their accusation is baseless, but unless you've seen the documentary, listened to the podcast or read the article, you can't know that. And it's definitely not the kind of thing that will get past KSB's censorship board. As far as their followers are concerned, catch her in one lie and you can't believe anything she says.

The very next day, there's yet another press release. This one is titled 'aQuellé – ALWAYS TRANSPARENT' (they love their all caps) and announces the members of said 'external panel'. But instead of the impressive line-up of 'legal, political, business and grassroots level individuals' we've come to expect, it appears they've only appointed two legal professionals to a two-person panel: Advocate Khumbu Shazi and attorney Peter Le Mottée. Arnott and Associates in Durban will handle the admin.

The press release also states that they're engaging with law enforcement to 'bring to book those engaged in the vicious false allegations'.

69

THE ACCUSATIONS MOUNT

As more people come forward, other news outlets start taking note. Journalist and columnist Sipho Hlongwane speaks to CapeTalk radio of his own memories of growing up at KSB – the severe beatings and psychological trauma. Sipho urges people to read the mission's response and the reports in the media. 'Compare the two,' he says. 'Compare how detailed the stories of these victims are, compare how passionately these people speak. Look at the fear that people still have, some having left the mission decades ago. These people have palpable fear up until today. And then look at the denial. Look how flimsy and flippant that denial is.'

Sipho asks listeners to take part, to investigate, to use their deductive reasoning.

Ever since I realised in therapy that my unresolved trauma had allowed me to welcome a malignant male into my home and bed, I've been reading up about trauma. And something Judith Lewis Herman wrote in her book *Trauma and Recovery: The Aftermath of Violence – from Domestic Abuse to Political Terror* has stayed with me, because it so accurately describes the situation we're facing with KSB:

To study psychological trauma is to come face to face both with human vulnerability in the natural world and with the capacity for evil in human nature. To study psychological trauma means bearing witness to horrible events. When the events are natural disasters or 'acts of God,' those who bear witness sympathize readily with the victim. But when the traumatic events are of human design, those who bear witness are caught in the conflict between victim and perpetrator. It is morally impossible to remain neutral in this conflict.

It is very tempting to take the side of the perpetrator. All the perpetrator asks is that the bystander do nothing. He appeals to the universal desire to see, hear, and speak no evil. The victim, on the contrary, asks the bystander to share the burden of the pain. The victim demands action, engagement, and remembering. [...]

In order to escape accountability for his crimes, the perpetrator does everything in his power to promote forgetting. Secrecy and silence are the perpetrator's first line of defense. If secrecy fails, the perpetrator attacks the credibility of his victim. If he cannot silence her absolutely, he tries to make sure that no one listens. To this end, he marshals an impressive array of arguments, from the most blatant denial to the most sophisticated and elegant rationalization. After every atrocity one can expect to hear the same predictable apologies: it never happened; the victim lies; the victim exaggerates; the victim brought it upon herself; and in any case it is time to forget the past and move on. The more powerful the perpetrator, the greater is his prerogative to name and define reality, and the more completely his arguments prevail. [New York: Basic Books, 1997, pp. 7–8]

This particular perpetrator is indeed powerful, but it is floundering because it does not know how to navigate a world in which it is not lord and master. On 1 October, KSB calls a press conference where they say they will be answering questions. It's the pandemic, so they do everything over Zoom. I log on about fifteen minutes early and am astounded to see one of Erlo's daughters, Ruth Combrink, rehearsing her lines. She's the spokesperson for KwaSizabantu. I remember her as a sweet young girl. I'm not sure who gets the bigger fright, me or them. I log off quickly, and when I return at the allotted time, there is no press conference. Just a pre-recorded video of Ruth with no Q&As, nothing.

The statement is quite something, though. It's an about-turn for KSB. For ten days, they've denied there's truth to our allegations. But now Ruth urges those with grievances to share them with the 'independent' panel 'to ensure that their story is told and that justice may be served [...] It is our absolute intention to work to rectify any proven wrongs and we are committed to taking whatever actions are necessary to bring restorations within these circumstances.'

So much fluff. 'Proven wrongs' indeed. Here's how I know that they still live on a different planet: she says they hope 'News24 will assist us to facilitate this on behalf of all those named in the programme'. Come off it, Ruth. My mother and sister both have my contact details. You don't need News24 to reach out to me or any of the others. You know who we are. Proper journalists don't compromise their sources – you'd know that if you lived in the real world.

Let's get real. This can only be about money. 'To this end, we open our hearts to everybody, including our retail clients, to reassure them of our commitment to transparency and to upholding of strong ethical values and morals that we are renowned for.'

There it is: Please buy our water and our fresh produce again, South Africa. We promise we'll be good.

'Our hearts bleed for any individual who has experienced the trauma and pain of abuse – this is closer to our hearts than many can imagine,' Ruth continues. 'We offer them our support and invite them to reach out to us in this regard.'

No, Ruth, I will not be reaching out to you any time soon. You want the hundreds of kids KSB is accused of having systematically beaten up, traumatised and humiliated to come to *you* for reconciliation? Please. I believe you just want your retail customers back; you have no genuine interest in any of us survivors. You were a child there too. At the very least, you must have witnessed countless beatings.

KwaSizabantu is not that familiar with social media, and its supporters on Twitter keep scoring own goals – I feel quite bad sometimes, it's like shooting fish in a barrel. (Check out #KwaSizabantu in October and November 2020, though many of them have now deleted their tweets and accounts.) But it's great fun. And then, KSB takes the first intelligent action since the story broke. They appoint PR guru Bridget von Holdt as their spokesperson. Suddenly, all the KSB apologists disappear off Twitter, bar one or two who cease their attacks on survivors. KSB changes their homepage, too, and now it appears as though none of this has happened. Gone are the upfront denials. It's business as usual.

But Bridget isn't fast enough. Before she intervenes, KSB posts their submission to the panel that they're paying, including all the accompanying affidavits, front and centre on their homepage. The mind boggles. There it is for anyone to download. And that's how I get to read what my mother and my sister have said about me under oath.

70

A LESSON IN GASLIGHTING

A week before my family signs their affidavits, my sister records a video and sends it via WhatsApp to our extended family. It is 21 September, just two days after Exodus dropped.

It's not even lunchtime, but I fortify myself with a glass of wine before I press play. It's a Vrede en Lust Jess rosé – I figure I need a favourite in my glass for this.

Hanna has lots to say about me – twelve minutes' worth. I guess I should be thankful that only the first episode of the podcast had aired when she recorded this, otherwise it would have been much longer. Her face is devoid of emotion. Her eyes move from side to side as she reads from a script on the screen in front of her. She begins by glorifying Erlo and saying people shouldn't believe what I say about him. Around the four-minute mark is where it gets interesting.

The second point I want to address is Erika's assertion that she was just a shell of her previous outgoing self after thirteen years of so-called terror. I lived with Erika. I shared a room with her. She's entirely mistaken if she really believes that.

Her family saw one side of her, while the outside world saw another. We knew her moodiness and her anger when she was opposed. From when she was small, I didn't find it easy living with her – I presume she didn't find it easy with me either. But the outside world saw the sunshine and the gregarious nature. To be sure, we did also have wonderful and good times. But there was a side to Erika, which made it challenging to be her sister. Erika's sunshine was no different when she left than when she arrived, except that other aspects of her character just became more pronounced.

I know Erika as somebody who brooks no opposition when she has set her mind on something, but she also expects you will agree with her. If you don't, you will lose her friendship and love. Erika will not rest until Mom submits to her view. And it is clear to me that she believes the end justifies the means. This type of totalitarian and intolerant view where everyone must agree with her or else bear the consequences precludes any discussion. It is impossible to have any conversation with Erika as she has shut the door on us. The only way she will open the door again is if we will govern our thoughts on her terms. And that means the door she closed remains shut.

Wow. Percy taught me a lot about gaslighting because he was so very good at it. One way you mess with someone's perception of reality is by accusing them of the same thing you are guilty of. Percy would accuse me of being secretive when he was the one keeping secrets from me. Should I ever doubt it, I have a host of people, including my brother, who can confirm that I'm not the one with the totalitarian and intolerant views. There are KSB's own YouTube videos. And the *Voorblad* episode too, of course. There was a time when I might have fallen for this narrative and started doubting myself, but that time has passed.

Hanna then talks about the abuse I 'suffered because of Muzi Kunene'. She says that for Erika 'to imply that the culture of the mission made her submit to him because he was deemed a man of God is creating a false impression of culpability on the part of the mission. Whatever evil was perpetrated by Muzi Kunene was done by himself as an individual and was not sanctioned in any way by the mission. Erika remains silent on the measures taken by my mother to protect her and her own unwillingness to submit to these measures. She creates a narrative where Reverend Stegen is to blame. This is a false narrative, and one which she needs to reassess. By shifting the blame onto the innocent people, she removes herself from those who could have helped her.'

This is news to me. My mother did nothing to help me. She denied for years that anything untoward had happened between Muzi and me. I wasn't unwilling to submit to her measures – I was completely ignorant of them because they did not exist. Also, I believe Erlo has been shown to be far from innocent. What has emerged in the News24 investigation is personal accounts of how he told girls and women who came to him about sexual assault to never speak of it again. How he asked them to apologise for making a man of God stumble. And how he told men who came to talk to him about women being abused to be quiet. Innocent, my arse.

Hanna accuses me of having 'waged a one-sided war' against my mother for twenty years:

> It seems to me that this is the narrative of someone who became a disillusioned and bitter adult, and then revisited her childhood projecting this hurt, pain, anger and other emotions onto an otherwise happy life with a normal, ordinary family. The stories are often only shells of what really happened. And she has put so much malice and cruelty into her retelling of it that it seems as if it happened in another world.

She details the love and care my mother lavished on me and says what I've done is a travesty. She says that despite all the mud I've slung at my mother, she's only ever spoken about me with love and compassion in their home. (No mention of the pulpit, of course.) 'I hope that Erika will discover what a treasure she has discarded before it's too late.'

Hanna ends the video by giving the first hint of the KSB narrative that will

214

unfold over the course of the next few months: that there's a group using the media to take control of the mission's businesses – this is also how I know for sure that she didn't write this statement on her own. KSB will go on to claim that their accusers are 'disgruntled' ex-members trying to take over their multibillion-rand water-bottling plant, aQuellé. It's all a big conspiracy and a smear campaign. 'To participate in the intimidation of people who only do good to others is a terrible thing,' Hanna intones. 'I can only come to the conclusion that Mr Greeff and co. are determined to ruin the good work here for financial gain. I cannot see what else justifies their irrational and cruel actions. And as Erika's sister, I only hope she is not a tool in their hands.'

I watch the video repeatedly, trying to find a glimpse of my sister. I can't. I cannot reconcile this detached woman reading this script with the sister I once knew. My heart aches for her, but even more for her three daughters who will never know the vibrant woman she was once destined to be. I cannot know her state of mind or whether she is truly content with her lot in life. Somehow, she believes the statement she has just read. Maybe she did even write it herself. I used to love you, Hanna. How I wish things were different.

Chris asks me not to make the video public and I honour his request. I do show it to the News24 team, because it arrives as we're still recording the last episodes of the podcast. And because they've become more than journalists reporting on the story. They've become family. Even more so now, as they're just about the only people I see during lockdown. As has happened so often in the past months, Deon's words to me on the Zoom call help enormously.

'I can say with entire conviction you're one of the most positive, sunniest people I know. No reasonable person can look at any of this and find you the dark one.' I know this about myself, but it really helps to hear it from someone I look up to.

71

A CLUMSY CHILD

Affidavits are weirdly very hard to write. I found it so, as did the others who submitted theirs to the investigating team. I wonder how it was for my family.

My mother's recollection of that fire back in Estcourt differs from mine. In an affidavit dated 30 September 2020 (eleven days after *Exodus* launched, with only the first two episodes of the podcast available), she says she had bought certain clothes and shoes while in a relationship with a man who was not my father. 'I did not feel free wearing them anymore, neither had I peace to give them away to someone else,' she explains. 'Consulting my husband, we set fire to the items one night while the children were asleep [...] Our children knew nothing about it until I later told them about it in my testimony of what the Lord had done for me. I do not recall ever burning my children's clothes.'

What is not in dispute is that my mother burned some clothes. My memory of that day is so vivid – the acrid black smoke, the note in my pocket – that I cannot reconcile it with my mother's account.

As for my telling of how Erlo forbade me from talking to my mother about Muzi, she has this to say: 'I am unaware of any hurtful way Reverend Stegen spoke to Erika at the time, nor that she was not allowed to speak to me. She never shared this disappointment with me. I am convicted [*sic*] that what she said, is not the truth.'

Whatever, mother, don't mince your words. You've already denounced me as a liar from the pulpit, so it's hardly a surprise that you don't think I'm telling the truth. Let me give you the floor again – if I've got it all so wrong, tell us in your words what happened on that awful day your husband died.

Regarding Erika's allegations around the death of my husband. Erika claims that the way Rev Stegen spoke to her on that day was very hurtful, and that she was not allowed to see me. [...]

I went along with the doctor and others, taking my husband to the hospital, and asked Mr Friedel Stegen to let Erika know what had happened. My husband had a second attack and died en route to the hospital. Because the storm had damaged the telephone lines, we could not inform the mission about his death.

I do not recollect what happened upon our return. Possibly Rev Stegen told Erika about her father's death, which, as our pastor, would be a normal thing for him to do. What I clearly remember is that he took me and Erika in his car to his brother's farm where there was still telephone connection, so that I could inform our relatives of the passing away of my husband. I remember his comforting words, and the song he sang with us upon returning from the farm.

No, it's not normal for a pastor to tell a young girl that her father has died, not when her mother is right there. You didn't even try to tell me that my beloved father had died; you sent someone I barely knew – and it wasn't Erlo. So what do you actually know about what happened to me that day? I have not experienced the death of a husband; I can only imagine your grief. But what mother drives past her child to go to another house and then sends some random man to inform her daughter that her dad has died? Am I judging you too harshly, Mother?

My sister has a fair amount to say about that day too, even though she was in Pretoria and has no way of knowing who said what to me. She affirms what my mother says happened and then adds: 'At no stage in all the time from my arrival until I returned to Pretoria after the funeral did Reverend Stegen or any other person on the Mission speak to me in the way Erika alleges Reverend Stegen spoke to her [...] At no time was I confronted by any person at the Mission during those days that I had to confess my sins or that I would not see my father in heaven again unless I toed the line.'

Good for you, Hanna. Not all siblings have the same experiences just because they share the same blood and space.

Hanna has lots more to say about me, including my sunny disposition. She's a bit more circumspect about my character defects in her affidavit than she was in the video. 'I have no recollection of Erika becoming silent and withdrawn. I recall her as always popular with her peers and adults. I recall discussing with my brother how our identity in the eyes of others was often just to be known as Erika's siblings even though she was the youngest. My perspective on this never changed in the years that we stayed together on the mission.'

But she's not done. 'Erika makes a few factual errors in her retelling of our visits to the mission and of our home situation.' She has this to say about me bemoaning the end of my athletic career because my mother burned my shorts: 'Erika was very unathletic. She was a clumsy child who did not enjoy physical activities and did not enjoy participating in sport and did not participate because she did not want to.' She's right, I didn't enjoy having to jump over things and I often sported bruises. But I enjoyed running. And I was good enough at it. It's not only the people who come first who enjoy sport.

Here's more from her signed statement:

Erika alleges that we were trained not to question our parents or to ask questions. I never experienced this. I recall being raised in an environment of intellectual freedom. We had ready access to our family's extensive library, which contained a wide variety of fiction and non-fiction material. We were given free reign [*sic*] in every local library in every town we lived in. I particularly recall going to the library at Estcourt every Saturday, with my siblings, where we would take out four books each. I do not recall ever having my reading censored or checked. We had debates and discussions and were free to ask questions on any and every topic, if we chose to do so. What I do recall was that we were expected to treat our parents with respect and this was the norm in our house.

I'm grateful for my brother – this gaslighting won't work, because he remembers what I remember. Our parents *did* censor our books. They allowed – and encouraged – us to read extensively, but not everything we brought back from the library was permitted. Hanna will repeat a lot of this in her testimony before the CRL Rights Commission in October, which Chris and I watch on Facebook Live. We will agree that she experienced a different childhood from the one we remember.

My mother, who until our chat in Montagu had rebuked me for lying about Muzi, has now changed her tune somewhat. Convenient. He's left KSB and is sitting in jail, so there's no need to defend him any more:

Regarding Erika's allegations that she was sexually abused by Mr. Muzi Kunene:
I remember that her friendship with the family of Muzi Kunene began through her interest in their handicapped daughter, with whom she spent many enjoyable hours. I was unaware of any close contact between her and Mr Kunene. I never had cause for suspicion that there was something not right. I knew that she had great respect for his intelligence, and his ability to debate. We took him and his family as our friends, and invited them for meals in our rondavel. I particularly do not recall Erika ever being called late at night from the rondavel to the Kunenes' room. As we stayed together, I would have known that.
I remember returning from school one afternoon, and found Mr Kunene, a married man, sitting unusually close to my daughter in our home, it was after her matric year; I think she was 19 years old at the time. To me this was very disturbing and unusual. I went immediately to Reverend Stegen to tell him about my concern and ask for his advice in the matter. Reverend Stegen acted immediately and told me the next day that he had asked Erika not to go to the Kunenes' room any longer but to use another counsellor.

This must be what my sister meant in her video when she spoke about the 'measures' my mother took to protect me. But what a sad indictment on her mothering that she claims she spoke to Erlo about her concerns instead of her daughter. That's vintage KwaSizabantu. Family means nothing, leadership everything. I doubt the truth of the anecdote, though. Muzi and I were alone in the rondavel only once, that day he asked me to undress. Also, it was the conversation between Erlo, Muzi and me that led him to ban contact between us.

To say she was 'unaware of any close contact' is ridiculous – she knew full well he was my counsellor, as did many other people who lived at the mission. Then again, lies are allowed – even encouraged – when they serve to protect the god of KwaSizabantu. First, they lie to you, then they lie about you. Also, note how my mother is at pains to stipulate my age. This will not be the last time the mission will bend over backwards to specify I was an adult throughout the period Muzi and I spent time together.

Both my mother's and my sister's affidavits paint me as a happy child who became inexplicably embittered after leaving the mission and proceeded to lie about my experiences there. My mother details several meetings with me (with several factual errors) and reveals that I told her on two occasions that I forgive her (this is true). She ends her affidavit by stating: 'I have been the topic in many talks that Erika has had with the media, including the program *Carte Blanche*, from which is clear that, rather than her alleged forgiveness, she is carrying a grudge, causing a destructive root of bitterness in her against me and against the Mission.'

It was *Voorblad*, not *Carte Blanche*, Mother – and you were right there next to me. Also, I can forgive you for what you did to me as my mother and still hold you and KSB accountable for what you've done. The one does not preclude the other.

This public airing of our family's dirty laundry is as distasteful to me today as it was twenty years ago, but it's the only way I know how to expose the rot that is at the heart of KSB. I cannot divorce my family's story from my own.

I wish I could spare my niece, though. Her parents upload videos of her refuting my claims that she had been kept against her will. My sister even goes so far as to lodge a complaint on her behalf with the Press Council against Media24. The ombud finds no malpractice with regards to how she is featured, or that *Exodus* distorted her words. My sister seeks leave to appeal, which is refused. My nieces did not ask for this life and all I want to say to them is that they must please, please find a way to contact Chris or me should they ever want to leave. We'll help them get out, but it must be their decision.

The mission would love all the focus to be on the Bornman family 'feud' and not on their doctrines, teachings and malpractices. But it is exactly those doctrines that have fractured our family – and countless other families – beyond repair.

72

'MACHINE-GUN ATTACK'

Nothing could have prepared me for the horror of what the *Sowetan* calls 'spine-chilling testimonies from KwaSizabantu' at the CRL Rights Commission hearings held in October 2020. Some of the testimonies are televised, some are on YouTube, others are held without any media present – all are heart-breaking. They kick off in Durban on Monday 5 October, and in the first two days the commission hears of families allegedly being pushed off their land – land that now belongs to KSB. They hear of people apparently being beaten so badly that they peed their pants. There is so much pain in these testimonies: child abuse, sexual abuse and rape, physical abuse, human-rights violations.

'The presentations were very … painful, they were very agonising, some of the victims were crying, weeping and of course willing to share with us their pain,' the commission chair, Professor David Luka Mosoma, tells Azarrah Karrim of News24 after the first day.

KwaZulu-Natal MEC for human settlements and public works Neliswa Nkonyeni kicks off day two and tells the panel that her department is looking into several allegations.

'I can't hide the fact that people have been complaining over a period of time,' she says.

Then it's Celimpilo's turn. She's followed by a woman who wishes to remain anonymous. She was raped, she tells the commission, and Erlo swore her to silence. 'The Lord has forgiven you, we don't talk about it any more,' he told her. Note the Lord's forgiveness and how it's graciously extended to the rape victim.

KSB's turn comes on day three, and they've acquired a champion: an advocate named Keith Matthee. The first I hear of him is when I see him in action on the video taken of KwaSizabantu's appearance before the CRL Rights Commission.

I find Matthee's approach, when he accuses Professor Mosoma of bias, to be belligerent right off the bat. He says the chair is profoundly compromised because, among other things, he gave an interview the previous day in which he called the people who testified 'victims'. Matthee maintains Mosoma has fundamentally com-promised himself and the commission by prejudging KSB and demands that he recuse himself. He pontificates for some length in the entertaining hour that ensues, lecturing the commission about their role and who they are and what they're sup-posed to do.

I applaud Professor Mosoma, Advocate Botha and the other commissioners who rightfully stand up to Matthee's bullying tactics. They school him in what the commission is about, and what a cohesive society is about, and what is required of institutions to build such societies. Mosoma refuses to recuse himself and the KSB contingent walk out in a huff. This, coupled with the disrespectful way Matthee addressed the commission, is a disgraceful display that clearly shows their contempt for anyone who is not one of them. They're not used to people not listening to them. How I wish I could have been a fly on the wall in the Upper Room that night!

Matthee clearly likes the sound of his own voice, and he particularly loves certain phrases he's coined. For example, KSB stands accused of 'multiple ongoing rapes'. He believes that if these allegations of 'multiple ongoing rapes', specifically those made by Koos Greeff and me, can be shown to be false, then the entire *Exodus* investigation should be thrown out.

'If it's found that it is baseless, then those witnesses who come to you, how on earth can you believe anything else they say?' Matthee asks. 'Because then they've used an incredibly cynical method to sensationalise their story.'

Neither Koos nor I used the words 'multiple' or 'ongoing' when discussing rape at KwaSizabantu. I said I'm sure abuse still happens there, seeing as there are rapists still walking around. I know of more than one man who has been accused of rape and faced zero consequences. They are all still preaching and teaching. I'll be happy to name them in court. Koos asked if *he* knew of so many cases, how many more must there be?

In the coming months, Matthee will use every opportunity to attack me and the others who have spoken out. He's as scathing when it comes to Adriaan and the News24 reporters, calling their integrity into question too.

Another recurring phrase in his strident rhetoric is that KSB faces a 'machine-gun attack'. In one of their earlier press releases, 'aQuellé – THE REAL VICTIM', KwaSizabantu lamented being 'the subject of a severe onslaught of allegations, including rape, sexual assault, money laundering and being a cult. Most of the allegations are vague, lacking any real particularity [...] The obvious intention of this machine gun attack strategy is to make it difficult to cover every aspect of the attack.' It's a refrain with which we will all become familiar as KSB seeks to recast itself as the victim.

73

REIGN OF TERROR REVISITED

As I listen to the testimonies of the KSB survivors at the CRL Rights Commission, I'm reminded of what Kyle Stephens said in 2018 to disgraced former US gymnastics coach Larry Nassar at his sentencing hearing for sexually abusing hundreds of young girls in his care.

'Perhaps you have figured it out by now, but little girls don't stay little forever. They grow into strong women that return to destroy your world.'

Some former Domino Servite pupils have drawn up a questionnaire for those who can't make it to the hearings or who don't want to appear in public. Sibonelo Cele was a few years below me at school. He is now a lawyer, and he has been helping KSB victims for many years. He and I undertake to be the keepers of the testimonies from former pupils, workers and preachers – some of whom joined KSB back in the 1960s and others who were there as recently as 2019.

The two weeks I spend going through the more than seventy responses is without a doubt the most difficult time in this entire journey. It is a deep dive into utter depravity, a look into the long-lasting psychic wounds KSB has inflicted on us. Many still feel worthless, still don't know how to be a part of society, still carry the shame and fear the mission instilled.

I spend my days weeping at my computer, calling up old schoolfriends and emailing others. There's a part of me that's upset that News24 didn't have access to these stories when they were compiling *Exodus*, but I am heartened that so many of us are coming forward and speaking up. I realise that I truly was one of the lucky ones – I had it so easy. When I think of the shame and fear I walked around with for so long, I cannot imagine what it's been like for the writers of these stories.

None could have asked for a better spokesperson, though. Sibonelo gives powerful testimony before the commission:

We are aware of, and in fact, [there] are victims of many instances of sexual abuse that happened at KwaSizabantu. These allegations came to my knowledge directly from victims, who are afraid to have their ordeals known to the world and their children out of shame.

In addition to the sexual violation's odious nature and the stigma it comes with, this fear is exacerbated by an oppressive response from KwaSizabantu authorities.

When these crimes were reported to the mission leadership, they were covered up, or the victims themselves were blamed and expelled from the mission and/or the school [...] In most instances, proper medical care was not provided – and the rapes and sexual abuse were not reported to the authorities [...]

That rapes and sexual abuse took place is beyond dispute. Two important issues are of concern. First is the response of the mission when it receives reports. Second is the admission and release of unrehabilitated drug [abusers] and offenders among mission residents.

The people Sibonelo refers to here are among the addicts who have flocked to KSB for their much-touted 'restoration programme', run by the Concerned Young People of South Africa. It is an unaccredited programme that relies on the power of prayer rather than trained medical staff or mental-health professionals. News24 has reported on men being kept against their will and severely beaten, and one heart-breaking account of a family who have not heard from their son since he checked in.

I spoke to the man's brother, who told me how eager his brother had been to get help for his alcoholism. The whole family believed this place to be a rehabilitation centre. The man's brother said goodbye to him there on 28 September 2019. No one has heard from him since 2 October 2019, when a security guard his brother had befriended alerted him to the fact that his brother was missing. According to him, KSB simply shrugged their shoulders and told the family he ran away. If he did, he did so wearing only one shoe (the other was found by a tall fence), and without his ID, cash or other belongings. Where is he now? KwaSizabantu doesn't care, and has apparently given the family no assistance whatsoever in finding their missing son. His missing-person docket remains open.

Sibonelo tells the commission how some of the men who had gone through this unregistered, twenty-one-day programme were allowed to exercise the authority of boarding masters over Domino Servite School pupils and, as such, allegedly 'mercilessly tormented young boys and girls alike'.

One of these individuals arranged young boys into a choir and sodomised them. When this was brought to the attention of school authorities at DSS and Mr Erlo Stegen, he dismissed the reports as a detraction of the good work of the Lord. When KSB later found out, they quietly removed him from KSB and never assisted the traumatised schoolboys.

KwaSizabantu reportedly allowed a known paedophile to leave quietly – free to go and abuse other children in other places. This is not the only time they were accused of turning a blind eye to paedophilia. I know of two other men who faced no consequences after mission leadership was informed that they were abusing kids – in the one case, it was the man's twelve-year-old daughter, in the other, a five-year-old girl. When confronted years later, the man who sodomised the five-year-old said, 'I'm surprised she remembers, she was so little.' He is now buried at KSB. When I think of men like him, I wish I did believe in hell.

We've gathered enough testimonies by now to back up what we all knew. Despite KSB's statements and sworn affidavits that claim corporal punishment was abolished in 1996, learners at Domino Servite 'continued to receive corporal punishment well beyond 1996'.

> This was carried out by subterfuge. Parents were compelled to give parental authority to KwaSizabantu to administer corporal punishment if they wanted their children to continue schooling at the mission. Alternatively, DSS will expel the child for even inconsequential misdemeanours.
> Beatings were administered with a plumbing plastic pipe. Often you did not know how many lashes you were going to get. Furthermore, these would be for nebulous conduct such as an allegation that you are obstinate, bad influence, walked cocky, or you have not confessed sins in a while.

Sibonelo is not telling one person's story here, he's speaking for hundreds. And, as we all know by now, these beatings were not the only humiliation the black girls suffered.

> We have, in response to a questionnaire, confirmed that – the act of virginity testing was widespread at DSS; and that it was discriminatory in terms of race and sex; only African girls were tested.

One of the girls in my English class tells me that they were all lined up as well. They were five years old and having their vaginas examined to make sure their hymens were intact! She is now a grown woman and a mother and still can't quite get herself to talk about what that was like for her. Celimpilo says it's a travesty that KSB hides behind virginity testing as 'Zulu culture', as the way they do it bears almost no resemblance to tradition. KSB turns what should be an uplifting, life-affirming experience – a celebration of womanhood with the older women of your tribe – into a repulsive and demeaning experience.

In the *Exodus* documentary, Celimpilo describes what happened every time she returned to school after being home for the holidays. In the presence of three old women, she would lie with her legs up and open, everything exposed.

> One would wash her hands and then touch you and they would look and the others would come and witness. 'Oh, it is still alright'; 'It is not right.' And it would be, 'Alright now, you can put on your panties and stand up and go.' So, if unfortunately you have been found to be tampered with then you would

know and you would be put aside in your corner and most of the time would be expelled.

KSB maintains they 'allowed' virginity testing because the Zulu parents insisted on it and that they stopped the practice in 2002. Many of the girls refute this. Parents were told that girls had to be tested as a prerequisite for attending the school; they did not ask for it. And, according to some respondents of our questionnaire, it went on beyond 2002.

Only girls who have reached the age of puberty may be tested [in Zulu culture]. Girls as young as five years old would have their private parts inspected as a condition for their continued presence at the school. We assert that this was racist, sexual and emotional abuse.

Sibonelo is not done. He calls on KSB to account for allegedly playing an active role in helping the apartheid regime retain its grip on South Africa. Again, he has the testimony of countless ex-members to back up his claims. 'KwaSizabantu must account for the receipt of funds, equipment, vehicles and unlicensed firearms in return for violating the sanctity of confession – in other words, by giving up people who were opposed to the apartheid regime.' He ends his testimony with the following:

We believe it is the duty of the duly appointed legal entities to investigate these practices and, where applicable, seek justice for the victims of these crimes. It is time for the KwaSizabantu Mission's leadership to acknowledge everything that has been revealed to date and will continue to emerge in the future.

However, their continued denial and dismissal of all the serious allegations that have emerged give us no hope that justice can be done without outside intervention.

The commission hears from KSB members too, including my sister, but no one from the leadership appears again (at least not by the time this book goes to print – the investigation is ongoing, and I have yet to testify). Their minions all sing from the same hymn sheet. Everything at KSB is rosy and glorious, and these 'disgruntled' ex-members should be disregarded. I believe several are lying. I know they witnessed beatings. Even Jenny, the one who told David to fetch the butcher's knife before Jessie was brutally beaten, says everything is all sunshine and roses at KSB.

Anita, a resident and teacher at Domino Servite School, tells the commission that KSB saved her from her abusive father. I had read her affidavit after it was posted to the KSB website and remember being dumbfounded that they had allowed it to be published. And now here she is telling that same story to the commission. Anita's sister, Marietjie Bothma, is a brave woman who has spoken about her abuse in the media for many years – her story is truly horrific. Like Hanna, Anita's role is to discredit her sister. She is here to say that KSB bears no responsibility for the abuse she and her siblings suffered.

But here's why it's so surprising that KSB allowed Anita's testimony to be made public: it is a devastating glimpse into how the mission coddles the abusers in their midst. Anita says her mother found a note she had written to her father when she was around twelve years old, begging him to stop sexually abusing her. Subsequent to this, three of the leaders – including Erlo – came to talk to her father and she says he never touched her again. This is how they 'saved' Anita and her two sisters and their young brother. By allowing a known paedophile to stay with his family.

The horror I felt when I read Anita's affidavit intensifies as I listen to her speak to the commission. She genuinely believes that the mission saved her. Her father left of his own volition some months later and has since died. Two of Anita's siblings tell me that his abuse only stopped after he left. I simply cannot get over the fact that KSB allowed him to stay with his family. He should have been locked up. Had the leadership reported him, he would have spent his last years in prison rather than in comfort. Who knows what access he had to little girls before he died?

74

PINK PANTIES

'I made sure I always wore nice panties on a Saturday, just in case my name was called.'

I'm chatting on the phone to a schoolfriend, whom I'll call Thandi. I'm asking her about something that has come up as more people have started speaking about their experiences at KSB. What's the deal with the Saturday beatings? I always knew the Zulu kids got beaten a lot more than the white kids, and that they had services we didn't attend – in fact, we were sometimes told to leave a service while the black children stayed behind. But it's becoming increasingly clear to me that I don't know the full story. I hear about grown men and women who today walk around with scars on their backs, buttocks and thighs from the beatings they got when they were schoolchildren at KSB. Add to this an element of Sibonelo's testimony that the various news outlets haven't reported. He told the commission that children were beaten in public after being stripped naked. 'Buck naked' is the phrase he used. I call him and ask him why he thinks the media has failed to report on it, and I agree with his assessment. Sibonelo thinks the horror is simply incomprehensible to the average human. It sounds too far-fetched to be true. Adults stripping kids naked in public – in front of their peers and other adults – and beating them till they bled? Surely that couldn't happen?

It could, and by all accounts it did. Sometimes they were allowed to keep their underpants on, Sibonelo tells me. I don't understand this at all. KwaSizabantu is so against boys and girls even talking to one another, how could they possibly justify stripping the kids naked in the presence of members of the opposite sex? The beatings are horrific in themselves, but this nakedness is something I was taught to avoid at all costs and adds an entirely new element to my understanding of what my friends experienced.

So I call Thandi.

I ask her to tell me more about the Saturday meetings. She confirms what I know by now – these meetings happened almost every Saturday, in that infernal Upper Room. The kids would be called to the room and made to sit down. The adults would then take a confession of one of the children to a co-worker, who would announce it to the gathered assembly. The confession would be openly discussed, and a co-worker would preach, 'so that if you were hiding a sin, you would feel so guilty', Thandi recalls. 'And then one of the children would stand up and start

227

telling on other pupils. And then it would go from there. A chain reaction. Another would say something, and so on.'

Often, children made up stories, possibly to deflect punishment from themselves. Thandi tells me about one incident in which she was involved. She had politely asked her classmates not to leave their dirty dishes in front of reception when they'd eaten there. The following Saturday, a boy stood up and accused her of 'telling him in a cheeky way to pick up his dishes'. It was grounds for a beating, never mind that it wasn't true and that she wasn't given a chance to defend herself.

When you were named, when the finger was pointed at you, you were beaten.

'Once your name was mentioned, you had no right to say anything; they didn't even wait,' Thandi tells me.

This happened almost every Saturday. I am appalled.

Thandi is crying now, and so am I. I am responsible for opening all these old wounds. I wish there was a different way to hold KSB accountable, but there isn't. People's pain is all that can stop them.

And it gets worse.

'They stripped the kids naked, and you were left in your underwear, and they would beat you in front of the whole school,' Thandi continues.

I am incredulous. Girls were stripped to their bra and panties?

'No, no bra,' Thandi clarifies for me. 'You have to take off everything except your panties. And then you lie down to get beaten in front of the whole school.'

I cannot imagine the humiliation.

'Every time we were called, we'd run to quickly change into a nice pair of panties, colourful ones, you know, because you might be stripped naked. Until one day, one of the mamas was there. And there was this girl. She was grown, and she had a beautiful body. She was beautiful. We were sitting there, the whole school, and she was right at the back. They called her name, and she stood up and she stripped right there where she was standing, at the back. And she walked slowly to the front wearing only lacy pink panties to her beating. And after that, we were allowed to keep our clothes on.'

I call Celimpilo next. I tell her how sorry I am, that I didn't know the full extent of the abuse the black children experienced. I ask her what happened to the girl in the pink panties.

'They beat her and then they expelled her,' Celimpilo tells me.

This is a common story. They didn't just expel the schoolchildren. They first beat them and *then* they expelled them. I am incandescent with rage and consumed by grief for my friends.

Back in 2000, KSB denied using corporal punishment. Then they admitted that the parents beat the kids on their premises. In September 2020, in their 'aQuellé – THE REAL VICTIM' press release, they say:

Response about physical abuse: It was the practice of the Mission school, since its inception in 1986, to use reasonable and moderate corporal punishment in line with all other schools in South Africa at the time. In 1994, a year before the Department of Education banned the practice of corporal punishment, the school suspended it. In early 1996 it was officially banned by the school at a special meeting for parents.

There were aberrations and excesses of corporal correction before 1994, which were dealt with by Church discipline and teaching. (As we have said in the past, we say again: If there are still any outstanding issues pre-1994 regarding corporal correction, the individuals concerned should please come forward so that reconciliation can be facilitated).

Some of those men are dead. They cannot be held to account, not any more. But many of the other perpetrators are still alive. I don't know what rage, what bloodlust they were expressing, but what they did to the defenceless children in their care is unforgiveable.

Michael Ngubane is still alive. Michael Ngubane is still a member of the school board. Michael Ngubane is on the board of aQuellé, 'the real victim'. This is all he has to say about corporal punishment in his affidavit, dated 30 September 2020 and made in his capacity as chairperson of the board of Domino Servite School:

I confirm that it has been the practice of the school (as was acceptable at the time, and practiced in all other schools in South African [sic]) to use reasonable and moderate spanking as a form of discipline.

From my enquiries, I have learned that the school suspended corporal punishment before 1994. Both the chairperson of the board and the principal at the time that corporal punishment was banned are now deceased. To my knowledge, corporal punishment has not been used since 1994 as a form of discipline.

Tell that to the people walking around with the 'reasonable and moderate' scars KSB inflicted. On their bodies. On their minds. On their psyches.

75

PUTTING THE DENT
IN INDEPENDENT

KwaSizabantu knows the truth, and they know there are many who can attest to it. And our number is growing by the day as more and more people come forward.

What KSB can do, however, is to try to influence public perception. The public who buys their products. And the public who are the decision-makers for the retailers that stock their products. And I believe that's where this panel they call 'independent' comes in.

I refuse to recognise the panel's legitimacy – I actually advocate against people cooperating with them. In my opinion, their aim is to whitewash, nothing else. Would anyone with any common sense believe the veracity of an organisation who conducts a self-investigation? I don't trust them, but because it's unprecedented for the mission to engage in such a process, I'm eventually persuaded to put aside my reservations. It's mainly out of concern for my mother, sister and nieces, because I don't want to reach the end of my life knowing that I didn't do all I could to help them escape. Also, as people point out to me, we can't call it a whitewash if we don't give them our side of the story.

And so I agree to talk to Khumbu Shazi and Peter Le Mottée. Andrew Arnott of Arnott and Associates sets it up. I open our chat by saying I do not trust a panel that is being paid by KwaSizabantu. Then I ask them who will have access to their final report. Peter responds that their mandate is to make the report available to whomever they deem appropriate. 'It won't be a hush-hush report,' he says.

Later, I'll realise that he's prevaricating, but right now I take them at their word and cooperate fully. For the next hour and a half, I answer every question they ask. It's 24 October, thirty-five days after *Exodus*'s launch.

I'm one of many survivors who cooperate. Afterwards, everyone I speak to says they feel confident that it won't be a whitewash. Those two have put our minds at ease, for sure. They are independent. Whew. Except then we don't hear from them again. They were supposed to deliver their findings after two weeks. It takes closer to three months, and during that time Andrew assures us that we'll see the report. KSB has also promised complete transparency – on national TV – and that the report will be made available to all.

It is Friday 20 November, just before three o'clock in the afternoon, when I get a WhatsApp from a friend. 'KSB is holding a press conference at 3pm to discuss findings of report!'

The press conference is meant to be on their website, but their website is down. Eventually, by now frantic, I find Keith Matthee pontificating on the KSB YouTube channel around ten minutes after the start. (For people who decry social media, they sure do make use of it. 'If your name is on Facebook, it is not in the Book of Life,' Erlo preaches.)

Around twenty minutes in, Keith starts laying into me. Bear in mind, I've not seen the report or what was written about me – or anyone else for that matter. So much for transparency.

I want to touch on the integrity of Mr Basson as a journalist. If one watches the *Exodus* video, at one point, Ms Bornman, Erika Bornman, creates the impression that as a young sixteen-year-old girl, in Standard 8, for a relatively minor infraction, was expelled from the school at the mission. Her mother supported the expulsion. And she, in the video, she still says, 'Imagine a young girl of sixteen, with a suitcase, just being let out into the world.' If one looks at the video, that's the clear impression created. This was put to Ms Bornman by the panellists. And the response of Ms Bornman to the panellists was as follows: Ms Bornman's account of the story in the News24 was edited to appear as if she was expelled from the mission, at fifteen.

I listen in stunned disbelief. It's all a lie. I can't breathe. The damn tremors are back; I'm shaking uncontrollably, and it takes enormous effort to stay in my body, to keep listening.

Because the truth is, and this is presented to the panel, is that Ms Bornman in fact matriculated at that school, and not only matriculated, but was one of the co-dux winners of her year and, in fact, returned the following year as an assistant teacher. And yet if you look at the video, the impression is clearly created, clearly created, there's no other impression that can be created if you listen to the video, that she was expelled as a fifteen, sixteen-year-old. Here she said she never told that to Mr Basson. And that it's Mr Basson who's edited. That's in effect what she's saying. Has edited what she said to create this impression.

I send a WhatsApp to the News24 team. That is not true, I tell them. I never said that about your editing.

I am completely distraught that the panel has so completely misrepresented what I said and that I can't even check what they've written – I have to take this man's word for it. And he's not done with me – or Adriaan – yet.

If I were judging this matter, simply that act by Mr Basson would lead me to the conclusion that I would have absolutely no further regard to anything else that was stated or done by him in that video or any other subsequent work. And there are other examples of this lack of integrity of Mr Basson. Linked to this integrity of Mr Basson, is also that of Ms Bornman and Mr Greeff. If you look at the video, the *Exodus* video, you will see they both make allegations of multiple ongoing rapes at the mission, and I'll get back to that, but you'll see that the panellists make a clear finding in that regard. And basically say there's not a scrap of truth when it comes to those allegations.

There is more, so much more. The way he rips apart the testimonies of the rape victims is awful to watch. I send Andrew Arnott a WhatsApp: 'Hi there, seeing as your panel has written extensively about me and quoted me, when will you give me the courtesy of being able to read it for myself?'

He responds that the terms of reference give the panel the power to decide who can see the report. But, he tells me, the panel has authorised him to release the report to the *Sunday Times* and he has sent it to them accordingly.

I recorded my entire conversation with the panellists. I find where we speak about my expulsion and send the clip to Adriaan and his team. The next day, I contact the *Sunday Times* and speak to two journalists. That same day, 21 November, Philani Nombembe publishes an article on the findings titled 'Lawyers' KwaSizabantu probe clears mission of string of allegations'. 'The embattled Kwa-Sizabantu Christian Mission has released a glowing report absolving itself of damning allegations — including rape – made by former members,' he writes.

The article quotes Dr Peet Botha, a former member who has been instrumental in the investigation: 'It's like former president Jacob Zuma setting up a parallel investigation to the Zondo commission, choosing his own judge and his own attorneys and they find nothing wrong on his part. And he says to the world, "See, I am innocent".'

I am also quoted, having told the journalist how the panel backtracked on their promise to release the report: 'It is utterly unfair to vilify us in public but deny us the opportunity to read what they wrote about us. It's unconscionable and highly questionable and re-victimises us all over again.'

The weekend passes in a blur. By cooperating with the panel, we played into their hands. We should have known better. I watch the video again and again, as odious as Keith is – I need to figure out how he could say the things he said about us. I find no answers.

On Monday morning, Andrew sends me a message.

Dear Erika
I confirm that as the work of the Independent Panel is now over, and they are now functus officio (or no longer empowered to deal with any queries relating

to their report), I have been authorized by those instructing me to release the main findings of the Panel in Section A of their report to you. Please confirm receipt of the findings as requested.

All further queries relating to this matter are to be directed to DW Attorneys who's [*sic*] email appears below as my duties as registrar to the Panel have likewise come to an end.

E-mail: mail@dwinc.co.za

Sincerely

Andrew

And just like that, the three lawyers wash their hands of whatever devastation their report has wrought. Section A of the report does a pretty good job of attempting to exonerate the mission, but raises more questions than it answers. Without the other sections, I'm still in the dark. In the meantime, I engage a legal transcription service to transcribe my interview with the panel.

Finally, at noon on the Tuesday, Andrew sends me sections A, B and C and all the annexures. He demands that I acknowledge receipt, but I ignore him. He's screwed me over enough.

I share the report far and wide. Anyone who asks for it, gets it. KwaSizabantu, Keith, Andrew, Khumbu and Peter are all on record saying that the report will be transparent and made available to everyone, so I'm merely fulfilling their well-documented promises.

76

A DUCK THAT IS NOT A DUCK

Khumbu and Peter had the power to help stop a great evil. They failed to do so.

I could fill an entire book about this sham report. I understand why KSB wants to keep it from the public – it most definitely does not exonerate them, despite what the panellists assert in Section A.

In my opinion, the report is a masterclass in the twisting of facts. Scientology has a practice called Fair Game. Anyone leaving the organisation who speaks out against it becomes – you guessed it – fair game. They do what they can to place the spotlight on the detractor to divert attention from their own heinous crimes and human-rights abuses. KwaSizabantu has taken this particular leaf straight from Scientology's playbook, and this report has further enabled them to do so.

I am sickened by the report. And heartsore. Not so much for me – though the way they've twisted my testimony angers me – but for the way they discredit, malign and vilify the survivors of sexual assault who were brave enough to come forward. For the way they seem to parrot the KSB narrative. I didn't expect much from Peter, but Khumbu? She's a woman, a sister. Her CV says she's worked with victims of sexual assault. It blows my mind that she could put her name to this.

Under 'Rape and sexual abuse', the panellists say: 'We found no substance to these allegations. The witnesses who spoke to us regarding this aspect mostly relied on hearsay and could not give primary accounts of any specific incident.' Say what? Whose hearsay am I relying on when I talk about what happened to me? I gave them a first-person, primary account. And based on the details in the report, I was not the only one. And surely, just because some of it is hearsay does not mean there is 'no substance' to it.

It defies logic. Perhaps it's because I don't have a law degree. The panellists say they don't have the qualifications to make 'final theological determinations regarding the practices and doctrine of a church or a cult', yet they go on to state that they find KSB is not a cult. And then they qualify that by saying that there are some practices they 'found concerning and [that] need to be addressed'. Further on in the report, they recommend that KwaSizabantu should dissolve their governing body and amend their constitution – basically encouraging them to dismantle their entire system. If I were KSB, I'd ask for my money back.

The panellists further state that they find no proof of money laundering. And yet: 'We were initially informed that Ms Dube did not have a personal bank account, but it transpired from our follow up interview that she actually did. We asked for the bank statements of the said account for the period 2015–2018. At the time of drafting the report we had not been furnished with the said bank statements.'

The panel is willing to conclude that there is no evidence of financial crimes without even looking at the bank statements of the person who apparently lied about not having a bank account.

Slipped into the section on the alleged money laundering are three sentences that tell you a whole lot of nothing that is actually something: 'The Reedneh Trust had an outstanding loan from the Mission of R23 million. The loan was impaired at the instruction of the Trustees. We did not investigate this aspect further, since we could not find any indication that this account had been used to move the money which was loaned [...]'

The Reedneh Trust belongs to Erlo and his six daughters. On the face of it, they were basically gifted R23 million, but that doesn't require further investigation?

The panel did, however, find that an amount of roughly R146 million was improperly loaned to a certain individual between November 2015 and December 2018. The loan was never repaid and was impaired in 2020, but this – the panel is at pains to report – 'does not amount to money laundering'. 'The Mission must immediately make efforts to recover the money [and] report this matter to the police for an investigation to be conducted.'

Whether the impaired loans are the result of criminal activity or not, the fact that these people can be allowed to continue to oversee the millions brought in by KSB's various business interests I find seriously questionable. Imagine how much good can be done with R169 million? Instead of abject poverty, the communities surrounding KSB could have proper hospitals with real doctors, schools, sanitation, roads. Where has all that money gone, and why has no one questioned it until now?

Unlike everyone else, the panellists were allowed to interview Erlo. 'At the Mission we interviewed Dr Abu [sic] van Eeden and Ruth Combrink about Rev Stegen's condition. We were informed that Rev Stegen was of sound mind, except that he had occasional forgetfulness which was related to old age.'

Except, maybe not … 'It became clear to us that the Mission had downplayed Rev Stegen's condition. We decided to not proceed with the interview as Rev Stegen was clearly not in a position to participate meaningfully.'

Those on the outside have known for a long time that Erlo has Alzheimer's, while the leadership denies it and shields him from the world. Erlo is still a trustee, despite being mentally impaired. He still has the power to sign away millions (or supposedly squirrel them into his own Reedneh Trust). And yet the panel does not question this further.

Interestingly, they take care not to impugn anyone on the evangelical panel that wrote that heartfelt report in 2000. They reserve their disbelief for those of us with little or no ecclesiastical standing – or connections to their retail clientele. They also make a big deal of the fact that they interviewed three scholars, among them Professor Henk Stoker of North West University's theology department. But in the entire report, I cannot find a single mention of what Professor Stoker said to them. Why is that? And yet they quote his scholarly writings unrelated to KwaSizabantu. This is disingenuous in my view, as it gives the impression that Professor Stoker agrees with their findings.

I'm quite vocal about KwaSizabantu on Twitter, but the tweet of the year belongs to user @JG77:

Regarding the 'cult' allegation, the report seems to say that it looks like a duck, walks like a duck and quacks like a duck but nonetheless concludes that it simply ain't a duck because those looking, walking and quacking like ducks claim they are not ducks.

77

BECOMING A
CONSCIOUS CONSUMER

I see out 2020 on a hopeful note. The CRL Rights Commission's investigation is ongoing, the Hawks are investigating allegations involving those missing millions, and the KSB report with all its contradictions is in my view so blatantly spurious, I can't imagine anyone taking it at face value.

Except every single major retailer in South Africa, it seems.

By February 2021, aQuellé is sold far and wide once more. To be fair, Shoprite and Checkers never took it off their shelves to begin with, and as a result I have not bought anything from those shelves since October 2020. But Food Lover's Market, Spar, Pick n Pay, Makro and Game did stop stocking the brand. And Woolworths stopped buying their fresh produce. And they all trumpeted the fact in 2020. Only to restock quietly in 2021. News24 investigates, and the majority confirm that they believe the investigations have cleared KSB. Clearly no one is prepared to wait for the official CRL Rights Commission report. But that they actually bought *this* report beggars belief.

I believe that they have not only failed us, the survivors, but their shareholders and their customers too. The buying public trusts their retailers to uphold certain ethics. They trust that the products they find on the shelves have not been produced by a company owned by a religious cult that has devastated hundreds of lives. And when such products reappear on the shelves after an absence, the assumption is that due diligence has been done and everything is all right.

It seems to me that these retailers have put profits before people. It's as simple as that. I would love to get the various directors in a room and read some of the testimonies to them. It's not necessary, of course – most are online anyway.

And if they'd actually read the report, here's what they'd learn about one of the directors of aQuellé: 'One of the senior leaders, Mr Michael Ngubane, who was accused of being particularly vicious in the manner that he used to apply corporal punishment, admitted to having frequently used a piece of rubber hose in administering the punishments, and he acknowledged that sometimes he may have "overdone" it.'

Show me one other company whose director is accused of something this heinous, admits to it, but then stays on the board – and not a single retail partner objects?

If they'd actually read the report, they'd notice that conspicuously absent from the list of interviewees are the actual workers at aQuellé and Emseni Farming. The people earning minimum wage while their directors squander tens of millions and fly around in four private planes, including a multimillion-rand Pilatus. There are no interviews with the retired people who now have nothing – not even enough, in the case of one woman, to buy life-saving medication. There is no interview with the former worker who could tell them about the alleged unfair human resources practices at aQuellé. For him, Khumbu and Peter didn't have the time.

I have not shopped at any of these stores for months now. I know my boycott makes not the tiniest bit of difference to any of them, but it does to me. It matters to me.

And yes, I run out of fresh milk every now and again. I miss my favourite ready-made meals. It's inconvenient not buying everything in one go under one roof or on one app. But I'm loving the journey of becoming a more conscious consumer. The fact that I live in Cape Town makes it easier, of course. If I lived in a one-horse town with one shop, my options would be severely limited. Instead, I have found the most amazing small suppliers to support. People who are passionate about their produce, their goods, their service. It feels good to support them instead.

I am sitting with a severe moral quandary, though. I'm a freelancer and my main source of income is editing a staff magazine for a certain company. I am contracted to a publishing house, but they are contracted by one of these retailers I'm boycotting. What if I don't find other work and I lose my house because I was trying to make a point no one else cares about anyway? I am looking for alternatives, but so far, the pickings have been slim. I genuinely love my colleagues at the publishing house, and I enjoy working on the account. I am so conflicted. Life is not black and white. Navigating the grey sometimes keeps me up at night.

78

SURVIVING IS NOT THRIVING

What might my life have been like, what would so many others' lives have been like, had we been free to thrive in our twenties and thirties? Instead, we struggled to survive while dealing with the debilitating wounds inflicted on us, without the necessary tools to cope.

We fought to reclaim ourselves, not understanding that our personal boundaries had been demolished. We tried to establish a different sense of self – one that was not evil and wicked and predisposed to being bad. We did not have the tools, but we did it, for the most part. Some of us are thriving, some are still merely surviving, and some are barely hanging on. Others are no longer with us.

And yes, I am saying 'we' and not just 'me'. Over the past year and a half, I have spoken to countless others and read the words of many more. I have wept for the desolation, the alienation, the devastation that KwaSizabantu has wrought in our lives, and continues to wreak for so many, even those who left long ago.

By all accounts, public beatings don't happen at KwaSizabantu any more. Good. We've achieved something at least in the past two decades. Kids are still allegedly getting hidings there, only now it's not at school but in their homes. And perhaps you think that's okay. 'Spare the rod, spoil the child.' But if it's illegal to assault an adult, why would you model assault as a form of discipline for children? Much less a child in your care whom you, hopefully, love? Corporal punishment is a sure-fire way to obliterate a child's healthy personal boundaries.

KwaSizabantu has not shown an ounce of remorse. They want us to move on. They say they want their victims to contact them for reconciliation. Why? They have school records and presumably the contact details of the parents of most of their past pupils. Why is the onus on *us* to go to *them*? They are the ones who beat my peers to a pulp, not the other way around. If they felt genuine remorse, they would be using their not-inconsiderable resources to find the people whose backs, buttocks, thighs and psyches still bear the marks of KSB to this day. Hey, they could even ask News24 to publish a public apology if they don't want to go to the trouble of tracking us all down.

This desire to have people move on is typical of abusers. They want their victims to let it go already. No. We will not be moving on any time soon. And do you know why? Because without genuine remorse, without reparations to victims and without a stated intention to change behaviour, they will do it again when given the chance. Abusers stop abusing when under scrutiny. When the scrutiny goes away, they pick right up where they left off. And therefore the scrutiny cannot be lifted until they have been held fully accountable. Until they have publicly acknowledged how they abused people and how they covered up that abuse. How they knowingly allowed abusers to live among them, or quietly asked them to leave without protecting the most innocent among them.

The leaders at KwaSizabantu refuse to recognise that they have done anything wrong. It's the odd individual, they say. They can't control everything that happens there. It's a 'family matter', and 'we don't comment on those'. Bullshit. I believe it is their institutionalised doctrine that is the problem, not individuals. They have not renounced their belief that you must break the spirit of a child by the age of three. They do not see their use of violent movies as wrong. They do not see the destructiveness of imprinting the fear of hell on a child. If left unchecked, these children may in turn become the abusers, because they know no different and they know no better. KSB still encourages pupils to snitch on one another. There is no recognition of wrongdoing and no remorse.

KwaSizabantu has done nothing to heal the countless families they have fractured with their divisive doctrine. They continue to deny that they encourage family members to break contact with those who leave. And yes, even in 2021, families are still being ruptured because of their doctrine. There is no remorse.

KwaSizabantu has done nothing to help repair the damage done by the sexual predators they have harboured and protected. They refuse to acknowledge that they covered up sexual abuse and continue to vilify the survivors who have been brave enough to tell their stories. They continue to shame the victims for not filing police reports when they are the ones who silenced them. No remorse. No reparations.

Here is my solemn vow: I will continue to be a voice for those who have been silenced by KwaSizabantu. I will be a thorn in their side until they stop breaking the spirits of the children in their care. My voice may not be loud, but together with the voices of countless other survivors, I hope it becomes a rousing call. Together we form our own Choir Number One – a choir for change. I really hope the world will listen to us and help us save the children of KwaSizabantu.

79

MY HAPPY ENDING

Every story has a beginning, a middle and an end. I would have so loved to conclude this book with a truly happy ending. One where the perpetrators of evil have been removed from power. Where the millions generated by their businesses are being used for good. Where kids are free to grow their hair, read whatever books they want, discover the world. Alas. Maybe that day will come, maybe not.

I've always considered myself lucky. I'm a *kurkproppie*. I've always thought how fortunate I am to have escaped KwaSizabantu relatively unscathed. But that's not entirely true. I was badly scathed, and I only realised the extent of the damage once my marriage ended, twenty-seven years after running away.

I was definitely luckier than some, but I was still harmed. I don't think anyone leaves there intact. And I feel for the people living there – the majority of whom are good people wanting to do good. The damage is pervasive. It is destructive and insidious.

In our final podcast interview, Deon asks me how I've found the whole process and what I've learned about myself. I mix an awful lot of metaphors as I paint him a picture: many years ago, I put all my demons and skeletons in a box and I buried that box in a very, very deep hole. I had to in order to survive, because I did not have the tools to deal with them. They didn't stay in that buried box, of course; they managed to claw their way out and crawl through the soil. They left that box and started terrorising me, these demons and skeletons.

And the demons looked at me with red-hot coals for eyes and the skeletons shook their bones around. For so many years, their visits petrified me because I couldn't deal with them, I didn't know how. I just wanted to run away from them, and I would beg them to please just get back in their box or find a cupboard or something and just leave me alone.

And then I grew stronger. Now, when a demon arrives, I look at it and say, 'Okay, you're here. Let's chat. What have you got to teach me? Teach me, tell me, and then fuck off.' And the demons have diminished in number – they teach me what they came to teach me and then they disappear into thin air or, I don't know, maybe become angels. Who knows what happens to them?

The skeletons are a little bit trickier, because they represent my shame. When addressing them, I confront the shame I still carry inside me. I haven't wanted people to know about certain things, because if they know, they're going to judge me. During the earlier podcast recordings, I had this vision of flinging open my cupboard doors and saying to these collections of bones: 'Come out, let's dance. Who wants to waltz? Who wants to salsa? Let's dance.'

When I stop fearing them, they turn from scary to almost friendly, almost paternal and maternal, almost caring – if bony fingers can be caring. We dance, and I realise yet again that I can't salsa. They teach me some steps, I teach them a step or two, and then they disappear. Right now, there are still some skeletons left in my cupboard. I'll dance with them one day, when I'm ready.

And what is the most important lesson I've learned about myself?

That's simple: Garrakachok, I *am* my den.

ACKNOWLEDGEMENTS

In telling my story, I have not done full justice to my fellow warriors. The ones who gathered evidence and witnesses; the ones who bravely shared their stories with the media in the hope that they could effect change; the ones who counselled so many wounded souls. I salute you.

This book would not exist without three incredible women at Penguin Random House. Marlene Fryer, my publisher, thank you for believing me – and for believing in me. I will forever be grateful. Every writer should be lucky enough to have Bronwen Maynier as their editor. Thank you, Bronwen, for the care with which you treated my words and the many, many ways you improved them. Thank you also for your wisdom in dealing with those passages I found so hard to write. Ronel Richter-Herbert, managing editor extraordinaire, thank you for your wise counsel and encouragement, and sorry for all those deadlines I missed. And to the rest of the Penguin Random House Non-fiction team: typesetter Monique van den Berg, publicist Ian Dennewill and everyone else – heartfelt thanks!

I hope people judge this book by its cover. And I have my friend Sean Robertson to thank for that. We first met at Struik Publishers in 2003 and have been colleagues intermittently over the years, and friends the whole time. Thank you, Sean, for 'getting' me and helping me express it so beautifully.

My deepest gratitude goes to Adriaan Basson, Tammy Petersen, Nokuthula Manyathi, Aljoscha Kohlstock, Azarrah Karrim, Mpho Raborife, Sharlene Rood and the rest of the News24 team who produced *Exodus: Uncovering a Cult in KwaZulu-Natal* and for continuing the investigation to this day. Deon Wiggett, what an honour to have you tell my story in the podcast; you've been an inspiration and a solace. Institutions and people around the world are held to account thanks to intrepid journalists like all of you. Think of the *Boston Globe*'s investigation into the Catholic Church, the #metoo movement and so many more. *Exodus* sparked investigations by South African authorities and for that I will be forever in your debt.

I also want to thank my aunts and uncles who helped me escape KwaSizabantu, first physically, but then also its mental and emotional confines. Thank you, Iris, for giving me refuge and being my guiding light all these years – even today. Chris and Janet, I would not have escaped – I would not be here – if it weren't for you. Like Iris, you showed me unconditional love and the meaning of family. My gratitude also goes to Herman and Melanie, and my cousins Maureen, Bennie and Karin.

I'm with Frank Sinatra about having too few regrets to mention. I also have too many friends to mention here. Special people who have encouraged and loved and comforted and cheered me on. You've been a safe space for me, a warm blanket to wrap around me when confronting the chill of my childhood. You've been the bubbles in the many glasses we've shared while celebrating life. Thank you. You are my family.

Thank you also to the therapists who have helped me uncover the beauty of my life and handed me the tools to navigate and clear my trauma minefield.

Books have always been my lifeline, and again there are too many to mention. In 2003, *Under the Banner of Heaven: A Story of Violent Faith* by Jon Krakauer helped me understand what had happened to me in a way no other book had done before. Dr Edith Eger's *The Choice* and *The Gift* are two books everyone in the world should read. For me, memoirs written by survivors of the Fundamentalist Church of Jesus Christ of Latter-Day Saints struck a particular chord, especially *The Witness Wore Red* by Rebecca Musser and *Lost Boy* by Brent Jeffs and Maia Szalavitz. Keele Burgin's *Wholly Unravelled* is another more recent masterful memoir that helped me to let go of all the shame I've carried for so long. *Unfollow* by Megan Phelps-Roper helped me enormously – especially in guiding my Twitter responses to KSB apologists. I have to stop there, but there are so many, many more!

Speaking of Twitter, @JoLuehmann, @C_Stroop and @monaeltahawy are three powerhouse women whose incisive commentary and insights had me falling in love with the platform all over again. I came late to podcasts, only really discovering them in late 2019. *Let's Talk About Sects* by Sarah Steel and *A Little Bit Culty* by Sarah Edmondson and Anthony 'Nippy' Ames are two podcasts I listen to religiously, pun intended.

During the writing of this book, I drew on the support of many friends, even though we were all locked away in our own homes for the most part. Michelle, you're an angel in disguise. There are so many ex-KSB members who helped me tremendously, but I'd like to single out Celimpilo, Jessie, Greg, and Koos and his family, in particular Monika and Annemarie. There are many more, of course, and thank you to everyone who was only a phone call or a message away.

And Chris, my beloved brother. I have no words with which to express my love and gratitude to you. Everything I write is so inadequate that I delete it immediately. You have my whole heart, brother dearest. I watch you with your sons and I am so proud of how you've broken the cycle. They, and I, are so lucky to have you in our lives.

To the two little beings who can't read these words, but who share my life and home and give me so much succour: Troy and Matilda, love you to the moon and back.

Thank you also to the many people I have never met who sent me messages of support after the launch of *Exodus* – your encouragement means the world and often moved me to tears. May we all consciously build a world that is filled with compassion, not condemnation; understanding, not denunciation. And accountability for all.

MENTAL-HEALTH SUPPORT

If this book has raised difficult memories and issues for you, here are two toll-free South African helplines to call for support:

- Lifeline 0800-150-150 (lifelinesa.co.za)
- The South African Depression and Anxiety Group 0800-567-567 (sadag.org)

Please don't suffer alone.